Gallery Books
Editor Peter Fallon
SELECTED PROSE

Derek Mahon

SELECTED PROSE

Gallery Books

Selected Prose
is first published
simultaneously in paperback
and in a clothbound edition
on 31 March 2012.

The Gallery Press
Loughcrew
Oldcastle
County Meath
Ireland

www.gallerypress.com

*All rights reserved. For permission
to reprint or broadcast this work,
write to The Gallery Press.*

© Derek Mahon 2012

ISBN 978 1 85235 528 9 *paperback*
      978 1 85235 529 6 *clothbound*

A CIP catalogue record for this book
is available from the British Library.

Contents

Author's Note page 11
Huts and Sheds 13
The Poetry Nonsense: A Docudrama 24
Dark of the Moon 34
The Theatre of the World 44
The Road to Highgate 56
Yeats and the Lights of Dublin 64
Ghosts in the Sunlight 76
Bridging the Gap 81
Bowen on the Box 87
Wind and Limb 95
Sad Wings 106
An Open Secret 115
The Strings are False 121
MacNeice, 'the War' and the BBC 127
Human Resources 135
Olivia Manning 142
Dying to Get Home 146
Prospects of the Sea 149
Whale and Pelican 160
Paws 165
The Sadness Lurks So Deep 170
Against the Snow 175
A Given World 179
An Unflinching Gaze 185
Gin and Cloud 190
Life as Story Told 197
Wild Bunches 200
J. G. Farrell 209
Everything for Keeps 211
A House Remembers 215
If Only 220
War and Peace 224
The Coleraine Triangle 229
Dublin in the Sixties 234
A Ghostly Rumble among the Drums 237
Icarus in the Ignorance Age 241

Anne Madden: A Retrospective 244
The Mystery Intact 252
The Pied Piper 260
Going the Distance 264
Indian Ink 268

for Terence Brown and Gerald Dawe

Author's Note

When *Journalism* (1996) came out from The Gallery Press the novelist Aidan Higgins wrote to offer, with characteristic subtlety, congratulations on 'a fine vein of captious equivocation'. Praise indeed; but, as we know, old-fashioned literary journalism is on the way out, what with the internet and so on. We salvage what we can. Some of these pieces have expanded from review to essay length. Others — Swift, Dylan Thomas — were written as introductions in the Faber Poet to Poet series. The Jaccottet piece introduced *Words in the Air*, a translated selection of his work, the MacDonogh piece (re)introduced his *Poems*: both of them Gallery books, 1998 and 2001 respectively. 'The Strings are False' prefaced a reissue (Faber 2007) of Louis MacNeice's book of the same title. But the present selection is not about writing only: photography, art and travel are here too. It could even be read as random fragments of autobiography. As it took shape I realized it was starting to look like a book of memoirs.

Huts and Sheds

There used to be jokes about North-South checkpoints and customs huts in Fermanagh and South Armagh, stories based on the physical absence of an actual Border. (This was before things started getting rough in the late 1960s.) Teenage cycling days proved the point. The phantom frontier was topographically non-existent yet somehow present. The huts or sheds were often deserted, during the local 'rush' hour for example. Only briefly disturbed by a strangely sinister air they seemed to emanate, you sailed blithely past on your Rudge or Raleigh into the other jurisdiction; but these huts inscribed themselves photographically on the memory. Even at the time they symbolized their period, like the air-raid shelters and empty airfield hangars left over from the 'last' war. So too the ready-made structures thrown up to accommodate Belfast families made homeless by the Luftwaffe in the spring of 1941. The prefabs on the Shore Road, site offices in High Street, nightwatchmen's shelters on waste ground, each with its charcoal brazier: huts and sheds of all shapes and sizes were a significant part of the landscape for some years and provoked a peculiar excitement over and above their drab functionalism. They spoke of recent disaster and an indeterminate future. As children we didn't think about the future of course. We lived in the day, roaming among the broken bricks and rubble, gleeful amid the ruins. The provisional was our world, and we loved it. Soon there were other kinds of hut: the hen-houses behind 'Hilltop', my grandparents' crazy retirement farmhouse, since demolished, high up on the eastern, seaward-facing slope of the Cave Hill, and the Girl Guide 'hall' behind St Peter's Church on the Antrim Road, abode of mysteries; school bicycle sheds and supposedly temporary wooden annexes where languages were taught at Belfast 'Inst'; changing rooms, caddie shacks, phone boxes.

According to RTÉ News, another man has been 'shot to death' in

Derek Mahon

Dublin. Not just shot dead, mark you, but thoroughly shot to death. Now *The Irish Times* (1/4/11), in equally uncompromising transatlantic mode, reports that the Dún Laoghaire golf club is to be 'torn' down. Not taken down or even knocked down, but positively *torn* down: 'Demolition of the old Golf Club pavilion, which dates from 1910, has been approved as part of the next phase of housing development on the former course.' There will be new 'homes'; also offices and 'retail units'. (As if to pre-empt the conservationists, it has since been 'maliciously' *burnt* down, early on a Sunday morning wouldn't you know.) I've never set eyes on the place but I can imagine it, and I feel a pang of vicarious nostalgia. I've known these old clubhouses since my teens, when I walked with my father the fairways of Antrim and Down. (Golf, in those days, wasn't the showy, expensive business it later became.) The low-ceilinged buildings were always pleasantly shabby, though of more interest to a boy were the huts and sheds, wood and tin, added as living quarters for machinery, spades, tyres and hoses, scythes and shears, repair kits and spare parts of various kinds, oil cans, odd spiky shoes, gnarled gloves and retired or injured woods and irons, some with the grips unwinding. But these were privileged glimpses. Mostly these places, these tiny palaces, were kept locked and were the more mysterious in that condition, too basic even for asbestos, much less the imbricated pantiles and elaborate weatherboards of more sophisticated structures. I'm not talking here about red-cedar gazebos and plastic summer houses or the unaesthetic materials on show in contemporary garden centres, though no doubt these will take on patina in time. No, I mean your old-fashioned hermetic box unknown to the catalogues, so unadorned as to seem like a reproach to anything comfortable or decorative. Not just 'garden furniture', these real old-style huts and sheds aren't made any more but they're still around, behind houses, up lanes, on beaches and in open fields.

The difference between a hut and a shed? A hut you could live in, a shed not, though both foster extraneous reflection. Reverie, says Gaston Bachelard in *The Poetics of Space (La poétique de l'espace*, tr. Maria Jolas, 1964), is 'not a mental vacuum; it is rather the gift of an hour which knows the plenitude of the soul'. Sites of reverie: sun porches, empty houses, windows, rivers, 'mobile homes' on

Huts and Sheds

bricks, huts and sheds. Other places too, anywhere really; but the hut, the shed, are refuge and escape. Known or unknown unknowns, immune to market forces, they offer their own spatial poetics. Bachelard again: 'The hut, a centre of legend, can receive none of the riches "of this world"; it possesses the felicity of intense poverty.' They have been with us, in one form or another, since Diogenes. Christ was born in a shed. Beloved, outside and in, by artists and writers, farmers and groundsmen, swimmers and lovers, their mysterious presence recurs in the art of the ages. The Giotto fresco known as 'Joachim's Dream' features a strikingly modern-looking hut. There are good sheds in Bruegel and Giorgione. American art, enamoured of the provisional, is full of them, and related structures, from log cabins and barns to Hopper's roadside filling station. The camera loves them, including the film camera. Westerns make ample use of them. Does Chaplin's wobbly cabin in *The Gold Rush* qualify? The memory of hard times seems never to have left them; they remember Eumaeus the Swineherd's hut where Odysseus found shelter, and the mountain retreats of the T'ang poets. Sometimes they retain vestiges of religious significance, still potent today, like the monastic 'beehive' huts on Sceilg Mhichíl. Or of pagan significance, like opaque Heidegger's *Dasein* thinking 'hut' (in fact a substantial chalet) in the Black Forest, and the gamekeeper's hut in *Lady Chatterley's Lover*: 'a secret little clearing, and a secret little hut made of rustic poles'; Dick's 'work house' in *Tender is the Night,* a converted stable in the garden at Tarmes where he can be alone and write his book. Dylan Thomas's widow Caitlin described his famous workplace as 'a humble shed nesting high above the estuary' at Laugharne. Interesting things happen in huts and sheds; don't spoil it with phones and digitry.

We approach them with curiosity, with trepidation, even with reverence. Michael Longley's poem 'The Hut' describes, in an evident paradox, 'A windy, wide-open snug, a shrine to daylight'. (He writes elsewhere of a 'subconscious cottage'.) This is the exterior we're looking at, the isolated, visible framework. It promises homecoming and simplicity. The materials must be old: ideally knotty, stained planks or corrugated iron with patches of blistered olive paint and rust around the edges. The inside is a different story, there might be danger there. Bothy and trailer; beach huts of Essex and Brittany;

Derek Mahon

thatched huts of India, as once of Connemara, Raj compounds where wind dances with the ghosts of Inniskillings and Black Watch. Shanty towns, African huts. An Achebe character reclines 'on a mud bed in his hut, playing the flute'. Ngũgĩ wa Thiong'o speaks of 'the oilskin of the house' and describes a shed hospital where 'black soot hung from the roof in strings as if ready to fall'. Greenhouses, kiosks, vans broken down and permanently at rest; shipping containers the size of buses; shipping containers *for* buses, half the size of ships: these, we are told, are 'memes'. OED, latest edition, *meme*: 'An element of a culture transmissible by non-genetic means, e.g. by imitation.' Or is it just a trendy word for custom, a flip relation of phoneme? A hut, together with its analogues, is mimetic, memetic, of domestic space and perhaps most dramatic when it really is a domestic space — as in Jennifer Johnston's novel *The Old Jest*, to which I'll return. It hoards the privacy and mystery of domestic spaces, but we appreciate it first from the outside. I'm looking at a picture by Angie Shanahan called 'A Disused Shed in Co Cork', acrylic on canvas. It shows a country road near Clonakilty, pine trees, a few square yards of rough grass and an olive-green corrugated-iron shed, one tin gable-end dead centre, the roof shining with pale afternoon sunlight. Down in a corner is a Castrol drum, probably empty. It's quite a big shed, perhaps 20 x 10 ft., but no more than 10 ft. high; wider than it's long, it has the general air of a garage. It was once a milk depot. The door is shut and I see no lock or handle, but they must be at least notionally there. Bachelard, in his chapter 'The Dialectics of Outside and Inside', emphasizes the importance of doors, each one in life an image of 'hesitation, temptation, desire, security, welcome and respect'. But outside is about inside, the silent drama, 'intimate immensity'.

A cave dream. Claustrophobic, I'm required to enter a natural tunnel in the side of a cliff. The tunnel narrows till I have to crawl on hands and knees, the ceiling inches above my head. (I hate this, but it has to be done.) I 'think', in the dream, of mineshafts, coalfaces, of Delphi or Cumae or somewhere like that (my, what an erudite dream!), and the tumuli at Newgrange and Loughcrew, but you can be upright there. Not here. After some minutes of terror I emerge into an inner chamber, room-size, much better, where a circle of unidentified folks is sitting round a fire talking. What's going on?

Huts and Sheds

An extended family get-together? A religious rite? Group therapy? They're wearing furs and hides. Are they eating, drinking? They look round at me curiously, and there the dream ends. I know that, much against my will, I have to join in and talk to these people. Nothing short of complete candour will do. There's obviously something primitive and archetypal about this, and no doubt a Freudian interpretation would explain a lot, none of it flattering. Besides the mineshafts and so on I think, later, of Plato's Cave; but my cave people had a knowing air, they were under no illusions. Presumably we talked and then I left to get on with my life — that tunnel again! — a changed life perhaps. I know I was meant to learn something important.

sitôt sorti de l'ermitage
ce fut le calme après l'orage

Beckett's couplet involves a witticism: the calm not before but *after* the storm. The hermit emerges with a lighter heart, or at least peace of mind; but what was the inner storm about? Huts evolved from the example of the cave, I suppose, and something of the cave remains with them. They invite us to mine, to mind, our human resources and put ourselves in order.

In search of peace and quiet, and with a 'firm purpose of amendment', I once spent a Christmas of recreational seclusion at a Cistercian monastery in Co Waterford. I started badly by presenting the abbot with a bottle of Hennessy. 'We'll save it for when the bishop comes,' he said, not very pleased. I was told about the refectory and given a slammer with a hard bed watched over by a reproduction of Leonardo's St Anne. I'd intended staying a fortnight but left after a week, the noisiest week I've ever spent. Bells rang day and night to call the monks to prayer; there was scarcely a wink of sleep to be had. Soon as I got to town I drank a large gin and felt better at once. So much for the firm purpose of amendment; so much for communal spirituality. No, you have to be on your own for that sort of thing, you have to be Protestant about it. I went back to the temporal world, not having fooled the Cistercians for one minute. A hut is the answer, or in this case a stable loft over an old coach house, within sight of the sea. The sea because it's the

Derek Mahon

opposite of a hut — not a mansion, but the sea. Seclusion is more expressive next to the oceanic, as the old poets knew:

> *A thonnsa thíos is airde géim go hard,*
> *meabhair mo chinnse cloíte ód bhéiceach tá.*
>
> *(High wave below there howling the whole night long,*
> *you drive me crazy with your plaintive song.)*

Another of Angie's pictures shows a ramshackle boatyard shack, in a terminal state of disrepair, facing into the same sunlight as her 'Shed' — light, on the point of decline, shining off the sea with a late-afternoon poignancy. Nothing lasts: soon, we know, the shack will be 'torn' down.

There's a different atmosphere inside a hut, mixed scents of creosote, paraffin, turpentine, sawdust and nicotine. Also a different soundtrack, a sanctuary silence or something by Ligeti: *Lux Aeterna? Clocks and Clouds?* You could spend days in there, reading and dreaming. Not mornings, perhaps, when the body wants to be active; but certainly afternoons, hut time, when the hours move slowly. A window, preferably grimy, is important, or better still a skylight with bird droppings and dead flies. Evenings could be a problem: as light fades the nerves grow restive, we turn to thoughts of society. A TV, unless ancient and worn out, would be incongruous, though a radio might help. (I'm assuming, for the moment, solitude.) The psycho-geography of huts and sheds. I lived for a year in that stable loft but haven't slept in a real hut or shed since I was young. Night, I remember, is a magical time. If moon or stars are visible so much the better, though wind and rain are no bad thing. In fact they can only contribute to the negative capability, the existential peace or void, whichever. Staring out of the dark like a dog in the dog-house, you can be consciously part of the universe, one with the forces of random, violent nature yet fairly safe. Safe enough to sleep, at any rate, and wake to whatever sort of morning it is as to a world made new, at any age:

> *The Soul's dark Cottage, batter'd and decay'd,*
> *Lets in new Light thro' chinks that Time hath made.*

Huts and Sheds

A fascination with huts and other modest interiors is a curious and recurrent feature of 20th-century 'Anglo-Irish' fiction and has complex sources. 'A house remembers,' says Edna O'Brien. 'An outhouse remembers.' While most were thinking in terms of better living conditions, offspring of the Big House, or at least of the biggish house, like Yeats and Synge, developed an intense emotional interest in the traditional cottage and subsidiary structures, often connected to the Big House as gate lodge or utility room. There was a touch of social voyeurism in this, together with an obscure longing for intimacy and absolution, as if grace and truth lay there and not in their own drawing rooms. Such places carried a powerful charge for some of these writers. The urge could be life-changing, sometimes problematic.

As recently as the sixties and seventies, though in flashback to an earlier time, 1920 and thereabouts, J. G. Farrell and Jennifer Johnston, to name but two, were still exploring the implications. Martin Sands, in Farrell's early novel *The Lung* (1965), remembers 'the door of a disused potting shed he had once opened and the long sickly white shoots racing each other interminably across the earth floor towards the minute bead of light from the keyhole. Tulips, or seed potatoes, or merely some anonymous weeds, it was impossible to tell. Perhaps by now one of them had reached the keyhole and, obstructing it, had condemned the others to death in darkness, only to expire itself in an unaccustomed blaze of sunshine.' Sands, like his author, has been singled out for a debilitating impediment. The passage is autobiographical, reflecting Farrell's experience of hospitals and serious medicine, but the historical resonances seem obvious enough. *The Lung* was set in England; *Troubles* (1970) is set in Ireland. Towards the end the protagonist, Brendan Archer ('the Major'), tours the kitchen garden and stables of the Big House he is soon to leave. 'They were empty, as were the garages and outhouses. The door of the barn was open, so he peered in ... Someone had been here recently. Dust hung in the air and, where the sun touched it, blazed like a furnace. On each side the towering banks of hay had a grey look, as if cut many years ago and abandoned. But there was no one here now.' Except there is, a man in hiding who knocks Brendan unconscious, drags him away and leaves him for dead: a 'Shinner' presumably, though never identified.

Derek Mahon

Another subversive hideout figures in Johnston's *The Old Jest* (1979), where young Nancy Gulliver (of the biggish house) discovers, half buried in sand, 'a rectangular wooden hut with a sloping roof' built by railway workers years before. She scrubs the floor, puts up bookshelves and oils the rusty door hinges: 'She had wondered about painting the walls but decided against it. Gentility was not her aim.' In flight from the gentility of her biggish house, she finds in the hut a clue to her life. Thought an orphan, she comes home to her lost father's den; for he, a noticeably urbane Shinner on the run, has moved in and made himself at home when she wasn't looking. There's a wealth of meaning here: the lost daughter, the father lost and found, their politically complicated relationship, the symbolism of the hut itself, the provisional nature of home.

Jim Farrell's biographer, Lavinia Greacen, writes to report a garden shed with 'a forgotten, padded double swing-seat stored inside' where as a girl she would sit for hours reading Poe 'to my detriment after dark ever since'; and she remembers 'a faint butterflies-in-the-tummy sensation' on approaching huts and sheds, derived from 'the lure of elderly sports sheds' at her Sussex school. The sensation remains, she says, 'visceral' — a key word in this context. A hut is to a man as a handbag is to a woman, said somebody once in the days of 'handbags'. The gender of huts? The human form has often been visualized as a house, stored with memories conscious and unconscious. A contemporary question: despite their ascetic reputation, are huts *sexy*? Do they, in fact, promise the snug enclosure of the womb? Are we dealing with the erotic here? With 'regression'? Agoraphobia? The death wish, 'As a man in spring desires to die in woman' (MacNeice)? Does a wooden hut represent at some level the cradle, the grave? In regressive dreams, says Freud, the thought fabric is resolved into its raw material by a revival of childhood perceptions. Behind this childhood lies 'a picture of the development of the human race' and its 'archaic heritage'. I've noticed these things too; probably most of us have. The hut, a true dream home, takes us back to the cave, the Platonic firelight and TV screen. We hide there from the noisy world as our ancestors hid from the wildlife. A house is trite; even in the age of the urban fox, it's too much insulated from nature, you don't get the thrill of the interface, the *precarious* safety of the edge. Intimations of sex 'n'

Huts and Sheds

violence, that's what we like. About tents I've nothing to say except that they blow away.

(These are sensitive areas.) It's been noted that the homes of the rural poor in 19th-century Ireland could compare unfavourably with slave quarters in the American South. While conditions must have varied greatly, old photographs and personal observation bear this out. At Jonesboro, Ga., ten miles or so from Atlanta and not far from where the fictional Tara 'stood' in Margaret Mitchell's *Gone with the Wind,* slave quarters have been preserved in a field behind a similar edifice, perhaps Mitchell's model, 'a whitewashed brick plantation house', nothing fancy as in the film. Slavery, the Peculiar Institution oddly described by John Crowe Ransom as 'monstrous in theory but humane enough in practice', seems to have provided, in this instance at least, tolerable (but only tolerable) sleeping arrangements. These consisted, consist, of a dozen or so wooden buildings resembling, at first glance, large raised family-size hen-houses. You might almost be looking at an abandoned holiday camp. Asylum seekers in Ireland were housed in the former Butlin's at Mosney, Co Meath, and seem to have liked it enough to resist dispersal; but Ransom's 'monstrosity' was just that, though no doubt some breezy Southern owners sought to beguile their Africans with the prospect of a new life on the plantations. Slave huts won't do, for obvious reasons. Nor will holiday camps. Institutionalized confinement and disorientation are the very opposite of what proper huts instil. That said, it's heartening to note, for example, Joseph Brodsky's feelings about his eighteen-month relegation to Norenskaya, which suited him fine at a critical point in his life. True, he got to pick his own hut, he could write and receive visitors. This wasn't the gulag, though intended as punishment for 'social parasitism'. A long sentence (initially seven years) to hard labour in sub-Arctic conditions is hardly a rest cure. Still, he came away fit and purposeful, and never complained. What doesn't kill you makes you stronger.

What sort of thoughts visit the hutted mind? Disgraceful thoughts, metaphysical thoughts, revolutionary thoughts like those of Rilke (yes, *Rilke*) in *The Notebook of Malte Laurids Brigge* (1910, Linton's translation 1930): 'I am learning to see. I don't know why, but

Derek Mahon

everything penetrates more deeply within me and no longer stops where, until now, it always used to finish. I possess an inner self of which I was ignorant . . . Here I sit in my little room, I, Brigge . . . I sit here and am nothing. And nevertheless this nothing begins to think, is it possible that nothing real or important has yet been seen or known or said? Is it possible that despite our culture, religion and worldly wisdom, we still remain on the surface of life? Is it possible that the whole history of the world has been misunderstood? Yes, it is possible . . . But if all this is possible then surely something must be done. The first comer, he who has had these disturbing thoughts, must begin to do some of the neglected things.' He's not in a hut, he's in a Paris hotel, but these are hutty thoughts, the rum thoughts of one who has lived in huts, read too many books, perhaps cast too cold an eye. (The flight from coldness can itself be cold.) Why is the beautiful world such an awful place in so many ways? Naive question. Original sin? Why can we never seem to get it right? Reality itself is at risk. Try putting it into words and the head spins, though we have to try. Or do we? One solution might be to refuse to doubt the real. Ignore the celebrity thinkers, the media, the triumph of virtuality. Get rid of the gadgets, ditch the digits. Resist conventional wisdom; in some sense start again. Not literally in mud huts perhaps (though there are those who prefer mud huts) but in primordial huts of the mind, in shady sheds of imagination thrown up outside the office blocks and hideous new developments. People before profit, please, art before artifice; and much less noise. We need a new, wittier music, 'outside the box', to replace the square, four-time, econometric pop currently dominant, with its pretence of insurrection. There are, or there used to be, better ways of doing it.

Historically we preferred a closed cosmos, one with walls and a starred ceiling. Unnerved or over-excited by chaos and infinity, and still at some level trusting in the 'argument from design', the imagination rests in structure, containment. An enclosed space offers both physical and emotional security. It's an archetype, perhaps *the* archetype, if often enough a sentimental one. It has the provocative fascination of the exclusive, the prestige of the seemingly impenetrable; it shuts us out or shuts others out. Answering to the need for spiritual privacy, it's a model of the anthropocentric universe. I'm not complaining. Berkeley's 'To be is to be perceived' falls short in the absence of a divine Supervisor; life goes on independently of mind. We know that at any given moment a wave is breaking, a tree dying; but besides the natural world we live in the human one, in a 'built environment'. We must attend to our own needs too, among them the need to hide and to make our own magic; and huts are magical. *You can't be seen.* Big Brother isn't watching you. Not even Google Earth can reach you — yet.

Build your own shed, your own hut house! A new outfit, one of many, offers for sale solar-powered, eco-friendly hut-size buildings to be used as workshops, studios, extra accommodation or 'sole residence', in the form of a kit or ready for occupancy. Benefits include low energy consumption and light ecological footprint (turf roof, *silence*); 'blends well into the natural environment'. Design your own *Dasein*! This isn't the kind of thing that advertises itself with fabrics in a range of colours and styles, with coordinated roof and window blinds and stylish lighting systems. No, this is an honest house, perhaps the house of the future when the mortgage will be a period curiosity; we are one step from the final hut which is the human frame itself, however imperfect or derelict. 'When one has lived a long time alone,' says the American poet Galway Kinnell, thinking of his place in Vermont, one indulges the other creatures, one hears the birds as inner voices; you realize you're there to 'hear them into shining'. How long is a long time? How long is a piece of string? 'Give me a break,' said a lady who stands no nonsense. 'He hasn't slept alone for twenty years.' But a day can be a long time on your own. The point is the solitude, the disposition it creates. In some it will induce cabin fever, in others peace of mind and enhanced concentration; one or two will be granted singular insight. The riches of this world will be found in a handful of dust or the faint stir of a cobweb. A hut is magical. When we leave it we take it with us, grateful and safe in the knowledge that, even if torn down, it is always there.

The Poetry Nonsense: A Docudrama

The Poetry Nonsense (Ire, 2010, 62 min). CarAnna Prods, *d* Roger Greene. *p* Donald Taylor Black. *sc* Derek Mahon. *ph* Nick O'Neill. *s* Darby Carroll. *ed* Maurice Healy. *cast* Seamus Heaney, Michael Longley, Patricia Craig etc.

'When are you going to give up the poetry nonsense?' my father used to ask. I can answer him now, in my seventieth year, by saying I've finally put it behind me or very nearly. The task is done, and now I can turn to prose with an easy mind. An easy mind? This film, made for TV, tells only a fraction of the story, but certain things stood out in the making of it, fascinating to do and fascinating to think about — 'for me', that is, in the egotistic locution recently prevalent. The opening sequence for example. Equipped with modest development funds from the Irish Arts Council and Film Board, we started in Portrush, Co Antrim, at one of the most beautiful buildings in Northern Ireland: the old Arcadia ballroom on the rocks overlooking the West Strand. The Arcadia is long past its heyday; in fact, it appears not to be a dancehall any more. It was once a famous venue, for locals and visitors both. Well-known bands played there in the fifties and sixties. At Easter and in the summer months young people flocked in their hundreds to bop to the music of Dave Glover and the like. ('Easter in Portrush' was always a potent phrase.) Now the neon sign is gone and the paint flaking in the sea air. The doors are heavily padlocked, in winter at least.

It was winter when we were there: November. We'd picked up the writer Patricia Craig to act as interlocutor. The biographer of Brian Moore among other things, Pat Craig is a historian of Ulster writing, with the added advantage of being good on TV. We walked along the strand into a biting wind while the team did their stuff, from the White Rocks to the Arcadia. Why the Arcadia? Once, as 'Writer in Residence' at the university in Coleraine, I'd had a flat

The Poetry Nonsense: A Docudrama

for a year in Craigvara House, just up the path, where I wrote a poem called 'Rock Music', read by the author in voice-over. The sea tumbled and crashed while Edna Longley, also in VO, explained the sea's importance as a symbol. It's a famous stretch of sea from there to Scotland, historic and picturesque with islands. Portrush, like everywhere picturesque, gets its share of aspiring writers; but the true culture hero in these parts was the poet James Simmons. Jimmy taught at the university. His vitality was everywhere in evidence. When he wasn't teaching he was producing plays or singing upstairs in the pubs with his Resistance Cabaret. His poetry makes good use of a long familiarity with the song repertoire from Thomas Moore to Irving Berlin to Joan Baez. Performative expectations gave his work that debonair virtuosity and insolent ease. An art-deco transport art of cars and trains, it seems to remember an old futurist belief in the superiority of the racing car over the Winged Victory of Samothrace. (Upmarket car design owes much to the Winged Victory.) Car rallies take place around here. Motorbike races too: the North West 200 is a great event each May, filling the air for days with the exciting fumes of Castrol GTX. But there's more to Simmons than the entertainment value of 'energy to burn'. His was a radical presence on the Ulster scene, combining the academic and the demotic as MacNeice so often did; and part of the fun lay in his grandiose, tongue-in-cheek assumption of provincial celebrity status:

> *I helped create the free hygienic mind*
> *rid of the guilt and infantile self-hate*
> *that we were subject to; but now I find*
> *this world too kindly to the second-rate.*

I'd wanted to pause in Cushendun, site of innocent young romance, but stormy weather made it impractical to film there, so we drove on down to Belfast where I 'grew up'. It was the first time I'd been in Salisbury Avenue for many years, so we lingered there for a bit. Not even the constant presence of the subject-narrator, looking older than previously thought, diminishes that moment ('for me'). We are opposite the old tram depot, where a lane runs off behind a row of houses. You can see up to the Cave Hill and down to the Antrim Road. There's a privet hedge there, undis-

Derek Mahon

turbed since 'the War', where our gang used to gather; young love has been inscribed on garage doors. We are on the edge of Brian Moore country, which stretches up this way from Donegall Street. I'm not thinking of *Judith Hearne*, set on the other side of town, off University Road, but of his other Belfast books — some of which, at least in part, take place in adjoining neighbourhoods. It was a 'mixed' area and our gang was mixed until we went to different schools and somehow, mysteriously, ceased to run around together. Nick O'Neill, his camera work remarkable for its unusual angles and serendipities, made a road movie as we drove into town and out east to the Harland & Wolff shipyard where my father once worked. Nick's camera watched the streets, picking up some of the twilight-zone dereliction Gerald Dawe calls 'a powerful local statement of a global condition', and found on the skyline the two immense yellow gantries, Samson and Goliath (Samson and Delilah, said Darby Carroll).

The present shipyard is in itself a powerful statement. Once employing 20,000, it now employs a tenth of that and, like so much else in the post-industrial world, is trying to turn itself into a retro 'experience' to draw tourists. With this in mind, a small area has been retained in something like its original form, externally at least, comprising the dry dock where the *Titanic* was fitted out and its adjoining Pump House, now a plasticky café for visitors. The Dry Dock, seen lengthwise at least, looks disappointingly short, though this is a trick of perspective. The great opening sequence of *A Night to Remember* (1958), produced by Bill McQuitty, a Bangor man, used old footage of the ninety tons of chain that scrambled after the hull as it slid into Belfast Lough. (This, not the Cameron tosh, was the real *Titanic* film, though everything was a bit too idealistic.) The yard is *clean* now and tidied up; there is no sense of work, and indeed there is little work to do. When my father showed me around in 1960, shocking me with a pin-up on his office wall, weeds choked the cracks and windows were dark with grime. Now, in a further refinement of *sic transit*, the place is as bright and shiny as a Belfast place can be, serving only to emphasize the vacuum and the attenuation of real historical memory. The men of the family trained here as marine engineers and spent the War Years, 1939-45, in merchant ships of the Head Line (*Torr Head* etc) of Belfast, and other freight companies, on the North

The Poetry Nonsense: A Docudrama

Atlantic convoys to Nova Scotia and points south. An uncle was torpedoed but not seriously. Some had been as far as China and Japan before the war. They never saw combat, properly speaking, but their uniform caps and jackets, navy and white, hung neglected and eloquent in domestic wardrobes after they 'came ashore'. My grandfather claimed to have slept through the Battle of Jutland (1916); otherwise there is no real heroism in the family record — which shamed me slightly with other boys whose fathers had flown with the RAF or served with 'Monty' in the desert.

Next stop the grave of Louis MacNeice at Christ Church (Church of Ireland), Carrowdore, hidden away up a quiet side road inland from Millisle, Co Down. I was there first in, I think, March of 1964. MacNeice had died the previous September. We'd driven down — Seamus Heaney, Mike Longley, Davy Hammond and myself, in Seamus's blue VW — to find a family headstone not yet bearing the name of Louis. A friend of MacNeice, the Belfast artist George McCann (Maguire in *Autumn Sequel*) was proposing to carve a blackbird there in low relief, and a line from Euripides (probably something from the *Bacchae*), but this was never done: perhaps there wasn't room. Instead there's an oddly inappropriate quote from one of MacNeice's own poems, 'The Suicide'. MacNeice didn't commit suicide; but the grotesquerie is of a piece with the Irish tradition of funerary confusion. George McCann was said to have mislaid, initially, the urn containing the ashes, in a London pub or perhaps at Heathrow. If so, he was only contributing to the graveyard comedy of lost remains and the like which goes back beyond Synge and Swift to medieval times at least. The 20th century provided a lingering doubt about the authenticity of Yeats's bones at Drumcliff, the fate of the hero's dust in Beckett's *Murphy* (another pub floor) and familial fights, involving moonlit interference, over the grave of Patrick Kavanagh. It's part of the merry history, a feature of Irish Gothic. The ashes of MacNeice's widow Hedli who, according to the incumbent rector, was drunk at her husband's interment, are there too. The church is handsome, the view spectacular. After our visit in the blue VW each of the three poets contemplated an elegy. I was the least busy with other things, so I got mine written first and gave it the title 'In Carrowdore Churchyard'. There was much wrong with it, especially in the second verse which suggested, erroneously, that there would be no

Derek Mahon

new publication of work from MacNeice's pen. Since then we've had, among other things, *The Strings are False* and expanded editions of the *Collected Poems*. The Maguire reference is unclear. The 'bombed-out town' seems to evoke Belfast at a later date, not the London Blitz as I intended. These things have been put right in the present version. This may displease some who know the original: which raises the question of revision, its ethics and aesthetics.

Some, like MacNeice, didn't and don't believe in revision; others, like Yeats and Auden (Auden to a sometimes ruinous extent), have seen a need for it in their own work. Samuel Daniel, the Elizabethan, put it like this:

> *And howsoever be it, well or ill,*
> *What I have done, it is mine own, I may*
> *Do whatsoever therewithal I will.*
> *   I may pull down, raise, and reedify.*
> *It is the building of my life, the fee*
> *Of Nature, all th'inheritance that I*
> *Shall leave to those which must come after me.*

The tone is a little off-putting. There is too much 'for me' about it, like those who say they write to please themselves, and the idea of poetry as *property* is an ungenerous one: 'intellectual property' (horrible phrase!) I suppose. Work with copyright in mind and you won't fly very high. (Daniel flies high elsewhere.) My work is not 'mine own', it belongs to its readers too, if any, and it's important to do one's best by the reader. So, whatever old friends may think, factual inaccuracies and unnecessary obscurities need clearing up; a poem will mostly be the better for it. Is it a sophistry to say that a poem is never finished, only abandoned? What if it hadn't been published in the first place? Except for that unfortunate quotation over MacNeice's grave, nothing is written in stone; we write not on stone but on paper. Coleridge would have agreed.

A serious criticism of the film script is that there isn't enough about the poetry nonsense itself: aside from a few smart remarks from academic friends and some reminiscent chat with the Longleys, the closest we get is a trip to Highgate. Sitting in the Yorkminster pub in Soho (the 'French House'), Hugh Haughton and I decided to take a look at Coleridge's place in Highgate Grove — James

The Poetry Nonsense: A Docudrama

Gillman's really (No. 3), where STC spent his last years. It was a misty day, appropriately: Coleridge described himself as a 'philosopher in a mist', and a mist hung over St Michael's Church. If anyone ever believed in the poetry nonsense it was he. Old J. B. Yeats, father of all the Yeatses, proclaimed, in a letter to his poet son, that the world would 'not be right' until life itself was recognized as poetry — a view poets instinctively, if secretly, endorse. Coleridge isn't buried at St Michael's, by the way, as I say in the film, but (like Marx and Freud) in Highgate Cemetery.

Nothing in the film about my time, formative I suspect, as a choirboy at St Peter's (Church of Ireland) in the shadow of the Cave Hill. We wore stiff collars and white surplices, had choir practice on Wednesday nights and 'sang' at Sunday morning and evening services. God had nothing to do with it; we were in it for the money such as it was: ten bob each for a wedding, that sort of thing. (Oscar Wilde, asked about his religion, said that he hadn't one, he was an Irish Protestant.) The prosperous Antrim Road congregation, with their Armstrong Siddeleys and tweed suits, were the local Unionist Party at prayer. The then rector, an austere figure name of Breen, would remind his parishioners from the pulpit (as if they needed reminding) to 'support the Government' at upcoming elections. But the hymns were great, and remain with me to this day: 'Be Thou My Vision', 'Praise, My Soul, the King of Heaven', 'Ye Holy Angels Bright' and many more. During sermons (boring, boring) we studied from various angles the incredibly filthy drawings executed by previous choristers in the endpapers of our Church Hymnals, but on one occasion I pricked up my ears when Breen mentioned the name Frank Sinatra. He was giving off about a song he'd heard on the 'wireless' that morning: 'I've Got the World on a String'. As it happens I now share his distaste for Sinatra, but his view seemed, at the time, notably stuffy. God alone, he said, had the world on a string. The medieval image lingered after I'd finished blinking at the idea of Dr Breen listening to Sinatra on the wireless. Seamus, of the blue VW, uses a similar image.

Another 'powerful local statement' was the inter-tribal conflict (three tribes including the Brits) that raged for so many years; but I wasn't there. We watched it on TV from our flat in London. I say 'we' because I was married by then. We, the Mahons, lived in Kensington, off Campden Hill Road; we, the film crew, went back there in a hired car and shuffled around the neighbourhood: Holland Street, Hyde Park. I'd first met Doreen when we were both students at Trinity College, Dublin, in the sixties, a very special time; but my script is at fault in spending too long in the grounds of Trinity. The undergraduate courses lasted four years but I'd lived in London, off and on, much longer than that. Ezra Pound, before the first world war, described Observatory Gardens as the ugliest row of houses in the city, though it's long since been superseded in that regard. It was an eyesore, in that pleasant neighbourhood, but the rent was low for a five-room duplex, and it was a great place to be. The Turret Bookshop in Church Walk, where Pound once lived, provided a social centre. At the frequent parties there you would run into other writers, media people and the like, some of them quite famous. The Liverpool poets — Patten, McGough, Henri — were regular visitors; less often Christopher Logue, Alex Trocchi or Lawrence Durrell put in an appearance. Diplomatic relations were in place with the Chelsea Arts Club, so we got some of them too.

'One day the old grow young,' said Pete Townshend — in this agreeing for once with Beckett, who took great pleasure in a second childhood, though he didn't put it quite like that. Whatever the creaks and groans, those of us who reach the seventy mark find ourselves walking with a lighter tread. Responsibilities drop away. The body, having survived the years of wear and tear, can perhaps be trusted not to let us down; and the mind comes into its own. A certain type of older man (Yeats called them 'golden codgers'), whether through sex, heredity, swimming or simple diet, seems to revel in a youthful old age. There are plenty of older women like this too. Louis-Napoleon's widow, Eugénie, learned to fly in her sixties and died falling from an apple tree in her nineties. The youth cult, promoted by the media for half a century now, blinds us to the geriatric delights. Those who sneer will themselves be sneered at in due course, and meanwhile there are more of us as time goes by and we live longer. I'm tempting fate here, we can drop dead at any minute or be struck down by a stroke, but it's surely better to face the inevitable with a grin than be dragged kicking and screaming. I'm new to old age, I haven't been here before; but it doesn't seem so bad. These chirpy thoughts are prompted by certain reminiscential scenes in the docudrama: the West Strand at Portrush, where as a boy I

The Poetry Nonsense: A Docudrama

found the skeleton of a seagull and understood, or thought I did, mortality; the Trinity cobbles where I knew so many beautiful people; the London places where for a few years Doreen and I, in a *folie à deux*, were hectic and thought ourselves happy. I've often considered, like many another, trying to write some kind of an autobiography; but we remember selectively, and there's too much to be ashamed of. This film is the nearest I've got and, as I say, it's only a fraction of the whole: a cover-up job, even. Nothing about parents, really; nothing about the children; nothing about the bad times, of which there were many. I spent five years in New York: nothing, or almost nothing, about New York.

A proposed trip there, and one to Paris, had to be shelved owing to budgetary constraints, so we did Dublin again. Not Trinity this time — enough, already! — but Fitzwilliam Square, where I'd spent five years after five in America. It was during this time, the nineties, that the city transformed itself from the delightful old dump it had always been into an enormous ATM, a coarse simulacrum of any post modern market-driven money machine. Suddenly everything was multinational, bright, shiny, hard-edged and bad-tempered. Some got fiercely rich; suicide rates soared. The building trade (the 'construction industry') boomed. The sky filled with high-rise cranes, the air with dust, curses, car alarms and yellow protective clothing. (This is one more 'global condition' of course: the whole world is a building site.) It became intolerable. I moved to Kinsale, where I'd lived briefly before. Even in the film the change is a relief. Suddenly we are out in the fresh air looking from Charles Fort over a crinkly evening sea with one yacht gliding below. Now that we inhabit a 'post-real' world, says my publisher Peter Fallon, 'I believe poetry prevails as a point of departure not *from* but *to* reality'; and that's what we're working on these days. It feels like a return to rhyme and reason, certainly rhyme, a light-switch quick and predictable to the touch. Be it epic or lyric, rock or rap, rhyme is the pre-linguistic drumbeat, a distant echo in the depths. It goes not only back but down, whence its peculiar potency, and can also help you find what you want to say, as in Henry King's 'Exequy' for his dead wife:

> *But hark! My pulse, like a soft drum,*
> *Beats my approach, tells thee I come;*

Derek Mahon

> *And slow howe'er my marches be*
> *I shall at last sit down by thee.*

Nabokov thought Pasternak's *Doctor Zhivago* a bad novel by a good poet. Perhaps it is, but there are fine things in it (the train journey to Yuriatin). His opinion of the film, if he ever saw it, is not recorded so far as I know. Never judge a book by its screen adaptation. Besides the more serious stuff, there were many such soppy movies in those days, soppy but oddly memorable: Jacques Demy's *Les Parapluies de Cherbourg*, Bo Widerberg's *Elvira Madigan*. We chuckled at the dafter bits in the *Zhivago* film (1965) but, as in the novel, there were good things too: Julie Christie, after all. One of the best moments was when, with Lara and the child asleep on a frosty night, Yury sits down to write poetry. He writes without hesitation, starting with a title, and, Maurice Jarre's too rich soundtrack rising to the occasion, places his perfect lines on the page without strikings-out or second thoughts. (If only!) Curiously, it's also one of the best moments in Pasternak's text. It occurs in Part Two, Chapter 14, 'Again Varykino', section 8, pp. 478-481 in my old Fontana paperback, tr. Hayward and Harari. Lamplight and a full moon establish the mood as Yury sits at his desk. 'Careful to convey the living movement of his hand' as he warms to his task, he sets down some of the unwritten poems in his head, then, getting into his stride, starts on a new one. He has the world on a string. 'He experienced the approach of what is called inspiration. At such moments the correlation of the forces controlling the artist is, as it were, stood on its head. The ascendancy is no longer with the artist . . . but with language [which] itself begins to think and speak . . . by virtue of the power and momentum of its inward flow.' This is a strikingly post-modern idea, one in accord with contemporary linguistic theory. It's also empirically true; Pasternak knew what he was talking about. It's an experience familiar, I suspect, to many writers — to many real writers, I'm tempted to say. Not the writer, but the world, is doing the poetry, decides Yury before, distracted 'by a mournful, dismal sound', he steps out for a breather and notices wolves in the snow, four long shadows 'no thicker than pencil strokes'. This, or something like it, is how it's done, give or take a wolf or two.

Some are born to be poets and nothing else. Some have taught themselves to write poetry, and some are poets by default. We may have wished to be, like Byron, political figures or champion swimmers (he hated authors who were 'all author', or so he said), but poetry is the only thing we're any good at.

> *But now they only block the sun,*
> *Rain and snow on everyone.*
> *So many things I would have done*
> *But clouds got in my way.*
> — Joni Mitchell, 'Both Sides Now', 1971

'So many things I would have done'? Clouds got in my way, certainly, but I was never going to be a revolutionary, a pilot or a singer on the wireless. All author, and not a very prolific one, I've done my best — 'all I can manage, more than I could' — if never enough. Philippe Jaccottet speaks of the 'pure water-drop' of poetry, implicitly contrasting it with the muddy flow of critical theory and the obscure malice of deconstruction: 'Such nonsense (*niaiserie*) to set up against such knowledge, ingenuity, doctrine!' He's talking about the poetry nonsense, the vague, instinctual resistance to a world engineered for the maximum 'efficiency', competitive 'growth', 'global excellence' and 'world-class' foolishness of all kinds. The poetry nonsense sets itself up against regulation, system, utility. It's a last ditch of sanity in a naff world of exploitation and lies. It has no function and no exchange value, unlike art and music. It is indeterminate, marginal, unimportant; and therein lies its importance. What we need is a dimmer, dreamier universe.

Dark of the Moon

One of our set books, now out of print, was the old Everyman anthology entitled *Silver Poets of the Sixteenth Century* (1947), whose inspired editors chose 'silver' rather than 'minor' in order not to be disparaging: 'The least we can claim for them is a silver-tongued eloquence.' Why out of print? There was a reissue in 1992, but fashions and curricula change with the years and great names fall from favour, as the Elizabethans themselves knew to their cost. Now the argent ones, born in the 1550s and 1560s, provoke highly critical responses unknown to previous generations who took 'robust' policies and plaintive sentiments in their stride. We liked Wyatt ('They flee from me'; 'My lute have done') and Raleigh's puzzling 'Cynthia' — Marlowe and Spenser too, though they were something else, not *silver* really, and not in the book. Sidney was a special favourite, not only for the beauty of his verse and the personal note, but also for some unacademic remarks in his *Defence of Poesie*. Unsystematic, truant youth warmed to his argument that, unlike the philosopher, the poet 'beginneth not with obscure definitions, which must blur the margent with interpretations, and load the memory with doubtfulness; but he cometh to you with words set in delightful proportion, either accompanied with, or prepared for, the enchanting skill of music'. He goes back to the beginnings, the *sung* origins of poetry, and indeed one can easily imagine his own work — the songs from *Astrophel and Stella*, for example ('Who is it that this dark night') — set for strings by Dowland and best heard, perhaps, in a starlit garden: what he calls 'the planet-like music of poetry'. The prose poet and closet dramatist Plato, who wished to banish only certain kinds of poet, chiefly the 'imitative' playwright, was behind all this. He speaks of an old quarrel between poetry and philosophy, but this didn't bother the Elizabethans, who managed without philosophers. It was an age of song.

The adventurers, as the Everyman reminds us in the language of

Dark of the Moon

1947, 'combined a ferocious virility with habits which seem to us oddly effeminate, paraded in gorgeous colours and adorned themselves with rings and pearls'. Nor is the 'silver' epithet meta-phorical only. The search for real gold and silver was busily in hand in the Americas, and England's precious-metals race with Spain was a central preoccupation of the era. These minerals, precious owing to scarcity and once credited with magical properties, retained such very real magic that their literary potential imposed itself unignorably. Decorative yes, but almost numinous too, they acted (not for the first or last time) as measures of *spiritual* value. Elizabeth herself, to whom so much of the plunder found its way, was routinely credited with analogous attributes. The reign considered itself a golden age, and there was indeed gold (Spenser, Shakespeare), but silver talents also held the light: Sidney, Daniel, Drayton, Davies and many more. It's been estimated that there were at least thirty versifiers in and out of Elizabeth's court during her long reign, several of whom came to a bad end. The mischief started with *The Courtier* (1571), Thomas Hoby's translation of Castiglione's *Il Cortegiano*, that manual explaining how to get on at Court without really trying, or seeming to try; but your *sprezzatura* could get you into hot water if taken to extremes. Capricious, she liked her favourites bold and bad; she enjoyed a whiff of sulphur, up to a point. With level-headed *mediocrità* you were on safer ground, though Spenser's never did him much good. His aim in *The Faerie Queene* was too didactic: 'to fashion a gentleman or noble person in virtuous discipline', this from a well-known letter to Raleigh. (Was he telling his feral friend to behave himself?)

It would be nice to get the bad behaviour out of the way and concentrate on the poetry, as if they had no connection, except that they derived from the same sources: Plato, Castiglione, and the monarchical idea in its female form, the Protestant version of a proscribed devotion. Sometimes Elizabeth is the sun, sometimes the moon; always she is the receiver of homage, of verses, of tribute, of stolen goods. The gentlemen and noble persons, now often seen as little more than ruffians in ruffs, have had their literature marginalized by current educational wisdom, largely because they spent so much time stealing, or trying to steal, the land and natural mineral rights of the native peoples of what they called 'Virginia' and 'Guiana', now Carolina and Venezuela. Sidney died in the field at

Derek Mahon

Zutphen in 1586 and so had no hand in the later exploitation of the New World. This paragon, despite some soldiering, seems to have been a more peaceable and diplomatic figure than the contemporaries who revered his memory and wrote under his influence. Perhaps the Arcadian family home, Penshurst Place in Kent, had something to do with it. Many of the poems seem to be 'set' there or to be drawing on Penshurst imagery, especially the night pieces. The moon of these night poems, obverse of the golden sun of Elizabethan confidence and expansion — that flickering face there in the corner of the map — is ubiquitous, pervasive, in the poetry of the time. Sir Philip set the fashion:

> *Who is the same, which at my window peeps?*
> *Or whose is that fair face, that shines so bright?*
> *Is it not Cynthia, she that never sleeps*
> *But walks about high heaven all the night?*
> — Spenser, 'Epithalamion'

Sidney's nocturnes ('Come sleep O sleep', 'With how sad steps', but others too) make up a great series, each rhyming easily with light and bright though tortured in syntax, as in the psychological situations they describe. Dark and light, real and ideal, act together to make up a dialectic at once typical and symbolic of the Elizabethan double vision, its romance and violence. Wiltshire-born Davies, later MP for Fermanagh under James I, writes in the dance poem *Orchestra* (1594) about 'our rude age' and, a page later, 'our golden age'. It was both, screech owl and nightingale.

The strongest influence on the Elizabethan chorus was Petrarch, whose *Canzonieri* established a poetic model as Castiglione had provided a political one, and whose Courtly Love procedures they adopted. There were exceptions (Drayton, Harington, Raleigh), but this was the agreed template. Themes, tropes, conceits, figures of speech — jousts and Cupids, beds and ships, storms at sea — were imported from *treicento* Italy and naturalized by the English. When Sidney, for example, sketches his bedroom scenes, sites of pain and dream, he is remembering Petrarch who, apostrophizing his 'little room', previously a reliable port in a storm, bewails the fact that it's now a fountain of shameful tears he hides by day and sheds by night:

sfonte se' or di lagrime notturne
che'l dì celate per vergogna porto.

Within the convention, though, Sidney is his own man. Much of the tension and excitement of *Astrophel and Stella* lie in the resistance he puts up to Petrarch's perhaps too smoothly flowing precedent; the struggle between the courtly and the worldly, between art and life, is Astrophel's subject. Truth or fiction? There was the real Stella, Penelope Devereux to whom he had once been engaged. (Her unpleasant husband, Lord Rich, gets his come-uppance in Sonnet 24.) The truth of the human situation comes through in condensed, fractured lines and forceful departures from the polite norm. Euphuistic and colloquial, like his prose, as occasion dictates, the sonnets enact the authentic speech of an unhappy lover: 'look in thy heart and write.' Their force derives from a reworking of the conventions; and the need to free himself from constraint, formal and emotional, is written into a packed, fighting syntax that pushes at the limits of the sonnet form. (A sometimes baffling punctuation is crucial in sorting out the density.) The result is a vigorous, argumentative music that looks forward to Donne's peremptory tone and, curiously enough, the 'sprung rhythm' of Hopkins. Women readers are amused by the age-old argument of Sonnet 91 ('I'm really thinking of *you*, dear'):

> *Stella, while now by honour's cruel might*
> *I am from you, light of my life, misled*
> *And that fair you, my sun, thus overspread*
> *With absence' veil, I live in sorrow's night . . .*

'Misled' governs 'from you'. The fact of her marriage keeps them apart; he is alone in a dark place. If, as by candlelight, erotic images appear to him, she is not to be jealous (please be jealous), they're only poor copies of herself: 'Models such be wood-globes of glistering skies' — the wooden celestial globes we know, already long in production.

The first poem in *Astrophel*, 'Loving in truth and fain in verse my love to show', sets up a school for love based not on precedents ('study') but on 'Invention, Nature's child': 'look in thy *heart* and write.' His work won't be reliant upon 'poor Petrarch's longdeceasèd woes', he will write out of lived experience. He is spirited and sarcastic, going for 'dainty wits', Lord Rich, his own inadequate self, and derivative poets who 'into your poesie wring' the conventional properties unaltered; and don't imagine when I say Stella I mean some grand abstraction: 'With me those pains for God's sake do not take.' Asperity and optimism belong to the daylight hours when he mixes with coevals or catches sight of her amid the Thames river traffic: 'The boat for joy could not to dance forbear.' 'Most irksome night' brings other things: his 'dungeon dark', 'black horror'. He remembers her 'rhubarb words' (*sic*) and talks to the moon as an equal in suffering (as above, so below). The insomnia poems culminate in Sonnet 99, 'When far-spent night':

> *With windows ope then most my mind doth lie*
> *Viewing the shape of darkness, and delight*
> *Takes in that sad hue which with th'inward night*
> *Of his maz'd powers keeps parfit harmony.*

The shape of darkness! The phrase suggests a moonless night, the 'dark of the moon'.

Raleigh too attended night school; haughty as Lucifer, he walked on the dark side. When Oberon, in *A Midsummer Night's Dream* (II.i.162), praises Elizabeth, her eyes 'the chast beams of the wat'ry Moon', the line contains a pun. She is chaste, and chased by many suitors — Raleigh among them when he had ceased to be a favourite and, as the novelist Robert Nye tells it in *The Voyage of the Destiny* (1995), her frustrated 'lover'. Perhaps picking up on his Devon pronunciation, the royal tease called him Sir 'Water', which would prove, in time, to be a *poetic* favour. (All these sirs: Elizabeth had a Camelot complex.) The 17th-century diarist John Aubrey remembered him as 'a tall, handsome and bold man but . . . damnable proud'. To judge from the 1585 miniature portrait done in his 'dandled days' by Nicholas Hilliard, he was indeed 'ferociously virile', raffish and rather grim; but he had 'presence' and panache. There were many tributes to Sidney after his early death, and Raleigh joined the chorus:

> *There didst thou vanquish shame and tedious age,*
> *Grief, sorrow, sickness, and base fortune's might;*

Dark of the Moon

The rising day saw never mournful night
But passed with praise from off this worldly stage.

Base fortune and mournful night would preoccupy Raleigh to the end, and to him the world was indeed a stage: 'God, who is the author of all our tragedies, hath appointed all the parts we are to play.' His life and work are best understood in theatrical terms. The dramatic sense of life, the theatre of the world: the story is told once again by Mark Nicholls and Penry Williams in *Sir Walter Raleigh in Life and Legend* (Continuum, 2011), the first serious life of the man for many years.

A pushy, self-promoting sort of fellow, arrogant, opportunistic, a bit of a cad, he nonetheless took the long view — though his *History of the World* ('To write the story of all ages past'), begun in the Tower on a trumped-up charge of treason, only gets as far as the Roman Empire. Despite his nautical reputation (Spenser called him the 'shepherd of the ocean') he was an unhappy sailor, say Nicholls and Williams, and never visited 'Virginia', leaving the Roanoke project to others in his employ and acting only as financier. He did visit the Orinoco, twice, both times disastrously, in his quest for gold and silver. His previous soldiering experience consisted of trips to France during Oxford vacations for the religious wars, and a ferociously virile role in Munster during the Desmond Rebellion — notoriously at Smerwick Harbour, west of Dingle, where he performed some 'rough work' for the Lord Deputy, Grey de Wilton. He was rewarded for this with 40,000 acres of confiscated Desmond land and a fine house at Youghal, Myrtle Grove, still privately occupied, where he worked at a famous oriel window. (Spenser, Grey's secretary at Smerwick, who killed no one as far as we know, got only 3,000 acres at Kilcolman.) 'To seek new worlds, for gold, for praise, for glory', Raleigh was released from the Tower, still technically under sentence of death, for one last trip to the Orinoco with a motley crew, and there they sat like birds in the wilderness, down in Demerara. The San Tomé mine they coveted — a name later adapted by Conrad for the silver mine in *Nostromo* (1904) — was in Spanish hands and so remained. The *Destiny* called at Kinsale on the way back but Raleigh, unlike some of his men, proceeded to Plymouth and so to the scaffold under James, who disapproved of smoking. Mountjoy, the victor

Derek Mahon

of Kinsale (1601), another tobacconist, who later took up with Penelope Rich, displeased James for the same reason.

Raleigh, vain, morose, a 'bounder' in many respects, was nevertheless a remarkable poet, in part perhaps because his self-belief was so extreme. Sidney's professed unhappiness in love was evidently tolerable, Raleigh's not. Both were married men, by the way. Though far from prolific (the poetical works don't exceed fifty pages), and despite questions of attribution, Raleigh has had a stimulating effect on much later poets. 'The Ocean to Cynthia', that one strange poem alone, extends the imaginative field at a single bound. Exploration is the key. Though not really such a brilliant explorer in his travels, as Nicholls and Williams explain, he explores psychic conditions more extreme than those usually acknowledged; also the poetic landscape, which with him becomes horizontal as well as vertical. A 'great chemist', according to Aubrey, he transmutes 'base fortune' and personal misery into a bracing and exhilarating new idiom. It was maybe thoughts of the Cornish tin mines of his youth, in which his father had an interest (though Raleigh senior too had invested in expeditions), that put the idea of gold mines into his head; but these concluded instead with the discovery of silver in the shape of a highly personal and idiosyncratic form of poetic address. His work is a series of glyptic improvisations on the love theme — like the diamond-scribbled window rhymes he and Elizabeth exchanged in the early days of his ascendancy. The reworkings of old ballads ('Walsingham', the 'Pilgrimage': the image reformation didn't happen overnight), his farewells to the Court ('My Broken Pipes', 'The Lie'), which 'shines like rotten wood', if this one *is* by Raleigh, can be read as companion pieces to 'Cynthia'. She, moon and tide, has cast him adrift; he, her devoted Ocean, while still within her sphere of influence, beweeps his outcast state. This poem, or series of fragments, is a most un-Petrarchan and un-courtierlike storm of self-pity and rage, and none the worse for that. Exasperated but awed, you almost feel sorry for this unpopular figure who treated everyone else so badly. 'Mind' is the subject of 'writes'; he apostrophizes his heart:

> So, my forsaken heart, my wither'd mind,
> widow of all the joys it once possessed,
> my hopes clean out of sight with forcèd wind,

Dark of the Moon

> *to kingdoms strange, to lands far-off address'd,*
> *alone, forgotten, friendless, on the shore*
> *with many wounds, with death's cold pangs embrac'd,*
> *writes in the dust, as one that could no more,*
> *whom love, and time, and fortune, had defac'd.*

An active man constrained to long periods of enforced contemplation, he was an inspired amateur at the poetry game, writing only when the spirit moved him and only for intensely personal reasons; he was also reluctant to publish in his lifetime. After his eclipse he adopted the traditional rejected-lover roles of hermit and pilgrim: 'Like as a hermit poor in place obscure'; 'Give me my scallop shell of quiet'. (The scallop shell was a badge of pilgrimage.) 'Cynthia' is remarkable for its combination of ceremony and simple diction, grandeur and straight, even rude, talk. Its frequent reliance on the monosyllable ('writes in the dust, as one that could no more') gives it a raw spontaneity; it is intense and rambling both, full of strong lines ('Our ocean seas are but tempestuous waves'), some worthy of Marlowe:

> *On Sestos' shore, Leander's late resort,*
> *Hero hath left no lamp to guide her love.*

Sidney's father, who tried to subdue Ulster (Sonnet 30), can you imagine, had a predictably hard time of it. Sir Henry, says Seán Ó Faoláin, 'having long cursed the beastly country to which misfortune had consigned him', returned in 1571 to Ludlow and Penshurst, taking with him as foster-child (a custom of the time) the young Hugh O'Neill, who would therefore have known Philip. Directly or indirectly, all the Silver Poets had some experience of Ireland — in part a rehearsal for the Americas; in part, as they saw it, a strategic necessity should Spain try to invade. They saw correctly. The Spanish squadron under Don Juan del Aguila landed at Kinsale, with what results we know. (The truly dark side is evident in Ralph Birkenshaw's *Discourse*, 1602, a coarse and sadistic long 'poem' in celebration of Mountjoy's victory over the unfortunate Irish 'trusting to dreams and feignèd prophecies'.) History takes a long time to disperse, if it ever really does. The Orinoco adventures, and others of their kind, are remembered in Derek Walcott's 'Oceano Nox'

Derek Mahon

(1985), where the St Lucia poet speaks at last of a psychological liberation in this regard. Cynthia has finally ceded her place to 'a local moon, full of its own importance'. An admirer of 'high Marlovian clouds', Walcott takes his leave of the demanding old lady (Raleigh's senior by twenty years) with a courtly gesture worthy of Castiglione:

> *A different age is whispering to the ocean,*
> *the fronds will take the old moon by the hand*
> *and lead her gently into a cloud's grave.*

It's been estimated that Myrtle Grove, a 15th-century presbytery in origin, may be the oldest continually occupied house in Ireland: 'Almost the only completely unfortified house to have survived intact in anything like its original state,' says Mark Bence-Jones in *A Guide to Irish Country Houses* (Constable, 1988). The same can't be said for Kilcolman Castle. The place is a ruin, but at least it's a ruin; at least it's there. Its natural advantages, drawn on by Spenser, especially the local trout ('Those trouts and pikes all others do excel'), have made it a modern-day nature reserve. A 15th-century tower house on the road to Doneraile, it's known for the abundance of the local streams. Spenser did most of his best work here before being burnt out in 1598. His Anglo-Irish pastoral mode (he clearly loved the place in his own fashion) accommodated both a medieval ideal of fairyland and a working reality; the trout rose to a Platonic idea of trout. Which doesn't mean he was liked, though he tried to make his own kind of contact with the Gael. He had some bardic verse translated, we don't know whose, but decided it lacked 'the goodly ornaments of poetry, though sprinkled with some pretty flowers of their own natural device'. Some pretty flowers. Did he condescend to his own acres in the same manner? Did he dream of English gardens? The 17th century, beginning with the reign of James, saw such dreams realized — also the 'shiring' of Ireland, so that we can now start to speak of counties: Waterford, Cork and so on.

Something of that century is still visible in these parts. Kinsale, for example, has the Dutch gables and oriel windows, and the Restoration period saw two great forts arise, named for James I and for Charles II, to dominate the harbour mouth. Thoughts of history present themselves constantly. What version of history do we accept, though, if any? 'Chaos clouds the globe,' says Walcott. Some twenty years ago Kinsale still enjoyed a raffish culture in a direct line of descent from the age of Raleigh. History, global or local, is a chaotic living system, and the raffishness has moved on. We're left with our oceanic micro-climate and a quiet life; but, even at the dark of the moon, the modestly lighted *corniche* road to Summercove and Charles Fort retains a bit of antique glamour. Traces of old style and turbulence persist into a vastly different era. The 'Indian' peoples of South America get to elect, at last, governments they hope can protect them and their resources — oil, copper, soothing leaves — from the kind of 'material interests' exposed by Conrad in *Nostromo* and represented by Raleigh at an earlier time. But the past is cloudy too, and there's no contradiction in ruffians writing poetry of a high order. Swift said something of the sort: never judge a book by its author.

The Theatre of the World

Even now a myth persists about Swift's 'madness', as if no one in his right mind could take such a dim view of human nature. Which means that even now he is relevant — perhaps especially now, when so many features of the Age of Reason are again discernible, not to say obtrusive: strident economic 'growth', a mechanistic model of the universe, a constant expectation of imminent 'chaos'. The madness rumour started in his lifetime and achieved specious authority at the hands of later writers who deplored his alleged misanthropy — a term he himself used to mean 'philosophical pessimism'. It's now recognized that his problems were physiological in origin. The madness theory has been discredited, yet its spectral residue may have contributed to an interesting development, the rediscovery of Swift the poet. Widely perceived as a sort of anti-poet and critically disregarded for two centuries as offering nothing very dense or visionary to the scholarly mind or the inquiring spirit, he has since been read anew as one of the great eccentrics; for, despite his aspiration to a tough-minded detachment, there is great emotion in his work, great turmoil under the hard, glittering surface. Admirers of Augustan elegance and post-modern 'cool' will find him a remarkably hot-headed figure, a flamboyant character as colourful in his way as Wilde or Yeats; indeed the personality goes far towards explaining the continuing fascination of his verse which, unlike the prose satires, presented a recurrent means of dramatic self-projection. The enigmatic persona thus created, austere yet kindly — that of the 'Dean', the 'Drapier', 'Dr Swift' — spoke with a distinctive Anglo-Irish voice, liberal, witty and vertiginously ironical, whose echo is still audible even now.

The complete poems run to several hundred pages. Only 'A Description of the Morning' and 'A Description of a City Shower' were published before his appointment to the Deanery of St Patrick's Cathedral, Dublin, in 1713, at the age of forty-six. *Gulliver's Travels*, and the bulk of the verse, were written after this date — in Ireland, for the most part, though often with an English readership in mind. We are to picture a solitary though gregarious middle-aged bachelor of medium height, notable for piercing blue eyes and a formidable asperity of manner, alternately jocular and despondent, who passes his leisure hours with a circle of devoted admirers, male and female; who walks and rides a great deal, and who spends too much time alone, morosely contemplating the Hanoverian succession, the triumph of Whiggery and his own exile from the ministerial ambience where he once shone. Dublin is his native city and he has mixed feelings about it. There are two principal women in his life, Esther Johnson and Esther Vanhomrigh. The former, 'Stella', obscurely related, perhaps his niece, is a neighbour and frequent visitor, one of his inner circle, indeed his oldest friend; the latter, 'Vanessa', twenty years his junior, lives importunately in lodgings and in her house at Celbridge on the Liffey, twelve miles from town. Good girl, bad girl — though Vanessa, of course, was a good girl too. Edgily aware of each other, these women provide the emotional stimulus and repose in a seemingly sardonic, and often splenetic, existence. Other friends include Thomas Sheridan, schoolmaster and grandfather of the playwright, who has a property at Quilca, Co Cavan, and the Achesons of Market Hill, Co Armagh, where he is a frequent guest. The parish of Laracor, near Trim, a living he retained to the end of his days, where he built his own house and planted willows, provides peace and quiet, when required, among the thoughtful horses of Co Meath.

Gulliver reports of the Houyhnhnms: 'In poetry they must be allowed to excel all other mortals: wherein the justice of their similes, and the minuteness, as well as the exactness of their descriptions, are indeed inimitable.' Of the Laputans he says: 'Imagination, fancy and invention, they are wholly strangers to, nor have any words in their language, by which those ideas can be expressed.' The first of these observations we might take to refer to Swift's friends Pope and Gay; and indeed to Swift himself. The second is more problematic: the creator of Lilliput and Brobdingnag has never been thought to lack fancy and invention, but Swift the poet has often been found wanting in 'imagination'. If we mean imagination in the Coleridgean sense, this is fair enough. There is not much of Shakespeare in him, though there is something of Dr John

Derek Mahon

Donne, Dean of St Paul's. Other precursors usually noted include Milton's 'Il Penseroso', whose octosyllabic couplet he adopted; the first Samuel Butler, author of *Hudibras*, whose comic rhymes he imitated and surpassed, and Rochester, whose aphoristic vituperation provided a bracing model of plain speech. Swift's directness and clarity of image, his unmediated transparency and colloquial vigour, have given rise to a situation where, seemingly yielding little to close analysis, he suffers (or perhaps enjoys) critical neglect — but knows, like Burns, popular immortality, especially in Ireland. Traces of his mystique are scattered throughout the culture. Nor is this attributable solely to *Gulliver*. There is a folk memory of the generously seditious *Drapier's Letters*; but it's remembered, above all, that he made provision in his will for a lunatic asylum which, established in due course as the prestigious St Patrick's Hospital, thrives to this day:

> *He gave the little Wealth he had,*
> *To build a House for Fools and Mad:*
> *And shew'd by one satiric Touch,*
> *No Nation wanted it so much:*
> *That Kingdom he hath left his Debtor,*
> *I wish it soon may have a Better.*

All his verse is in the strict sense occasional — in his own perhaps disingenuous words, 'trifles never intended for publick view'. Like Byron later, he wrote not as an artist but as a gentleman amateur, or so he liked to imply. The poems, technically simple but rhetorically complex, owe much of their effect to the known character of the author and his contemporary celebrity. Eliot once rebuked 'those who condemn or ignore *en bloc* the poetry of the eighteenth century on the ground that it is "prosaic" when most of it is not prosaic enough'. Swift, in theory and practice, is one of the great 'prosaic' poets. Dryden advised him in youth that he would 'never be a poet'; but this prediction was based on early exercises like 'Ode to the King' (William III), where the young practitioner still aspired to some version of the sublime. The mature poet, the Swift we think we know, took no interest in the sublime except as an object of derision. The author of trifles, *écrivant* rather than *écrivain*, amused scribbler rather than dedicated artist (or so he would have us believe), he set out his view of poetic vocation in the cynical rap 'On Poetry: A Rapsody' (*sic*), that the whole thing, in the circumstances pertaining, is a lot of trivial nonsense, in Grub Street or at Court. Given the intolerable, self-pleasing cant of the age, he found it hard, like Juvenal, 'not to write satire'. But if he was quick to recognize the ridiculous in the sublime, the idiotic in the heroic, he shared (and took very seriously) the low-level anxiety of his time in regard to 'chaos', whose 'dread empire' Pope evoked in *The Dunciad*. With Swift this was not only a cultural but a personal fear. Any lapse from a briskly rational standard, in sexual matters for instance, and Pandora's box might turn into a temple of the winds.

Owing perhaps to their genial tone, none of the poems was more popular in his lifetime than the two 'Descriptions'. Appearing first in *The Tatler* in 1709 and 1710 respectively, the 'Morning' and the 'Shower' established this Irish provincial as a poet of London, a thing of great importance to him then and later. The first, said Steele, introducing the poem, was 'not only a description of the morning but of the morning in town, nay, of the morning at this end of town, where my kinsman at present lodges' (i.e. the West End); and we notice at once a characteristic attention to detail. This is both loving and quizzical as he introduces a theme more fully developed later, that of dirt and waste disposal, already associated with sexuality:

> *Now Betty from her Masters bed had flown,*
> *And softly stole to discompose her own.*
> *The Slipshod Prentice from his Masters door,*
> *Had par'd the Dirt, and Sprinkled round the Floor.*

A townsman, urban if not always urbane, Swift delighted in the noise and squalor of city life, the 'dialogical polyphony' in Bakhtinian phrase (a delight still evident as late as 'Verses made for Women who cry Apples, &c.'): whatever about misanthropy and perceptual problems, he lent an appreciative ear, eye and nose (nose especially) to the physical facts of the world he knew. The tone is not satirical but tolerant, humorous, even enchanted. The dynamics of order and disorder are uninflected by anxiety or stricture; the unusual pentameter, later discarded, imposes a deadpan formality; the chaos control is barely perceptible. If dirt is matter in the wrong place Swift's 'proper words in proper places' is a principle of stylistic hygiene. 'Not cold but intense' is how Geoffrey Hill describes Swift's mode of perception, noting particularly a capacity 'to transform, say, autocratic disdain into a cherishing particularity', and the ambiguity of his attitude to the anarchic: 'In principle he abhorred all its aspects; poetically he reacted to it with a kindling of creative delight.' Autocratic disdain, though, was not a Swiftian mode; he never sneered at the generality of 'folks'.

As a poet he was slow to find his own distinctive voice, but the 'Shower' was an immediate hit: 'the best thing I ever writ; there never was such a shower since Danaë's'. Parodically derived from all previous floods — Genesis, Ovid — and sharing the social alertness of Pope and Gay (it was Swift who first suggested the idea of *The Beggar's Opera*), the 'Shower' overflows with a love of London and a love of life, even or perhaps especially in the boisterous final triplet designed to mock the Drydenesque pomposity of triplets. At this stage he went with the flow of the age, a time of rapid population growth and expanding newspaper readership — an inflationary age of financial speculation, sophisticated philistinism and harsh comedy, when Hobbes's version of the 'selfish gene' promoted a culture of winners and losers, the club and the street. These mock-pastoral genre pieces, like most of Swift, are best read with an eye to historical context, especially visual context. Brisk Susan and the Beau in his sedan chair, clothes and objects, the furniture of room and thoroughfare, create a theatrical space which has become, with time, almost the substantive content of the verse. Like Hogarth he is a narrative painter of the period, rich in material fact and vivid detail; he has inscribed, engraved even, certain aspects of early 18th-century experience indelibly on the historical memory, and not only the more scabrous and grotesque. His genuine interest in life below stairs, for example (see 'Mary the Cook-maid's Letter'), is in the same spirit as Hogarth's later group portrait of his own domestic servants.

'Cadenus and Vanessa', the title echoing Shakespeare's 'Venus and Adonis', its length and ingenuity testifying to the vitality of this relationship, was first drafted about 1713, shortly before his Dublin appointment. Inhabiting a theatrical space of the period, the erotic school-room, it's a closet Restoration comedy of manners, mistaken motives and sexual innuendo, owing much to his fellow Dublin graduates Congreve and Farquhar (also to Molière), its manipulative showmanship barely concealed by the baroque machinery. There was scandal on its unauthorized publication; a certain caddishness was deplored. Swift's friend Patrick Delany spoke sadly of the 'idle vanity' of 'these vile verses':

> *But what Success Vanessa met*
> *Is to the World a Secret yet:*
> *Whether the Nymph, to please her Swain,*
> *Talks in a high Romantick Strain;*
> *Or whether he at last descends*
> *To like with less Seraphick Ends;*
> *Or, to compound the Business, whether*
> *They temper Love and Books together;*
> *Must never to Mankind be told,*
> *Nor shall the conscious Muse unfold.*

'So bright a nymph to come unsought' in his caducity, the *ingénue* Vanessa, like Stella herself, was the talk of the town then and later; the story fairly crackles with sexuality. Vanessa followed him to Ireland against his wishes, endured isolation and neglect, died young, and left her property not to Swift but to Swift's friend the philosopher George Berkeley, Bishop of Cloyne, whom she hardly knew.

Stella, whose tutor he had been in the early days at Moor Park, Surrey, first appeared under that name (borrowed from Sidney) in the series of birthday poems he wrote for her in Ireland, starting when she was thirty-eight and he forty-six. A potent mixture of gallantry and naturalism, these lyrical exercises, consciously anti-idealistic yet equally distant from the cynical seduction verse of the previous century, recall the amorous ratiocination of Donne, the assumption being one of mutual equality and backchat, 'sense and wit'. It was Swift's opinion that modern love was a fraud based on unrealities at once grandiose and sordid, whereas he and Stella had achieved a complex, unillusioned relation founded on intimacy of mind as much as body. Goldsmith praised his 'boldness'; and Robert Graves, writing about what he calls the Age of Obsequiousness, remarked that among the poets of the period 'the only personal

Derek Mahon

Muse I can recall is Swift's Stella'. Swift was unusual in this as in so much else, and the warmth and realism, fresh insight and startling candour of these extraordinary love poems make them unique for their time. 'Not the gravest of divines', he specializes in what he called 'raillery', the teasing familiarity and back-handed compliment he established, unilaterally and no doubt a little tiresomely, as their private language; but regular 'lapses' into plangency and charm, as in the delightful 'Stella at Woodpark', or the turbulent stoicism of the last birthday poem (1727), give the emotional game away:

> *O then, whatever Heav'n intends,*
> *Take Pity on your pitying Friends:*
> *Nor let your Ills affect your Mind,*
> *To fancy they can be unkind.*
> *Me, surely, me you ought to spare,*
> *Who gladly would your Suff'rings share;*
> *Or give my Scrap of Life to you,*
> *And think it far beneath your Due;*
> *You, to whose Care so oft I owe,*
> *That I'm alive to tell you so.*

Not too much need be made, at this stage, of the scatological poems, few in number, written in the period of disorientation following Stella's death. They might even be ascribed, paradoxically, to the good influence of her living presence, now withdrawn. Celia and Corinna are the unfortunate whipping-girls of Swift's bereavement and despair; the rage is cosmic, the sadism a kind of blasphemy. Irvin Ehrenpreis speaks of 'the comedy of sexual prosthesis' and points out that the voyeuristic boudoir visit and discovery of cosmetic aids were practically a *topos* of the period, with a literary genealogy going back, once again, to Ovid. The satirist isn't getting at the girls, he suggests, much less the female economy as such, but at the vanity fair of high society, 'the social imposition of a preconceived sexual idealism' and, in Swift's phrase, 'that ridiculous passion which hath no being but in play-books and romances'. W. J. McCormack sees his 'excesses' and 'obsessions' in this regard as less a 'biographical oddity' than a 'cultural symptom'; and Victoria Glendinning, while deploring Swift's 'peculiar and impertinent treatment of women', charitably interprets the scatological writings, in psychiatric terms, as analytical 'work' on 'a universal neurosis'. Everything in historical context, everything 'situational'; anachronistic modern attitudes won't help us here:

> *Thus finishing his grand Survey,*
> *The Swain disgusted slunk away,*
> *Repeating in his amorous Fits:*
> *'Oh!* Celia, Celia, Celia *shits!'*

The second couplet, delicately omitted by George Faulkner from his 1735 edition, and even by Herbert Davis from his old-spelling 1967 edition of the *Poetical Works*, has its comical and unpathological equivalent in *Directions to Servants*, where Swift advises the Chamber Maid as follows: 'Do not carry down the necessary Vessels for the Fellows to see, but empty them out of the Window, for your Lady's Credit. It is highly improper for Men Servants to know that fine Ladies have Occasion for such Utensils.' The misfortunes of Celia and Corinna must be balanced not only by the Stella poems but by Swift's more characteristic relishing of the physical, and his benign influence on the circle of strong-minded, witty women, poets among them, who were a constant presence in his Dublin life: Mary Barber, Constantia Grierson, Laetitia Pilkington. To Mary Delany, while praising her eyes, he complains of 'a pernicious heresy . . . that it is the duty of your sex to be fools in every article except what is merely domestic'. He was, in his own fashion, a ladies' man — a fact noticed by the exuberant heroine of Erica Jong's *Fanny* (1980), who hits it off with him: '. . . a curious fellow, the cleverest man I e'er had met . . . and, I believe, much misunderstood'. There's a certain breezy, play-acting misogyny sometimes but, unlike most of his male contemporaries, he takes women seriously, and the complexity of his attitude merely reflects the actual complexity of real-life gender relations.

The Anglo-Ireland to which he returned in 1714, after the death of Queen Anne and the fall of the Tories, was a rackety place. Roy Foster speaks of its 'gamey flavour' and 'ruthless but ironic pursuit of style'; the words 'savagery' and 'ferocity' also occur. Protestant hegemony was absolute, the majority legislated into subjection while 'civil' society toasted 'the glorious, pious and immortal memory of the great and good King William, who redeemed us from popery,

Derek Mahon

slavery, arbitrary power, brass money and wooden shoes'. Swift, out of favour with government and suspected of Jacobitism, cut a solitary figure in this ripe milieu, though by no means an invisible one. No one was ever invisible in Dublin, which encourages the performative instinct: see and be seen. The psychology of Berkeley's *New Theory of Vision* (1709), and his later notion that 'to be is to be perceived', must have owed something to these conditions. Both within and beyond his chosen coterie Swift was a cynosure at all times, incorporating this as an imaginative principle into the work. He lived in an age of insectology and optical science, but had no need of Gulliver's spectacles and pocket telescope, or of Celia's magnifying glass, to tell him he was under constant, closed-circuit observation; even his introspection was extroverted: 'When a true genius appears in the world you may know him by this sign, that the dunces are all in confederacy against him.' Paranoia perhaps — though, as Delmore Schwartz observed, paranoia can be justified. Politically marginalized, his correspondence opened for evidence of sedition, Swift had good reason to think himself persecuted:

> Had he but spar'd his Tongue and Pen,
> He might have rose like other Men.

He inhabited a social and linguistic ghetto, albeit a privileged one. Beyond the English 'Pale', and even within it, lay the alternative, indeed the original 'native Irish' culture, largely invisible to the urban eye; though Dublin itself was a bilingual city, with Irish-speaking poets in residence. Swift would have known no Irish, or a *cúpla focal* at most, but something of the Gaelic spirit got through to him. Through Sheridan he met the great, blind composer Turlough Ó Carolan, who is said to have played the harp in the Deanery. Tradition attributes to Carolan the air and the English version of Hugh MacGowran's 'Pléaráca na Ruarcach' ('O'Rourke's Revel') on which Swift based 'The Description of an Irish Feast'. He had an affinity with the Gaelic poets, particularly in the vehemence of his satire. It may not be entirely fanciful to trace an analogy between his own extremity and that of Gaeldom's great elegist, his near-contemporary Aodhagán Ó Rathaille (c.1670-1729); and, sure enough, folklore records or imagines a spirited encounter between the Dean and the Kerry poet in the summer of 1723, when

The Theatre of the World

Swift toured Munster.

His gift to subsequent Irish writers, to speak only of Ireland, has been immense. With him the principal themes are already in place: 'race' and religion, cabin and Big House, famine and genocide, internal exile, sexual neurosis, the language question, and a complicated attitude towards the imperial neighbour. Representations of the body in Joyce and Beckett owe much to him, as does the 'savage indignation' of Yeats and Kavanagh. Beckett's taxonomy of laughter in *Watt* is decidedly Swiftian; somewhere behind it lie the ontological predicament of the Yahoos and the scrupulous grotesquerie of *A Modest Proposal*. Beckett identifies three laughs, all known to Swift, the bitter, the hollow and the mirthless: 'The bitter laugh laughs at that which is not good, it is the ethical laugh. The hollow laugh laughs at that which is not true, it is the intellectual laugh. Not good! Not true! Well well. But the mirthless laugh . . . is the laugh of laughs, the *risus purus*, the laugh laughing at the laugh, the beholding, the saluting of the highest joke, in a word the laugh that laughs — silence please — at that which is unhappy.' Swift laughed bitterly and hollowly at the misgovernment of Ireland, of England indeed, and mirthlessly at our existential situation. As for his satirical panache, we can look back on it now with nostalgia: as Adorno pointed out, the mode has been made redundant. How do you satirize achieved nihilism or an absolute consensus?

Anxiously awaiting the mail-boat at Holyhead in 1727, after his last visit to England, he wrote:

> I never was in haste before
> To reach that slavish hateful shore.
> Before, I always found the wind
> To me was most malicious kind.

He railed often enough against the 'slavish hateful shore', the 'land of slaves' where he was obliged to live and where he expected to die 'like a rat in a hole', while privately conceding that 'in truth, I have no discontent at living here'. If a sense of grievance at his relegation to a fine house in a convivial capital full of friends and admirers seems exaggerated, it must be understood as a literary device. The air of life sentence he cultivated aligned him imaginatively with the marginalized and persecuted, and placed him at a creatively

Derek Mahon

useful distance from the centre of power — yet he looked constantly to London, the scene of his conspicuous early years, where the larger reputations were made. Despite his audacity and hauteur, reputation mattered greatly to him; and his best-known poem, 'Verses on the Death of Dr Swift', written in the 1730s during his sixties and intended for posthumous publication, was a bid to pre-empt and control how he would be seen by posterity. A bid that didn't wholly fail: he is often taken at his word, and the 'impartial' panegyric constituting the final section accepted as simple fact. Aside from its biographical interest we can now see that the distinction of the poem lies in its remarkable technique, its pro-active grasp and embodiment of gossip and transience; Swift's voice is only one among many, albeit one aiming for the last word. 'History is gossip,' says Gore Vidal, also guilty of 'the sin of wit', and Swift's poems are full of gossip, his own and others'; they throng with people and voices, so that the private play takes place in the theatre of the world:

> *My female Friends, whose tender Hearts*
> *Have better learn'd to act their Parts,*
> *Receive the News in doleful Dumps,*
> *'The Dean is dead, (and what is Trumps?).'*

Swift's is a Rabelaisian and a Brechtian world, a thieves' kitchen, a site of vice and predation embracing pickpockets and politicians, Gin Lane and the royal Court. His nausea, vertigo and 'excremental vision', synecdoche of the body politic, compare with those of Baudelaire, yet he has something Baudelaire lacks, a vernacular zest (see, for example, 'Tom Clinch'): far from being a misanthrope in the usual sense, he revelled in life's feast. Street cries, music to his ears till he grew deaf, echo throughout. He has a ludic taste for popular forms and idioms; indeed, the only noticeable 'development' in technique, once he gets into his stride, is the adoption of an increasingly racy, conversational style often incorporating 'Irish' rhymes and turns of phrase. Folk song he preferred to Italian opera, street ballads to Handel and Purcell. At his best he is a light, fast, indeed *swift* poet, again like Byron, riding helter-skelter a current of kinetic energy with streamlined fluency. The virtuosity is extraordinary — though, strangely, the magical or visionary vein is reserved for the science fiction and invisible cities of *Gulliver*. 'On Dreams', for example, is strictly deterministic.

No one, said Hazlitt, had written 'so many lackadaisical, slipshod, tedious, trifling, foolish, fantastical verses as he, which are so little an imputation on the wisdom of the writer; and which, in fact, only shew his readiness to oblige others, and to forget himself'. This aleatoric aspect of his poetic practice extends to the publishing history, a shambles of confusing devices including anonymous and involuntary publication, variant texts and disputed authorship. The poems seem to offer themselves as provisional drafts rather than finished compositions. Often we are dealing with a joint project, as with Stella who 'collected' and perhaps co-wrote some of the poems, or with one part of a cooperative venture involving Delany, Sheridan or Anne Acheson. Audience participation is encouraged; referred attitudes and opinions are everywhere, friendly or hostile responses anticipated. Eminently situational, Swift is a gift to reception theory. How we read him now depends very largely on our own response to a singular personality and the enduring psychodrama he so graphically projects.

The Road to Highgate

'If a man could pass through Paradise in a dream, and have a flower presented to him as a pledge that his soul had really been there, and if he found that flower in his hand when he awoke — Aye! and what then?' (This, famously, from Coleridge's *Notebooks*, though the trope, or something like it, goes back to ancient times.) Well, like Coleridge, he would still have his life to live in the real world: a story best told in Richard Holmes's two-volume biography, *Early Visions* (1989) and *Darker Reflections* (1999). Holmes's Coleridge is not the almost exclusively bookish figure of some 20th-century scholarship (although the poet did describe himself as a 'library cormorant'); he is the walking, talking, living character, both childish and impressive, described at first hand by De Quincey, Hazlitt and others. *Early Visions* takes us up to the spring of 1804 when the poet, then thirty-one, with 'new boots, a sun-hat, and a pair of green solar spectacles (price one guinea)', took ship for Malta, there to act as secretary to the Governor and, he hoped, recover his shattered health: also, perhaps, to escape the shadow of Wordsworth. Much of his best work was behind him: the 'Conversation' poems, 'Kubla Khan', 'The Ancient Mariner', the unfinished 'Christabel' and, surprisingly, the 'Dejection Ode', which reads like the work of a man of forty-nine, not twenty-nine. Holmes, in a postscript to *Early Visions*, speculates as to how we would now think of Coleridge if he had died, as he himself half expected to do, soon after his departure from England: 'Suppose his grave now lay, not in the leafy confines of Highgate Cemetery, but in the volcanic foothills of Mount Etna? Suppose his life never actually had a part two? How would his reputation now stand?'

'We would,' he suggests, 'think of him as a Keats or a Byron, one who lived and died in a premature blaze of talents, his name unblemished by considerations of failure, plagiarism, political apostasy or even opium addiction.' And indeed, although he is one of the first generation of Romantic poets, the life described in *Early Visions* is more like that of a second generation Romantic in its idealism and turmoil, its impetuosity and sexual confusion, 'as if this earth in fast thick pants were breathing'. There was his self-rustication from Cambridge, his brief enlistment in the 15th Light Dragoons (discharged as 'insane'), the Pantisocracy, the nine-month abandonment of hearth and home for a second student life in Germany, the mad dashes up hill and down dale, the radical journalism, the many schemes proposed and as soon forgotten, the Italian adventures, the endless talk. His friends, who all testified to his hypnotic manner, conspired to protect him from harm, and even from inconvenience. He was at Göttingen when his second child Berkeley died in infancy but, amazingly, Sara Coleridge was dissuaded by his friends from writing to him; when she finally did, imploring him to come home, he postponed his return for several months. He is generally thought to have been an atrocious husband, and Holmes, in his deliberately impartial manner, offers no defence of his subject in this regard; but it's worth bearing in mind how young they all were, still in their twenties.

Coleridge, indeed, was in some ways younger still, little more than a child himself — a child of nature, if a spoilt child. The youngest of ten, he had a row, aged seven, with his brother Frank and, in a famous incident, ran out and spent a stormy night shivering in the open: an incident which gave rise to the rheumatic pains for which opium was later prescribed, and one to which he alluded frequently in adult life. It was soon followed by the death of his father, the break-up of the family and his being sent, as a poor scholar, to the 'Bluecoat' charity school, Christ's Hospital (London), where he felt himself to be an orphan: 'that it was my lot, and that it was best for me, to make or find my way in life as a detached individual, a *terrae filius* . . .' He was, says Holmes expansively, 'to be a solitary voyager, an archetypal son of the earth, an orphan of the storm, flung out to wander over the world in search of vision'. Yet he remained a child all his life, oral and dependent, perhaps because he had never really *been* a child. As he explained to his last protector, the surgeon and physiologist James Gillman: 'I had all the simplicity, all the docility of the little child, but none of the child's habits. I never thought as a child, never had the language of a child.' Holmes is excellent on this aspect of Coleridge, as he is on the historical background, seldom letting the reader forget that the period was dominated, in Britain, by a terror of Jacobinism and the elaborate security measures of William Pitt. Coleridge's radical views, expressed in lectures and newspaper columns, were courageous, and more than once he was arrested as a spy.

Holmes is excellent too on the Coleridge 'circle', deftly sketching cronies like Charles Lamb, with whom he would drink nightly in Covent Garden when in London; and Southey, a bit of a stick, whose dog Rover is nonetheless described as an enthusiastic Pantisocrat: more fast thick pants. Sara Hutchinson, however, remains something of a mystery, as perhaps she was in life. She was his real Muse, the 'Asra' of the poems, and it was as a verse letter to her that the 'Dejection Ode' was originally written. Discretion obliged Coleridge to cut it by half for publication; fortunately, fascinatingly, we have both versions. Holmes comments: 'However much "Dejection" is to be preferred as a finished work of art, the "Letter" draws more directly on Coleridge's true imaginative life. It is richer in, and closer to, those irrepressible sources of imagery which fill his notebooks and private correspondence: the wind and sunlight over the fells, the moon and stars, the seasonal energy of plants and birds, the life of his children, the longing for love, friendship and a happy home.' He is good on the poetry, not only in his identification of sources (including the topography of the Exmoor farm where 'Kubla Khan' was written) but in explication. The 'meaning' of 'Kubla Khan' he takes to be the ambiguous nature of imaginative power: 'Does the power finally anoint him as an emperor of the imagination, or destroy him as its slave and sacrifice?' The troubled history of 'Christabel' is succinctly documented, and the themes of 'The Ancient Mariner' — 'exile and homecoming, the problematic relationship between man and nature, the fascination with states of madness, dream and hallucination which encroach upon the normal, waking world' — are skilfully interwoven with the narrative throughout. 'Had Coleridge died young,' he concludes, 'we might be tempted to think of him, paradoxically, as already greater than the man he became.'

But he still had to live in the real world. *Darker Reflections* takes us there, starting in Malta where his dependency on laudanum (tincture of opium mixed with brandy) grew, if anything, worse. His recovery began only in 1816 when, aged forty-four, he first

The Road to Highgate

lodged at the Gillmans' house in Highgate. He remained with the Gillmans until his death eighteen years later, and during that time his opium-taking came slowly under control, though it never ceased entirely. There was no more bingeing; instead, he entered a phase of sustainable medication, his intake reduced to a minimal dosage. Gillman, one of the first in the field of addiction, saved Coleridge's life and reason. 'It is difficult, after knowing opium, to take earth seriously,' says Cocteau in *Opium* (1930), the diary of his own first partial cure; 'and unless one is a saint, it is difficult to live without taking earth seriously.' Coleridge had a saintly aspect certainly, but he took earth seriously too, even or especially during his later, Highgate years, when the Gillmans' tactful supervision helped him resolve the various difficulties his addiction had caused. (Holmes calls the Gillmans 'the unacknowledged patron saints of the modern detox clinics for media celebrities making a comeback'.) 'Coleridge sat on the brow of Highgate Hill in those years,' wrote Carlyle, 'looking down on London and its smoke-tumult, a sage escaped from the inanity, his oak grove whispering strange things, uncertain whether oracles or nonsense.' Hazlitt, who mocked Coleridge continually during his later years, compared him to a crumbling tower, 'unearthly, insubstantial'. 'The author of *Biographia Literaria* was already a ruined man,' says Eliot of the new, older Coleridge. 'Sometimes, however, to be a "ruined man" is itself a vocation.'

A predictable result of his own drug use, says De Quincey, was that it brought 'confusion to the reason', and one symptom of Coleridge's ruin, if such it was, would be the maddening confusion of the *Biographia*, written in haste and pretty much unedited; another his sad plagiarism of 'Continental' critics in the *Biographia* and the Shakespeare lectures. These 'Continental' critics were, in fact, German, notably Kant and the Shakespeare scholar A. W. Schlegel. Perhaps Coleridge, frantic at what seemed to him his own failing powers, anxious to fulfil his commitments, and thinking he could carry it off, chose to risk detection as he had risked so much else in life, not least his health and sanity. But he hardly 'chose' anything. So inwardly did he understand and share the German material that the drift from annotated draft to fair copy would more likely have been fast and fuzzy, with a certain provisional sleight of hand to help expedite matters and keep the conscience quiet, or partially so. Did he forget that he was remembering? What are called his plagiarisms are really opium-induced delusions of originality, cloud quotations, involuntary homages *in nubibus*, 'cryptomnesia', the druggy zone-out between pen and page, or simply due to 'his particular combination of warm responsiveness to other writers with lack of scholarly method', as Lucy Beckett suggests. The plagiarized passages have been minutely documented, but it's illuminating to see this aberration in the context of his work as a whole, where it represents a tiny fraction. The *Biographia* and the lectures are among his most prominent work, so his borrowings there seem the more culpable. The poems are another story, and here the Romantics (Scott, Byron, Keats) drew inspiration from *him*. One poem in particular can be read in part as a comment on, or explanation of, the parasitic impulse. If 'Kubla Khan' is a hymn to the pleasures of opium (its 'profound lightness', in Cocteau's phrase) and 'The Ancient Mariner' a parable of its pains, the 'Dejection Ode' is an exploration of a drug-related state of mind in which, trying to 'take earth seriously', Coleridge acknowledged to himself the baffling nature of his practice.

In a poem concerning what Holmes calls Coleridge's 'self-doubts about his own poetic authority' (paradoxically one of the finest poems in English), it would be surprising if he didn't recognize, if only half-consciously, the derivative admixture (the 'intertextuality'?) in his method, the artificial component, the tug of dependency. It's part of the larger picture, an aspect of the disjunction between subject and object which is his opening premise and which makes the poem so modern. And indeed, long before the *Biographia* or the lectures, he lets drop proleptic hints of future difficulties. 'And fruits and foliage, not my own, seemed mine.' Now his 'sole resource', his 'only plan', is 'haply by abstruse research to *steal* / From my own nature all the natural man'; and this 'is almost grown the habit of my soul'. The 'twining vine' of hope changes to 'viper thoughts that coil around my mind' (so often this ophidian imagery); creative work is 'infected' with soul-entangling 'wrong' (guilt). The alienation described in the 'Ode' is an important step in his self-diagnosis, his self-recognition as in some sense a 'patient', and his acceptance of the situation. This acceptance led in due course to what might almost be called his *collaboration* with Gillman, in an early form of psychoanalysis — a term invented by Coleridge, or Gillman, or both, and

The Road to Highgate

first recorded in Coleridge's *Notebooks*. (Coleridge invented many things, including what we would now call critical theory.) Shifting from reverie to analysis as he brought his addiction under control, he seems to have been groping towards an understanding of its causes and mechanics.

> *I have been cunning in mine overthrow,*
> *The careful pilot of my proper woe.*
> — Byron, 'Epistle to Augusta'

Coleridge, at some level, sought the parabola of tribulation and redemption — a true Romantic, he lived his own imaginative autobiography. Which takes us back to that childhood night in the open when he thought, 'with inward and gloomy satisfaction, how miserable my mother must be!' This features in the seventh section as 'another tale'.

'In looking at objects of Nature while I am thinking, as at yonder moon dim-glimmering through the dewy window-pane, I seem rather to be seeking, as it were *asking* for, a symbolical language for something within me that already and for ever exists, than observing anything new.' This Platonic intensity relates to the 'abstruse research' he speaks of in the 'Ode' and has been taken to mean opium, though it might equally be code for plagiarism. ('Please always be careful to call it research.' — Tom Lehrer) Perhaps it's both; perhaps it means his Kant and Berkeley studies, or his reading generally. He claimed to have 'read almost everything'. (When Keats met him walking at his 'alderman-after-dinner pace' on Hampstead Heath he talked, said the younger poet, about nightingales, poetry, metaphysics, dreams, monsters, mermaids: 'Southey believes in them. Southey's belief [is] too much diluted.') He had a special interest in Orphic and Cabbalistic writings — which, as Kathleen Raine once pointed out, contribute to the symbolism of 'Kubla Khan'. Perhaps the 'abstruse research' was simply his own self-communion and self-analysis, an experiment conducted *seriatim* in the *Notebooks* and in the 'Letter to Sara Hutchinson'.

'Coleridge's ship,' wrote Hazlitt in *The Spirit of the Age*, 'flutters its gaudy pennons in the air and glitters in the sun, but we wait in vain to hear of its arrival in the destined harbour.' Coleridge 'has found,' says Hazlitt, 'no abiding-place nor city of refuge'; and this

Derek Mahon

is said, I think, in a puzzled tone, half despairing, half admiring, in the context of others' adjustments to conventional 'success'. As lecturer and guru Coleridge did, too late, become a notable figure, one much visited 'on the brow of Highgate Hill', where he found his 'destined harbour', though without his family, upstairs at No. 3, The Grove — still there, a short walk from the pub and St Michael's Church, with a fine view westwards over the Heath. (Also a short walk from Mr Dunn's pharmacy, now an estate agent's.) There were tentative reconciliations all round in the fullness of time, and his daughter, also Sara, subsequently co-edited his work. His descendants have included judges and generals; there's a Lord Coleridge in Somerset and a Nicholas Coleridge at the fashionable end of London journalism.

Coleridge the poet, overshadowed by Wordsworth and even Southey, was never hugely fashionable in his lifetime. The lecturer was another matter, the 'philosopher' yet another. After the *Biographia* his political thinking moved to the right as he evolved, Burke-like, an 'organic' vision of society ('states are but families magnified') and returned to the established church of his origins. The organic principle, which inspires equally the traditional conservative and the anarchist, was there from the start in his idea of poetry, so he was quite consistent and in tune with the younger self who observed, 'Nothing can permanently please, which does not contain in itself the reason why it is so and not otherwise.' The whole body of his work — poetic, philosophical, critical, political — has, says Kathleen Raine, 'the coherence of a living organism'. On the analogy of plant life and other natural growth (but more intimately than analogy) he wished for a poetry that was itself perfectly natural: 'The art itself is nature' (*The Winter's Tale*). The natural was his sounding board, the mechanical a noisy distraction; the manufacturer and the radical were equally at fault. Hence his constant recourse to flower and water symbolism, and his insistence on sensuous particularity, 'that definiteness and articulation of image ... without which poetry ... evaporates into a hazy, unthoughtful day-dreaming'. No stranger to daydreams, he knew the dangers, none better; but his best work actively *fuses* (his own 'scientific' word) reality and dream in a single thought by means of 'that synthetic and magical power', imagination.

The *Biographia*, far from being an organic whole, is vitiated by abstractions and definitions, as if its author were anxious to dispel a reputation for mist and mystery with a show of rigorous method; but mystery, as he perhaps dimly realized, was his great strength, the diffuse his natural mode. Resolution and independence were not for him: 'Action is one, thought manifold.' Even the act of writing was problematic. (Talking was no problem, no indeed.) System, in the 'Continental' style, was really foreign to his nature — despite the metaphysics, despite the stiffening compensation of taxonomies. Why, for instance, does imagination have to be split into primary and secondary? Because he had a book to write? He must have known better at heart. Second only to the poems are the *Notebooks*, fragmentary and substantial both — his best resource, animated as they are by the spirit of chance, the flash of illumination, the unsought epiphany: 'Slanting pillars of light moved along under the sun hid by clouds'; 'The spring with the little tiny cone of loose sand ever rising and sinking at the bottom, but its surface without a wrinkle.' Did he, has he, set another example here? Now that the literary novel is marginalized, the theatre too often a time-serving charade, and poetry increasingly like a children's party game, perhaps it's time once more for the considered observation, the aphorism, the intimate journal and the reflective diary.

Yeats and the Lights of Dublin

J. W. ('Basher') Boyle taught us English at Belfast 'Inst'. Dr Boyle was a Dublin Protestant and a graduate of Trinity where, in the thirties, he knew the likes of Conor Cruise O'Brien and Owen Sheehy-Skeffington. 'Inst', founded in 1791, was and is a large city-centre grammar school best known for its old boys' rugby club, Instonians, which always provided at least one or two names in the Irish international XV. The school, though Unionist in ethos (the principal was always an Englishman), had a vaguely liberal tradition, and numbered among its former pupils the poets Ferguson and Allingham. More recent old boys included Charles Monteith, a director of Faber & Faber and a friend of Eliot. We knew about that because there were several books by Eliot in the school library signed 'for the boys of Inst' by the author himself; and the publishers' address, then 24 Russell Square, London WC1, in those rich, 'linen-bound' editions, left an authoritative imprint on those of us who took a precocious interest in such things.

'Basher' Boyle was so called not because he was physically violent (he wasn't) but because, though of gentlemanly appearance, he had the large frame and concave features of one who could fight his corner. (He should really have been nicknamed Orson, since he bore a striking resemblance to middle-period Orson Welles.) He was put in charge of our Upper Sixth scholarship class where the syllabus covered a number of canonical texts from Shakespeare to modern times including *King Lear*, *Tom Jones* and *Heart of Darkness*. It also included a volume of verse entitled *The Tower*; and so it was that we embarked for the first time, during the school year 1959-60, on a serious reading of Yeats. Boyle had an insider's knowledge of Dublin personality, folklore and anecdote, and his idea of teaching five hundred years of English Literature was to race through Shakespeare and the rest in the first term and spend the remaining two terms on a close study of Yeats. No doubt I exag-

gerate, but that's how it seems in retrospect. No:
O'Brien (soon to be in the news because of the
he had met the septuagenarian Maud Gonne. H
met Yeats but had occasionally seen him, and
time, in the streets of Dublin; so when he read

> *I have met them at close of day*
> *Coming with vivid faces*
> *From counter or desk among grey*
> *Eighteenth-century houses*

— a magically recent world sprang to life: the streets of Dublin, a hundred miles down the road! Our own Belfast streets were Victorian and gloomy; but the Georgian streets of Dublin, glimpsed on our early travels, housed, we knew, a different and more glamorous spirit. Enchanted, we didn't confine ourselves to *The Tower* but ranged freely over the *Collected Poems* in the old buff-coloured edition. I can still recall the excitement we felt as we turned to page 217 and the sonorous octaves of 'Sailing to Byzantium', a sublime gift from the gods far transcending contemporary poetry — except for pop songs, of course.

The contemporary poetry we knew at Inst in January 1960 was of three kinds: the Illustrious, the Local and the New English. (Of Clarke and Kavanagh, the Dublin poets, we as yet knew nothing.) The illustrious were Eliot, Graves and above all Dylan Thomas, whom we strove to imitate. The locals were MacNeice, Rodgers and Hewitt; and the New English, notably Larkin and Davie, were the ones we sometimes saw mentioned in the book pages of the London *Observer* — which, as young sophisticates, we knew we had to read or at least be seen with. MacNeice and Rodgers, far off in London, seemed local no more. Hewitt ran an art gallery in Coventry but was known to spend his summers in a cottage at Cushendall, Co Antrim, which made him seem more neighbourly. A regionalist, he spoke of the 'identity crisis' of that now familiar figure, the Ulster writer, and had written, in the magazine *Lagan* in 1945, that 'the Ulster writer must be a rooted man [sic], must carry the native tang of his idiom like the native dust on his sleeve; otherwise he is an airy internationalist, thistledown, a twig in the stream'. We came to like and respect John Hewitt when we made acquaintance later; but in those days, without knowing him, we thought of him as rather programmatic and authoritarian, even his admirable radicalism too methodical. To us airy twigs the real question was: what's happening in London, where they print the *Observer*? And the curious answer was that some of what was happening there was really happening, or had just happened, in Ireland.

Larkin, for example, was a former librarian at Queen's University; and Donald Davie had recently taught at Trinity. Somehow there came into our possession, at least for a time, Davie's volume *A Winter Talent* (1957), which we took as illustrative of the state of English poetry, and perhaps we weren't far wrong. It contained, among other modest achievements, 'Samuel Beckett's Dublin', 'The Mushroom Gatherers', 'The Fountain', 'Hearing Russian Spoken' and 'Rejoinder to a Critic'. There was at the time in England a circle who called themselves, or allowed themselves to be called, the 'Movement'; sometimes, adopting the title of Robert Conquest's anthology of Movement verse, they were known as the *New Lines* poets. Larkin was one, Davie was another; and 'Rejoinder to a Critic' is not only a typical but even, in its prohibitive constraint, an emblematic Movement poem; indeed it's virtually a Movement manifesto. A critic of the time, perhaps someone nostalgic for the glorious excesses of Dylan Thomas, had rebuked Davie for a lack of feeling, no doubt suggesting his poems were arid and academic. As if to prove it, Davie responded with a poem notable for strict form, argumentativeness, direct quotations from Coleridge and Donne, self-deprecating irony and an almost complete absence of imagery — except for the atomic mushroom cloud, a picture presented with the clinical detachment of a physicist in a lecture room:

> *Love's radio-active fall-out on a large*
> *Expanse around the point it bursts above.*

Davie, himself a Navy man during the second world war, clearly felt implicated in the destruction of Hiroshima and Nagasaki, and there is something of Adorno here in the suggestion that, after the atrocities of the period, there could be no more 'poetry' (a theory contemporaneously disproved — as Adorno later acknowledged — by Paul Celan, and indeed Dylan Thomas); or, at least, that one should 'appear concerned only to make it scan'. This and the last line, 'How dare we now be anything but numb?', were often quoted in those years, and these prescriptions contributed significantly to the rather glum rationalism (Whiggery, Yeats would have called it) of Movement aesthetics; while their pedagogical tone and lack of interest in imagery were reflected also in more bohemian circles like the long-ago London 'Group', to which I'll return.

Irony is a mode attributed to liberal Ulster Protestants generally, the tone having been set by MacNeice, as if to absolve us of responsibility for our reprehensible heritage: one might write a love poem, or a plea for the wretched of the earth, and someone would say, 'Oh, he's a liberal Ulster Protestant, he's being ironical.' No one could describe Yeats as ironical (sarcastic sometimes, never ironical); indeed, it was always part of his public persona, and his appeal to satirical spectators like George Moore, that he was, if anything, too much in earnest. It has been said that he had no sense of humour. The answer is that he wasn't interested in humour but in passion and in wit, a different thing. Humour he would have considered beneath him, or rather a waste of time (one of his Middleton relations he calls 'a humorous, unambitious man'). He had, though, like his brother Jack, a sense of fun, of the festive — and, of course, the grotesque. Also, I'm afraid, a deplorable taste in puns. Mrs French in 'The Tower', for example, whose manservant presents her with a pair of ears in 'a little covered dish', is later described as 'gifted with so fine an ear'. The question of wit, humour, irony and the like may seem unimportant, but it is really quite central. Gramsci, in the *Prison Notebooks*, called irony 'a disease of the interregnum', which makes it sound peculiarly excruciating. While the world got on with the business of history, specifically the mutation of societies, irony remained and perhaps remains a resource for rueful liberals, nostalgic humanists, and football hooligans, many addicted to the backward gaze. Yeats looked back too — to the 18th century, to Byzantium — but in order to understand the present and anticipate the future; for, despite his patrician airs and flirtation with fascism, he remains to this day a revolutionary figure, a proto-hippie, eco-feminist and prophet of the new world disorder: 'The arts lie dreaming of the life to come.' Nor was he 'patriarchal'. The women in his life were, like himself, active, independent and disputatious.

John Boyle's extramural activities involved him with left-wing

Derek Mahon

politics and a novel if shamefully middle-class cultural experiment off the Malone Road, where Mary O'Malley, a Dublin woman, and her psychiatrist husband Pearse, ran an amateur back-garden outfit called the Lyric Theatre. The Lyric is now one of Belfast's most venerable institutions, but in those days it subsisted on the energy and enthusiasm of a few, of whom Boyle was one. He sat on the board, as did John Hewitt and Austin Clarke. The Lyric specialized in the Yeatsian repertoire and brought out a quarterly magazine, *Threshold*, which published, among other things, work by Clarke and Rodgers, Hewitt and Montague. Yeats's attitude to the North, specifically to the Protestant North, had been unappreciative. He visited often enough — first as a boy, for there were relations in Co Down; later with the Abbey touring company; and later still to broadcast for the regional BBC. Politeness confined his frankest comments to the correspondence with Lady Gregory, to whom he remarked at the time of partition: 'I have long been of opinion that, if such disagreeable people shut the door, we should turn the key in the lock before they change their mind.'

We got our scholarships, drank a bottle of Guinness with John Boyle in the Crown Liquor Saloon, and went down to Trinity —not a place, according to Yeats, that produced 'artistic minds', though his own father was only one obvious exception. I'm sure the lectures were all very good, but we didn't go to lectures much except to hear Alec Reid, an endearingly helpless Englishman of Irish antecedents who, like Boyle with pre-Yeatsian English literature, took an oblique stance vis-à-vis the curriculum. He was that legendary figure, the inspiring teacher who stimulates the imagination; and he often conducted informal tutorials in O'Neill's Bar and Lounge, Suffolk Street. Trinity lecturers didn't publish much in those days, not the older lecturers anyway; perhaps it was thought a bit showy. The gentle R. B. D. French, for example, confined himself to a tasteful monograph on Wodehouse and contributed brief comic sketches annually to the Trinity Week undergraduate revue. Alec would go on to write a short but insightful study of Beckett's plays entitled *All I Can Manage, More Than I Could*; but at the time of which I speak he was the author only of some theatre reviews in *The Irish Times* and a handful of short poems, one of which he recited sonorously to us in its entirety during our first lecture:

Yeats and the Lights of Dublin

Remembering the eagle's high adventure
And eager to resume the ethereal search,
I sit in a suburban drawing room —
A clever parrot on a polished perch.

This memorable quatrain (note the subtle variation of 'e' sounds) first appeared on the first page of the first number of Trinity's literary magazine *Icarus*, founded by Alec ten years before, in 1950; and that simple, unadorned phrase, 'a suburban drawing room', opens up a whole era — for I remember Alec's drawing room in Knockbrack, where he and his wife Beatrice sometimes had us out for 'tea' (bottles of stout), and very nice it was too for a Belfast scholarship boy then kipping, unsupervised, in a back room of the unrenovated Brazen Head — unrenovated, it seemed, since Swiftian times. Dublin was full of drawing rooms in those days, all of them in Edwardian bungalows like Alec's or in pleasant Georgian houses with windows open to gardens and birdsong, where sunlight lay perpetually on shelves of dusty first editions. These drawing rooms were the property of older people, amateur poets and philosophers of private means like Arland Ussher, who had known Yeats or had moved in circles tangential to his; and, though we were happiest in O'Neill's with Alec booming away, we were conscious too of a continuity with the unpubbable Yeatsian past. Alec's holiday home was a disused lighthouse in Greece, though whether he had Yeatsian towers in mind when he chose it he never said.

Those of us who were at Trinity in the early sixties and starting to write contributed to *Icarus*, which we edited in rotation, so I think of us as 'the *Icarus* crowd'. 'We' included Michael Longley (a slightly older Instonian), Edna Broderick, Brendan Kennelly, Ronnie Wathen, Jeremy Lewis and Deborah de Vere White. Not all were Yeatsians necessarily. Longley and Wathen were Gravesians. Up at UCD in Earlsfort Terrace they were Kavanagh people, as well as Joyceans, and our contemporaries there — Michael Hartnett, Paul Durcan, Macdara Woods, Eamon Grennan — could sometimes even be seen sitting nervously at Kavanagh's table in McDaid's. One of the fun things about the *Icarus* crowd was its gregariousness. We were a mixed bunch, from everywhere including India and Nigeria, and knocked about together with the natural camaraderie of youth — while cultivating, of course, all sorts of privacies and solitudes of the soul. Something of that inclusiveness is evident in Brendan's later remarks about Yeats, where he praises his capacity 'to discover unity where so many before and since have perceived and perpetuated discord and division'. This is an obvious but valuable point, and one to be emphasized; for Yeats incorporated aspects of most known traditions into the imaginative structure and wove into the patchwork, together with oriental silks and 'grey Connemara cloth', a few threads from the sash some fathers wore.

Longley and I, like other Northerners in Dublin, returned regularly to Belfast and environs, where our families lived, and often hung out with students from Queen's, some of whom we'd known at school; so a typical Saturday night in Belfast, especially around Christmastime, would find us in Kelly's Cellars or Lavery's Back Bar (the 'Cobbles') off Shaftesbury Square, with our QUB opposite numbers. There we met student activists like Eamonn McCann and other literary types like James Simmons and Seamus Heaney. Belfast-fashion, there was much sectarian banter, idiotic in a place where so many have exogamous relations: my own non-Protestant auntie, Lily Lavery, I presumed to be related, however remotely, to the 'wine trade' and so to the great Sir John, husband of Hazel. There too we met a recently appointed lecturer at Queen's, Philip Hobsbaum, a Cambridge man who had known the London 'Group' and now established a Belfast branch. An exhilarating presence who fitted in very well to the rackety local milieu, he was a challenging, rambunctious figure, fond of drink and controversy, given to self-dramatizing pronouncements like 'Things happen wherever I go; fights break out' and 'I bet I could take Mahon's girlfriend away from him'. About the fights it was certainly true, and we cherished him for it; but in his critical attitudes he espoused a moral earnestness, an insistence on 'felt experience', and a literal-mindedness that was dogmatic and doctrinaire in the extreme. You didn't disagree with Philip, or not for long; you learned to listen to his opinion, think your own thoughts, and keep your own counsel. Much guff has been written about Philip's 'Group', whose combative meetings aroused limited interest. Though we hit it off in informal situations, I myself attended only once and never went back. 'Group' guff was an invention of English journalists, critics and commentators who had no idea of the local circumstances, and I think there's a reason for this, a political one. Conscious of a loosening grip, English culture (always retentive) seizes upon whatever it can claim, however residually, as its own — and so it has been with Ulster poetry. The Limerick-born actor Richard Harris used to say that if he won an award the London papers would run the headline 'British Actor Wins Award'; if he misbehaved they would say, 'Irish Actor Thrown out of Night Club'.

While Belfast discourse was cheerfully abrasive, a more polished variety was characteristic of Dublin, where the rhetorical arts still flourished. Famous windbags abounded, and self-appointed wits; extravagant gesture was much admired, parliamentary vehemence cultivated. The university debating societies, where aspiring barristers and politicians practised their oratory, flashed with attitude; everyone thought he was Edmund Burke. These performances were exclusively masculine and stylistically conservative. Women were not encouraged, not that any sane woman would have wanted to take part, though she might have found the spectacle revealing; for here, on noisy nights, one could hear the voice of authority being formed (or so they hoped) in the inflections of an earlier time. They were all longing for an opportunity to exclaim, 'Let no man write my epitaph!' or 'You have disgraced yourselves again!' The tradition died, however. The debating-society stuff was already archaic; for even in Ireland the sixties presaged new developments. We're all provincials of our own time, and the decade probably brought little that hadn't occurred before, in the forties or in the twenties; but it seemed evident to us that a new age had dawned, and one or two of the brighter hippies noticed a relevance to their own concerns in some of Yeats's prophetic utterances. Gyres and the like were bound to appeal to a generation devoted to Tao and *The Tibetan Book of the Dead*.

Yeats himself, in *A Vision*, describes his strange ideas as 'stylistic arrangements of experience' comparable to the cubes of Wyndham Lewis and the ovoids of Brancusi. If he has taken such ideas literally, he reports, 'my reason has soon recovered'. This is reassuring to us sceptics, and gives us the perfect excuse to pay minimal attention to his magical system. But perhaps we miss out on something by being too quick to ignore the implications; for *A Vision* is really a sort of political book. Yeats described it as mythology rather than philosophy, much as Graves later described *The White Goddess* as 'an historical grammar of poetic myth'. But both are political books, or perhaps I should say ecological books. I think it probable that Yeats considered *A Vision* to be in effect a Nietzschean prophecy like Spengler's now largely forgotten *Decline of the West*, so fashionable at the time; and he may have thought it better to publish a fanciful work than a pompous one. The gyres have come in for a lot of stick over the years; but they're really a way of asking questions like 'Is there a shape to history?' and 'Where do we go from here?' — questions not in themselves ridiculous. Besides, in his curiously practical fashion, Yeats was epistemologically sound. He always 'saved the phenomena', as scientists say.

Another problem area is the archaism: linguistic certainly; social too, but also what might be called environmental:

> *Beloved books that famous hands have bound,*
> *Old marble heads, old pictures everywhere.*

The tower itself is an ivory one, figuratively of course; he wishes to 'set eyes on nothing' not sanctified by time, like Sato's sword. A tall order in the modern world, and there's something painful about the great national poet staring with 'hatred' (his own word) at the lights of Dublin. He studiously ignored many modern developments; much had to be excluded from consciousness, especially if it had an electrical or mechanical origin. We know his philosophical aversion to mechanism. Perhaps in the long run he will be proved right, and some future post-industrial society will turn for endorsement to his ecological purism; but even so he misses out on an exciting feature of the period. Readers of the future, exploring the texture of 20th-century life, will find little of it in Yeats. True, the Middleton freighters sailed to Constantinople ('All my dreams were ships'); but there are no cinemas or aircraft in his work, the obvious exception being Robert Gregory's biplane in 'An Irish Airman Foresees His Death'. Even here, though, the plane is more like the picture of a plane — there's none of the 'oil-rinsed bearings' of Hart Crane's 'Cape Hatteras'. Crane, another Platonist, also writing in the twenties, likened the cinema to Plato's cave with 'multitudes bent toward some flashing screen'. Yeats preferred his eternity unadulterated; yet he recommends 'the baptism of the gutter' — an example of his ability to make words mean different things in different contexts. 'Arrogance' and 'bitterness', for example, can be good or bad depending on the persons involved. He is hostile to the notion (his own) that the 'abounding gutter' might be Helicon; while for many, himself included, this has been an article of faith. He talks about 'the book of the people' and 'the common tongue'; and one can easily imagine him, in another context, using a phrase like 'the abounding gutter' with a positive and even festive intention. The list of modern poets whose Helicon has been, precisely, the abounding gutter, *vox populi vox Dei*, is a long one, and I need only mention MacDiarmid, Brecht and Pasolini to show with what eloquence the idea has been celebrated. Yeats knew this too, of course, as later poems like 'Lapis Lazuli' go to show: everything is dialectic, truth and counter-truth.

Other objections might be that there is too much 'fury'; that his heroism is too relentless, that his standards of beauty and performance are too elevated to be humanly interesting. There is a singular character defect besides: the will to 'win'. He was too interested in winning; so it comes as no surprise that his brother Jack was the more winning personality and his father, in most ways, the wiser man. Yeats learned much, perhaps most, from his father, as a reading of the old man's letters to his son makes clear. Writing from New York in April 1913, JBY says, 'Rhetoric expresses other people's feelings, poetry one's own' — a remark which, duly pondered by the poet, emerges five years later in *Per Amica Silentia Lunae*: 'We make, out of the quarrel with others, rhetoric, out of the quarrel with ourselves, poetry'; and there are many such examples. 'The world will not be right,' says JBY, 'till poetry is pronounced to be life itself, our being but its shadow and poor imitation'; and in June 1921, eight months before his death, he again writes to Willie: 'It is easier to write poetry that is far from life, *but it is infinitely more exciting to write the poetry of life*, and that is what the whole world is crying out for. I bet it is what your wife wants — ask her. She will know what I mean and drive it home.'

The mask compels reductive curiosity: what was Yeats 'really' like? Who was the bundle of incoherence that sat down to breakfast? Did he ever play football, go for a swim? Had he a phone, a radio? Did he drive a car? He would have played football at school, though it seems like a 'mobbish' kind of game for a solitary; so it comes as no surprise to learn, from the *Autobiographies*, that as a boy he followed athletics, where individual excellence is the thing, not team spirit; where individuals compete against themselves, as in any form of art. He himself drew, or implied, the parallel: 'I followed the career of a certain professional runner for months, buying papers that would tell me if he had won or lost. I had seen him described as "the bright particular star of American athletics", and the wonderful phrase had thrown enchantment over him. Had he been called the particular bright star, I should have cared nothing for him. I didn't understand the symptom for years after...' He swam constantly in youth at Rosses Point (indeed, he swam into middle age when occasion offered); interestingly too, also in youth, he was a keen sailor, sometimes setting off at dawn in a cousin's boat and spending whole days on the water. We know that later he had a phone and a 'wireless', answering back to broadcast voices he disagreed with. As for driving, no, he took buses and trains, or was otherwise driven. Did he ever push a pram? I don't know that he ever pushed one, but I think he's at least minding one in 'A Prayer for My Daughter', one of the great pram poems together with Coleridge's 'Frost at Midnight'. Watching his baby daughter, he entertains thoughts of 'natural kindness'; and it's worth remembering that, for all his abstract urgency and hauteur, these ordinary things were central to him — indeed, they have much to do with the 'unity of being'.

We came to think of him as a monument, even as a statue. Yeats himself, like Pound, perfected 'the sculpture of rhyme', and had a taste for lapidary inscriptions: 'Swift's Epitaph', 'To Be Carved on a Stone at Thoor Ballylee', 'Cast a cold eye...' To be cold, somehow beyond human reach, especially 'the daily spite of this unmannerly town' (Dublin), became a personal necessity, though one which didn't rule out the 'passionate': on the contrary, the ideas fused in his mind. To be somehow beyond critical detraction was also a stylistic (and creative) imperative, and we came to think of him as unassailable where the poetry itself was concerned, if open to serious question in matters of politics and philosophy; but the scholarly snow precipitated by his own coldly passionate dreams disfigured his dream-statue in our minds; he 'became his admirers'. The myths took shape, the critical books piled up, and somehow the man himself ceased to exist. Such was the force and ingenuity of his self-creation (a trick learnt from Wilde), he seemed to have spirited himself away until only the work remained, a monument of its own magnificence. He really did seem to be 'out of nature', one who had never taken his bodily form from 'any natural thing' — a ludicrous thought when one considers his own emphasis on the physical. It was a triumph of masquerade, heroic in its intensity; but the deconstructionists came to Sligo, and now he is human again.

Montague, Simmons, all of us indeed, have echoed Yeats; Heaney, too, echoes Yeats echoing Shakespeare: 'Every wind that blows'; 'The end of art is peace'. All this intertextuality is nothing new: 'Works of art are always begotten by previous works of art.' We inherit his example, to use Seamus's word. What we haven't inherited, or only vestigially, is his deep structure; for we were born at a later time, into changed conditions, and have often felt it necessary to resist the Yeatsian charm and authority. He was, as we know, proud with a pride many called arrogance; but, though no 'wit' in the traditional sense, he obviously had a rich vein of fun, besides giving an important place to 'gaiety' in his hierarchy of values. Humour he recognized as an enemy of his kind of poetry, so he avoided it in verse almost entirely; but gaiety is a different thing, capable as it is of condoning madness, lust and rage. The Chinese sages in 'Lapis Lazuli', and the lords and ladies of Byzantium and Ben Bulben, are gay in that sense; and so too was Yeats, as the later photographs testify. No doubt he could be affected and insufferable, yet how come such a man had so many friends? As for the admirers he has become, they increase daily. He bequeathed us phrases like talismans, consolatory and inspiring ('A lonely impulse of delight'; 'our proper dark'), an ideal of audacity and empowerment, and a paradigm of transfiguration, personal and historical. His example shames and ennobles us all.

Ghosts in the Sunlight

There was a series of daring high-profile break-ins a couple of years ago in the Bel-Air and Beverly Hills neighbourhoods of Los Angeles. (Charlize Theron was one victim.) A police spokesman acknowledged 'an increase in burglaries in the area between Sunset Boulevard and Mulholland Drive', adding: 'The problem we have is the area is large and expansive. We have long dark streets, a lot of foliage, and a lot of service trades in and out of there.' It was always like that. No one can walk down a dark street in safety, said Raymond Chandler in 'The Simple Art of Murder', a famous magazine piece. His 'mean streets' weren't only in south-central Los Angeles but in swankier quarters too, where 'mean' could mean more than just underprivileged, though the same anarchic principle applies: 'The realist in murder writes of a world in which gangsters can rule cities and almost rule nations, in which a screen star can be the finger man for a mob and the mayor of your town may have condoned murder as an instrument of money-making.' There's a touching innocence here, but the innocence is implicitly attributed to the presumptive reader, a respectable citizen shocked to hear the system is corrupt; he himself had no illusions. He postulates, as an agent of redemption, the Philip Marlowe figure 'who is not himself mean, who is neither tarnished nor afraid, a common man and yet an unusual one', a 'shop-soiled Galahad' who possesses 'rude wit, a lively sense of the grotesque, a disgust for sham'; the story is his 'adventure in search of a hidden truth'.

Chandler's ambition was to write 'mysteries' that were at the same time 'real novels of character and atmosphere with an overtone of violence and fear'. As he wrote frankly to his London publisher Hamish Hamilton: 'I am not just a tough writer. I am the best there is in my line and the best there has ever been. I am tough only incidentally; substantially I am an original stylist with a very daring kind of imagination.' His best work is indeed as serious as he claims and even his toughness is literary: 'When I split an infinitive, God damn it, I split it so it will stay split.' Comparing 'English and American style' in the *Notebooks*, he writes quite snobbishly (this was the 1930s) that American English 'has no awareness of the continuing stream of culture', for which he blames 'the collapse of classical education' and 'a lack of the historical sense'. American education is a flop, he says: 'Such tradition as they [*sic*] have in the use of language is derived from English tradition, and there is just enough resentment about this to cause perverse use of ungrammaticalities, just to show 'em.' This reads datedly now, but demonstrates very forcefully how English were Chandler's own background and guidelines. Educated at Dulwich College, he started out as an English (and indeed Latin) poet, a student of the Elizabethans and the Romantics, and the deep structure of that inheritance gives body and weight to his steel-harsh and steel-bright romances. He would have read Malory and Spenser.

To say that Marlowe is a knight errant is not just a figure of speech; the phrase identifies in his work a ghostly cultural presence going back many centuries. But he knew Los Angeles too like the back of his hand, and kept an eye on the local news. 'Montemar Vista', for example, with its 280 steps up from the Pacific Coast Highway, first came to sinister prominence not in *Farewell, My Lovely* (1940) but in crime reports five years earlier about the death of the 'screen idol' Thelma Todd, a friend of Lucky Luciano. About this time the Hollywood *Citizen News* commented, 'The real causes of death of many well-known figures, past and present, will never be known because of cover-ups by an oligarchical community, police and citizens alike, protecting its own and the millions of dollars in revenue such knowledge could harm.' Todd was part-owner of 'Thelma Todd's Sidewalk Cafe' beside the steps, a joint that also features in the novel: 'I gave it my business to the extent of using its parking space.'

Each of the four great novels, first published between 1939 and 1953, has Marlowe as its protagonist. No 'development', technical or otherwise, takes place during the ten or a dozen years between *The Big Sleep* and *The Long Goodbye*. Marlowe remains the same sceptical, hard-drinking, solitary man in his thirties or forties, in whom we can divine some secret hurt — a self-employed private investigator who dislikes the rich in principle but is apt to be lenient in particular cases. He himself is poor, unmarried, and spends lonely evenings playing chess against himself — until the phone rings, or a blonde walks into the office. Typically a Chandler novel begins on the steps of a big house, where he has been summoned by an elderly person to sort out a family problem to do with blackmail or the like. Or he may run into trouble in a public place and get himself involved. In either case he finds himself working among the rich, some of them okay, some of them monsters; in the underworld, where he invariably gets knocked about; and in competition with the police, who treat him with derision or with grudging respect according to temperament. This is all pretty familiar stuff; but it must be remembered that it was Chandler who started it. All clichés were invented by someone: 'It was about eleven in the morning, mid-October, the sun not shining and a look of hard wet rain in the clearness of the foothills. I was wearing my powder-blue suit with dark blue shirt, tie and display handkerchief, black brogues, black wool socks with dark blue clocks on them. I was neat, clean, shaved and sober, and I didn't care who knew it. I was everything the well-dressed private detective ought to be. I was calling on four million dollars.'

I need to correct myself. To say there was no 'development' in the work, other than plot development, is not quite true. There's a development in Marlowe's own character, a development some found soppy and unbecoming in a solitary and self-reliant hero, but the fact is he falls chivalrously in love. It doesn't amount to more than an innocent romance, but it dispels his cynicism, if that's what it is, at least for a time. Always, you notice, a sucker for the serious, bespectacled 'librarian' type (though he claims to prefer 'smooth shiny girls, hard-boiled and loaded with sin'), he allows himself to dream of fireside slippers in the house of Anne Riordan, a second-generation Irish girl whose father got fired by the cops for honesty. He resists the attraction ('I've had too many women to deserve one like you'), though the attraction is real and obviously heartfelt: 'She had gray-blue eyes, dark red hair, and fine bones in her face.' But cynicism prevails: 'An occasional light winked from the hills through thick trees. The homes of screen stars. Screen stars, phooey. The veterans of a thousand beds. Hold it, Marlowe, you're not human tonight ... I drove on to the Oxnard cut-off and turned back along the ocean ... No moon, no fuss, hardly a sound

Ghosts in the Sunlight

of the surf. No smell. None of the harsh wild smell of the sea. A California ocean. California, the department-store state. The most of everything and the best of nothing. Here we go again. You're not human tonight, Marlowe' (*The Little Sister*). Despite their narrow focus and genre mannerisms, the Chandler books are so obviously more than thrillers: there's a rough poetry there, and a satirical edge, that make us want to know more about their creator. He did indeed write verse in his time. A promising classical scholar in youth, he wound up as an oil executive until a drink problem led to his resumption of literature. He married a woman twenty years his senior, kicked the booze, and led a life of almost valetudinarian seclusion until her death. His life thereafter was one of rapid alcoholic decline. It was during the reclusive years that he wrote his best work — a solitary, anomalous figure, a rather formal Englishman (albeit Chicago-born) in a swirl of California kitsch; a poet *manqué* in an ivory tower rising out of the meretricious and violent raw material of his art.

It was his declared intention to take the detective story into the street. He is initially deceptive. You think you're dealing with an innocent little matter of blackmail, theft or murder, and in no time at all you're up to your eyes in hard drugs, seriously kinky sex and phoney psychiatry. Only gradually, as a complex and generally bizarre situation is laid bare, does the full extent of it strike home. He was obsessed with evil, in particular with the corruption of innocence — a recurrent American theme, but one handled by him in a recognizably un-American manner. Nowhere does he suggest that it's American innocence which is at risk. On the contrary, Chandler's America (the mean streets of LA) is inherently evil, owing perhaps to its lack of constraint and surfeit of money. His innocents are either European or quasi-European: a stuffy New York publisher, a Norwegian sailor, a Filipino houseboy, Anne Riordan. There's also his sense of a European culture from which, as he saw it, so much of America had chosen to cut itself off, though he is always nice about ethnic minorities and the underprivileged generally, with a special soft spot for 'the poisoned kitten dying in agony behind the billboard'.

Cultural nostalgia is evident at a number of points: the Rembrandt self-portrait on the office calendar 'who looked as if he might do a little work in a while if somebody made a down payment'; the

Derek Mahon

reproduction of a balcony scene by some forgotten Italian artist in a Bel-Air mansion; the English origins of Terry Lennox, the disappearing murder suspect in *The Long Goodbye*. This one tells us, I think, a good deal about the author for whom Lennox seems to have been, not exactly an *alter ego*, but a shadow, an imaginary buddy, a ghost in the sunlight. Lennox is an elfin war hero, a drunken charmer, a weak man once strong, married to a rich tramp in the Chandler mode. She gets dead and Lennox, realizing the vulnerability of his position, takes the first plane to Mexico, where he fakes his own death, and I'll tell you no more in case you haven't read it. But present here are several aspects of Chandler himself, idealized to be sure: the alcoholism, the barely concealed homoeroticism, the marital eccentricity. Also the English origins, including the war record, carefully investigated by the English-sounding Marlowe — name of a playwright who, a mystery man like Lennox, liked to fight in bars and tended to lose. Also the death wish, whose presence is there somewhere at the heart of all Chandler's work; Keats-like, he was half in love with easeful death. This is true too of the Chandler screenplays, like *Double Indemnity* with its fatalistic voice-over.

There's a lyrical plangency about certain passages which reminds us that we are reading, not pulp, not even good pulp, but 'literature'. Rusty Regan was an Irishman murdered by . . . well, murdered, and sunk in oil: 'Me, I was part of the nastiness now; far more a part of it than Rusty Regan. But the old man didn't have to be. He could lie quiet in his canopied bed, his bloodless hands folded on the sheet, waiting. His heart was a brief, uncertain murmur; his thoughts were as gray as ashes. And in a little while he too, like Rusty Regan, would be sleeping the big sleep.'

Bridging the Gap

It's changed hands since and gone downmarket, but there used to be a terrific pub called the Lion's Head at the corner of New York's 7th Avenue and Sheridan Square. Owned and run by Michael Reardon and Judy Joyce, it had a vaguely Irish character, though by no means exclusively so. Well known to the West Village crowd, for whom it was a local, it attracted writers and journalists particularly and featured in several books, notably Pete Hamill's *The Drinking Life* (1994) and Jay McInerney's *Bright Lights, Big City* (1984), where the hero meets a Princeton girl reading Spinoza in a quiet corner. In due course they go up the steps to the street 'like Plato's pilgrims climbing out of the cave, from the shadow world of appearances towards things as they really are'. McInerney got the speakeasy atmosphere of the place, but he's being a little snooty here. The Head hosted many interesting people including media types, trade-union figures, ex-seamen, psychiatric nurses and renegade nuns. When talk turned to politics you found that what they all had in common was a left-wing orientation. There was a famous gay bar next door, but they didn't bother us and we didn't bother them. It was a great neighbourhood, and in those first Clinton years, before Giuliani and the Bush gang, New York seemed liberal in the best sense. To the eyes of a resident alien like myself, the old radical America was still in place. But the Village isn't America, and the radical tradition was one of the things that drew people from everywhere else. It had drawn them for a hundred years, and round about 1920 it drew the poet Hart Crane from Cleveland, Ohio.

Crane had more addresses in the Village than you could shake a stick at, notably 45 Grove Street, but later moved to a two-room apartment, front and back, at 110 Columbia Heights, Brooklyn. He wrote to his mother Grace Hart Crane in April, 1924: 'Just imagine looking out your window directly on the East River with nothing between your view of the Statue of Liberty, way down the harbor, and the marvellous beauty of Brooklyn Bridge close above you on your right. All the great new skyscrapers of lower Manhattan are directly across from you, and there is a constant stream of tugs, liners, sailboats etc.' He discovered that Roebling, the designer of Brooklyn Bridge, had his observation post forty years before in the same house, overlooking the construction site. Crane found the place through Emil Opffer, a seaman who lived upstairs. Opffer was Crane's special sexual partner; the 'Voyages' sequence was addressed to him. As for the Statue of Liberty, the novelist Mary Gordon reports in *Good Boys and Dead Girls* (1991) that the sculptor, Frédéric-Auguste Bartholdi, 'reacted with horror to the prospect of immigrants landing near his masterpiece; he called it "a monstrous plan". So much for Emma Lazarus.' Lazarus was the poet whose familiar lines about the 'huddled masses' appear at the base of the statue, properly speaking 'Liberty Enlightening the World'. It's not a bad old poem. She speaks of 'the air-bridged harbour that twin cities frame'. Air-bridged although the bridge (1883) predates the statue (1886) by three years. Previously the Brooklyn Ferry (see Whitman) connected the two boroughs, as the subway was to do. Whitman, wrote Crane in 'Modern Poetry', 'better than any other, was able to coordinate those forces in America which seem most intractable, fusing them into a universal vision which takes on additional significance as time goes by. He was a revolutionist . . . but his bequest is still to be realized in all its implications.'

The mid-twenties, his own and the century's, were the best time in Crane's short life. He was sexually active, drinking euphorically, working furiously, and considered by many to be the coming man. So much is evident in the seven 'Voyages', in 'Ave Maria', 'The Harbor Dawn' and 'Atlantis', the last section of *The Bridge* but the first to be written. 'How could mere toil align thy choiring strings!' he exclaims; and it's immediately obvious, here in the prologue, that he is some kind of religious poet — which he would remain to the end. His religion, an Orphic one, had nothing to do, except by reaction, with the Christian Science of his Cleveland home. On the contrary, he sometimes seems almost to re-enact the masochistic spiritual intensity of the Spanish mystics. Just another victim of the times, he was caught between vicarious rural nostalgia and an age of rapid urbanization and immigration, between 'My Old Kentucky

Home' and the 'din and slogans'. His best years coincided with the Harlem Renaissance; a syncopated, bluesy note is often audible in *The Bridge* and elsewhere. He was and is a poet of minorities, starting with the gay crowd. The poetry world itself is a tiny minority to be sure. To say that 'Native Americans' are also a tiny minority is true only of the United States and Canada, since they're there in their millions from the Rio Grande to Cape Horn. Crane, in his quest to understand 'America', not only included 'The Sad Indian' in his demographic, he made the indigenous cultures central to his vision with 'Powhatan's Daughter', the river-and-prairie sequence, haunted by the past, where 'the old gods of the rain lie wrapped in pools'. His vertiginous and ill-starred project of 'discovering' for himself the old heart of the continent, in Mexico, was an extension of this. He bit off more than he could chew, but 'Powhatan's Daughter' remains an important moment in American poetry when, unusually, the white man looked closely at the red man — or rather the red woman, for the continental earth is naturally figured as female (Pocahontas). There must have been a bit of a psychic jolt in this for many of his first readers. Europeans and Asians are used to thinking of the earth as female, but go-getting and still frontier-conscious Americans of the time must have felt it, at some level, as a reproach.

'The average American,' said Gore Vidal mischievously, 'has a historical sense stretching back approximately three days.' By this reckoning, the average American poet looks back about thirty years. Crane, though, occupied another, anthropological time frame: pre-Columbian cultures, the Spanish and British empires, Irving's Tarrytown, the 19th-century commerce of tea clipper and railroad, and 20th-century technologies, are all contemporaneous in *The Bridge*. He wanted to bridge the gap between past and present, ideal and real. In 'General Aims and Theories' he speaks of 'building a bridge between so-called classic experience and many divergent realities of our seething, confused cosmos of today', and 'the articulation of the contemporary human consciousness *sub specie aeternitatis*'. Hence, 'Faustus and Helen'; hence the epigraph and marginalia to 'Powhatan's Daughter' drawn from William Strachey's *History of Travaile in Virginia Britannia* (1615) and related sources, and the epic use of these in apposition to the glimpses of modern underprivileged life, the wage slaves and the hoboes:

Derek Mahon

> *So the 20th Century — so
> whizzed the Limited — roared by and left
> three men, still hungry on the tracks, ploddingly
> watching the tail lights wizen and converge, slipping gimleted and neatly out of sight.*

His radicalism, like Whitman's, lay in his inclusiveness, and in his Rimbaud-like determination to be 'absolutely modern'. The end of 'Cutty Sark' signals in two words, 'Taeping' and 'Ariel', the demise of the sailing ship and the triumph of modern communications. What we hear is the clatter of office typewriters; what we see is a pulsating radio mast as in old Movietone newsreels. This is genius. 'I've always thought *The Bridge* a triumph of sustained power, and wondered why the best critics . . . so badly gummed up its achievement,' wrote Robert Lowell in 1958; and it's true that among the American poets of the early 20th century only Crane, arguably the best of them, has never had his due — perhaps because he never fulfilled his potential, more likely because he wasn't to the taste of Academe. 'Posterity,' said Heywood Broun, 'can be as wrong as anybody else.'

Crane's principal objective was what he called 'absolute poetry' — the ecstatic, rapturous absolution of finished art; but impurities, the rough and tough, were vital to his design. Hazard, spontaneity and contingency modified and completed the work's integration. Documentary, newsreel and cartoon filled out his programme. It's noticeable how much sheer information he incorporates, how much human interest he conveys. Impressed though we are by the high-strung lyricism and formal tension of *The Bridge*, he has another, more relaxed register both there and elsewhere, especially in the later poems. 'The Broken Tower', his last, recovers the preferred mode, but 'Key West: An Island Sheaf' is much less hectic. When it is hectic, it's an objective agitation set off by real-life events. Instead of the familiar dense solipsism, he is often blithely observant, with a stereoscopic clarity. This secondary Crane, the Crane of starry floor and watery shore, was most at home in Cuba's Isle of Pines (now Isla de la Juventud) and with the folk culture of the Windward Islands, attentive to local life and customs. Some of this island work could qualify as 'eco-poetry':

Bridging the Gap

> ... *huge terrapin*
> *Each daybreak on the wharf, their brine-caked eyes;*
> *— Spiked, overturned; such thunder in their strain!*
> *And clenched beaks coughing for the surge again!*

'Island Quarry', 'Royal Palm', and 'The Air Plant' extract hidden meanings from the inanimate: from the quarry's 'goat path quivering to the right' in a heat haze, and the air plant's 'inverted octopus with heavenward arms'. These have the lightweight feel of holiday verse, but are none the worse for that. 'Key West' itself, which finds no shore 'where gold has not been sold and conscience tinned', gets downright journalistic; but, in love with violent excitement, what really turns him on is hurricanes. 'Eternity' is a masterpiece of disaster reportage:

> *The old woman and I foraged some drier clothes*
> *And left the house, or what was left of it;*
> *Parts of the roof reached Yucatan, I suppose.*

A 'frantic peacock' rummages 'amid heaped cans'. The storm's 'howling, sheeted light' and 'screaming rain' are clearly sources of deep satisfaction. Sonic and visual both, it would have made a terrific real-time news item, concluding of course with the arrival of paternalistic aid:

> *The President sent down a battleship that baked*
> *Something like two thousand loaves on the way.*
> *Doctors shot ahead from the deck in planes.*

They used to wonder what Keats would have done had he lived. Well, what if Crane hadn't jumped from the *Orizaba*? What if he'd got back to New York, sobered up, and tried again? Another patron might have helped, or another foundation. He might have ended up running some proto-Beat establishment like the later Jack Kerouac Institute of Disembodied Poetics in Boulder, Colorado. Perhaps, having been initiated by Peggy Cowley ('whose sweet mortality stirs latent power'), he might have got hitched to her or another and settled down. We might just about imagine him as a mature student specializing in Whitman and teaching at Columbia. And

Derek Mahon

what would his new poetry, if any, have been like? But he did jump. A myth was born, and canonization indefinitely postponed. America has never liked those who jump, who opt out, and she doesn't like 'losers'. Crane has never been an acceptable role model, to put it mildly. An uncooperative copywriter, a sort of noisy Bartleby, alcoholic, suicidal and queer, he also devised, from Elizabethan and Jacobean drama and from the Romantics, a highly wrought idiom at odds with loose-limbed American speech — though he thought of himself, some of the time, as writing jazz, 'striated with nuances, nervosities'. Hollywood film techniques ('Chaplinesque') and the industrial realism of artists like Charles Demuth were other evident 'influences'. It scarcely needs emphasizing that he was an all-American poet, in disposition as in avowed purpose, yet reservations about him linger to this day. In a curious way, and despite his admitted stature, he remains a cult figure. Although the author of some of the finest American poems, his example, for obvious reasons, is not one that Creative Writing students are urged to follow. Still, they might look again at Crane instead of Williams, so easy to imitate, while studying the medium — respect for which, said Crane, 'forces the subject to yield surprising illuminations and assertions new to our experience, additions to the total of our sensibilities'.

Bowen on the Box

Once in the 1950s London *Vogue* ran a nostalgic questionnaire. Readers were asked, *Vogue*-fashion, to recall things they *liked* about the War Years, 1939-1945. Some remembered the dances, some the petrol shortage and empty roads; and some chose the blackout, when the darkened cities of Britain saw the moon and stars with a forgotten clarity. Elizabeth Bowen gets this experience in her story 'Mysterious Kôr', to which I'll return. She loved the dark, she loved light, also the in-between times to which she was so uncannily attuned: 'It is about five o'clock in the evening that the first hour of spring strikes — autumn arrives in the early morning, but spring at the close of a winter day. The air, about to darken, quickens and is run through with mysterious white light' (*The Death of the Heart*, 1938). She goes on to say even more perceptive things about human reactions to this phenomenon; but let's stay with the light. Like her younger contemporary Louis MacNeice she liked dazzle, which may in part explain her curiously showy taste in bling. (A television interview circa 1970 shows her gleaming and sparkling as she stammers her replies.) It may explain too, when the lights were on, her fascination with *artificial* light, direct or reflected. The light theme, 'the war' and the *noir* conditions of London after dark recur throughout her work.

I've been looking again at her history of *The Shelbourne* (Harrap, 1951), reissued by Vintage. 'A Dublin child', born at 15 Herbert Place beside the Grand Canal, she thought the Shelbourne 'the prototype of all large hotels' and 'a mine of human experience'. Her first novel, set not in Dublin but on the Italian Riviera, was entitled *The Hotel* (1928) and hotels occur frequently throughout her work, as in that of her admired Henry James — a symptom, perhaps, of that sense of dislocation, of not really belonging anywhere, some of the Anglo-Irish used to admit to. She remembered the 'twanging' trams of childhood, and coaches at the Shelbourne's revolving door, but spent most of her grown-up life in England. During the thirties and later, when she lived in London, the Shelbourne was often a stopping-off point on her way to Bowen's Court, Co Cork. These visits were infrequent; but in 1940, with the war a year advanced, she suddenly started spending longer periods in Dublin, where she took a service flat to pursue what she called her 'activities'. These activities, for which she was paid £100 per annum, were designed, says Victoria Glendinning in her biography (there are others too by Hermione Lee and Patricia Craig), to ascertain Irish attitudes to the conflict. Using her married name, Mrs Alan Cameron, she arranged to meet a number of prominent politicians, clerics and the like; and, with the help of old friends, set about leading a busy social life so she might hear as many views as possible. She prepared written reports for the Dominions Office in London, some of which were kept and eventually made available for inspection. There she pleaded for a sensitive response to Irish neutrality, while lending support to the unrealistic suggestion, originating at Westminster, that the status of 'Ulster' might be renegotiated in exchange for British use of the so-called Treaty Ports in Donegal and Cork.

Nothing came of this, but she may have been instrumental in ensuring the British government's continued tolerance of Irish neutrality at a time when that government was greatly agitated by the loss of Allied shipping to U-Boat action in the Atlantic. Tolerance was mutual. Glendinning remarks on the 'nursery solicitude' of Shelbourne staff towards visitors from Britain: it was 'the rooted belief of all chambermaids,' she says, 'that those arriving from London were the victims of air-raids'. (This was sometimes so: Bowen herself was bombed out of her Regent's Park house for a time.) A Dublin journalist who talked with her in 1940 met her, naturally, in the Shelbourne, clearing-house for news, and found her 'the synthesis of all Holbein family portraits'. The following year, writing about 'Éire' in the London weekly *New Statesman*, she told her readers that 'Éire feels as strongly, one might say as religiously, about her neutrality as Britain feels about her part in the war; she has invested in it her natural consciousness' — memorable phrase! Bowen was nonetheless critical of Irish policy while castigating her own social group, the Anglo-Irish, for presenting themselves as England's stronghold in Ireland: 'If they merged their interests with those of the Irish people, they could make Ireland an easier country to deal with.' At a time of blackout in Britain, the lights of Dublin resembled, she says, the lights of Broadway; but she rebukes those who took cheap shots at neutral Ireland, 'butter and steaks given luscious prominence by English journalists who, on flying visits to Dublin, fail to obtain the desired interviews'. She concludes, in traditional Anglo-Irish fashion: 'Given the plain facts of history, I could wish the English kept history in mind more, that the Irish kept it in mind less.'

The Shelbourne, a commissioned job, is a very readable mixture of history and autobiography stiffened by her astringent wit and heightened by her lyrical apprehension of sensory experience. Thus the hotel, 'opaque' from the outside, is seen inside as a series of light-impressions, from the morning windows which 'receive sunshine, reflect sky, gaze toward the Dublin mountains', to the roof at evening, 'a space from which one may look around and see Ireland under a world of sky. Sea gleams in the distance; cloud shadows bowl slowly over the hills.' Uniforms change from khaki to olive green as history unfolds, then disappear; political developments are reflected in Empire furniture, Sèvres china and 'the dark-watery polish of old glass'. The total effect is poetic and on occasion novelistic — as when, during a week-long strike in 1921, she reports or imagines 'wild cats in the kitchen leaping off the tables, glaring out from the cold blackness over the extinct ranges, chaos personified'. She is best on the long reign of the despotic and capricious Mrs Jury, who died in 1904; on the Easter Rising when guests, besieged by Republican forces, led 'a ghostly shipboard existence' and precautionary revolvers were distributed by staff with the morning tea, and on Dublin in the Jazz Age. The place, and the idea of the place, shine for her with a more than serviceable glow: 'When lights blaze in the evening, when morning sunshine comes flashing in through the glass doors . . .' She loved cars too, taxis, and an almost human vehicle in *Eva Trout* (1969): 'The Jaguar, homing, had had the chagrin of finding itself superseded . . . This unfortunate Jaguar, though now for nearly three months on Thanet, had got to know little of the locality. Going well when given a chance, it remained dispirited.'

The love of light makes her novels and short stories peculiarly vulnerable to the film camera, though she wrote before fiction began

Derek Mahon

to be conceived as drafts for screenplays. The hack adaptation of books like hers for television resembles, far-fetched though it may seem, the 'translation' of poetry: like poems translated from another language, scripts based on novels and short stories retain only certain features of their originals. Some are more faithful than others; some pursue the letter, some the spirit. My own attempts, back in the eighties when there was still some literacy in broadcasting, tried to preserve both. The critics were kind to these attempts; they didn't disapprove too much of the end product, the object on the box, of which the script is only the score. So much depends on the director, the cast, and everyone else; these are the real adaptors. The script 'writer' merely mediates between the original text and those most directly involved in production. This was certainly my experience with the two Jennifer Johnston books I worked on. These lent themselves so readily to dramatization that I felt slightly fraudulent in accepting any credit whatsoever. An absolute beginner, I had no very clear idea of what 'shooting script' and 'storyboard' signified, but found this no hindrance. It wasn't for me to bother about dissolves and tracking shots, though I got a kick out of INT, CU, VO and FX, especially FX.

Jennifer, the daughter of a distinguished dramatist and herself a playwright, makes extensive use of dialogue in her work. She wrote an intense short novel called *Shadows on Our Skin* (1977), and the BBC made an intense short film of it. Somewhere in between I jotted down a few production notes, laid out the dramatically important passages and made some suggestions; most people in that line of work do the same. We ought to be ashamed of ourselves really, even if it means more people read the books. Ashamed too because, whatever about commercial considerations, the soul of a book is *used* instead of loved for what it is. *Traduttore, traditore.* We betray the bookness of the book; besides, it never really works. TV feature films are in a category of their own; somewhere between the 16mm and the 35mm falls the shadow. A fine made-for-TV film like *Langrishe, Go Down* (1979), screenplay by Harold Pinter from the novel by Aidan Higgins, starring Judi Dench and Jeremy Irons, floats off into cyberspace, more rumour than movie, where it's hard to reach. It was twice on the box thirty years ago but, despite its credentials, is now, it seems, of purely archival interest.

Graduating from Radio Drama, where I worked with Maurice

Leitch and Andrée Molyneux among others, I started in the TV game in 1980, when the Beeb was still the Beeb. My screenplay of Jennifer's *Shadows on Our Skin* was found acceptable; more demanding was *How Many Miles to Babylon?*, same author, a first world war story based on family diaries. This was made for BBC2 by Innes Lloyd and Moira Armstrong and filmed in Co Wicklow, which represented both itself and, with a few appropriate touches, somewhere behind the lines on the western front. Daniel Day-Lewis played Alex (one of his earliest roles) and Siân Phillips his imposing mother; this was the real thing. Made for the small screen, it took place mostly indoors (a country house, a field headquarters, a café) or in leafy lanes. The production was thought a success, and soon I found myself working on Elizabeth Bowen for Granada, part of the ITN network. The one I wanted to do was *The Heat of the Day* but Harold Pinter, a real screenwriter, wanted to do it too, so that was that. Instead I was given *The Death of the Heart*, a head-scratcher but a lot of fun.

They used to say TV corrupts and ITV corrupts absolutely, but that wasn't my experience of Granada. This channel actively sought literary material and employed remarkable directorial talents. Among these was modest, thoughtful Peter Hammond, a director with an inspired visual sense. He related imaginatively to Bowen's own visual sense and took special delight in her use of polished surfaces; water, glass, waxed furniture, shiny shoes. *The Death of the Heart* is full of polished surfaces: the Quaynes' house is itself a polished surface: as are their social life and conversational style, all gleaming with 1930s upper middle-class manner and hypocrisy. Bowen and her husband, who worked for the BBC in Portland Place a short walk away, lived for some years at 2 Clarence Terrace, NW1. 'Streams of clever friends and admirers came to visit Elizabeth,' says Patricia Craig. Alan, arriving home of an evening to be confronted by rows of Homburgs hanging in the hall, gave his wife's callers the collective title of 'Black Hats', some of them evidently quite bad hats too. This is the milieu of the novel, where the querulous Quaynes 'entertain' the queer black-hatted author St Quentin Miller, the meretricious Eddie and the puzzled Portia, an orphaned teenage relative. The casting, with one exception, proved ideal: Patricia Hodge as Anna Quayne, all furs and pearls; the great Wendy Hiller as the wise old servant Matchett; Miranda Richardson, a newcomer, as rowdy Daphne when Portia goes for a seaside holiday in the South Coast bungalow 'Waikiki'. The 'sounding box' of Waikiki was brilliantly done. When Daphne ran her bath out at high tide, 'hoarse with shingle', precipitating Portia's 'roaring and gurgling' watery nightmare, Peter cut rapidly from sea to bath to sea and back again in about two seconds; water crashed, Portia cried out as if drowning. The result was terrific.

Other projects: John Montague's 'The Cry', from *Death of a Chieftain* (BBC1), and Turgenev's *First Love*, an RTÉ-Channel 4 co-production. 'The Cry' ran into trouble on location in Ballymena, where local people objected, and had to be filmed instead in Cushendall. (I myself, at my father's funeral, got a rap on the knuckles for this one.) To the Turgenev story, in Isaiah Berlin's translation, we gave the Wodehousian title (as we realized too late) *Summer Lightning*, since the series of which it formed a part had the generic title 'First Love'. Paul Joyce, who directed, wanted it moved from Czarist Russia to pre-Famine Ireland, so it joined the list of works derived from that fashionable equivalence. Paul Scofield was in this one (a favour to his friend Joyce) but it was not a success, though notorious for several years at RTÉ for its prodigious budget. I wanted to do Brian Moore's *The Mangan Inheritance* and Jim Farrell's *Troubles*, but both were already optioned elsewhere. Another that came to nothing was Moore's *A Moment of Love* (paperback title of *The Feast of Lupercal*). This unrealized project was initiated by an independent American producer, Sidney Glazier, an intriguing figure who started out driving trucks for the Philadelphia mob during Prohibition and later diversified. He had successfully filmed another Moore story, *Catholics*, with Trevor Howard — like *Langrishe*, a triumph of that literate era.

Before turning to other things I worked once more on Bowen with Peter Hammond. This time it was a scary yarn, 'The Demon Lover', the one that gave the title to her wartime collection, first published in 1945, about the effects of the Blitz. Clarence Terrace was damaged, but she and Alan stayed on in London while others left for the country. 'The violent destruction of solid things,' she writes in a postscript to the volume, 'the explosion of the illusion that prestige, power and permanence attach to bulk and weight, left all of us, equally, heady and disembodied . . . We all lived in a state of lucid abnormality.' 'All of us, equally': the war democratized her. The story, ostensibly about a forgotten suitor who returns after thirty years, is one more study in the 'lucid abnormality' of wartime London, the sense that anything could happen. There's something Gothic about it (the eerie house, the mysterious letter), but psychologically it's entirely of its time. As though straining to explain her predicament realistically, the heroine's baffled thoughts find a keyed-up syntax to put themselves in order: 'The caretaker (even if he *were* back) did not know that she was due in London today ... so his negligence in the matter of this letter, leaving it to wait in the dusk and dust, annoyed her ... On the supernatural side of the letter's entrance she was not permitting her mind to dwell. Who, in London, knew she meant to call at the house today? Evidently, however, this had been known ...' The story, a mere nine and a bit pages in the old Penguin edition, needed filling out for the fifty minutes of screen time required by the 'Shades of Darkness' series, so besides much atmospheric and tension-building photography, we invented some other characters she could talk to — her husband in the country, for instance, to whom she expounded some of the war thoughts contained in Bowen's postscript (to the annoyance of at least one critic) — and incorporated material from other stories in the collection: 'In the Square', 'Careless Talk' and 'Mysterious Kôr', the most magical and far-reaching. This last title comes from Andrew Lang's poetical coda, quoted here by Pepita, to early editions of Rider Haggard's *She*, a book Bowen must have known as a girl:

> *Mysterious Kôr, thy walls forsaken stand,*
> *Thy lonely towers beneath the lonely moon ...*

'No human eye' watches 'the prosaic woman' (Dorothy Tutin) in 'The Demon Lover'; but the Granada movie camera watched her as she 'gave the door, which had warped, a push with her knee' and explored her own, strange-seeming house. *Traduttore, traditore*. We had, so to speak, no right to be there; we were betraying a secret, an intimacy — though Bowen herself was interested in betrayal. Eddie, in *The Death of the Heart*, betrays Portia with Daphne; Robert betrays England in *The Heat of the Day*. Bowen, at some level, must have felt she was betraying Ireland with her wartime info-gathering 'activities' in Dublin. I used the word Gothic, and I think we can include hers in the list of Anglo-Irish names who come under that rubric, Le Fanu and the rest. She too kept a psychic record of the 'desuetude' (her word) of a governing class, in her case that of the pre-war upper middles with their pompous, frivolous, anxious assumptions and complacencies. (She had done the Anglo-Irish in *The Last September*, 1929). On a school trip in 1951, six years after the war, we looked at the Festival of Britain showgrounds on the South Bank of the Thames and queued at a Lyons Corner House in the Strand, where I heard a posh lady reprimand a cheeky 'nippy' behind the counter: 'I find your manner very rude.' 'No ruder than yours, madam,' said the girl brightly; and even then I knew I was watching history.

Wind and Limb

Patrick MacDonogh (1902-1961), a contemporary of MacNeice and Kavanagh but, unlike them, out of print for a generation, published five collections of poems between 1927 and 1958 and was highly regarded during his lifetime, with a modest international reputation based on a handful of recurrent anthology choices. Not an immensely prolific output and, despite what amounts to a cult following, he has recently seemed in danger of slipping through the cracks of literary history, which is one of the reasons he needs to be reissued. He is also a very fine poet indeed, which is its own argument. The five collections were: *Flirtation* (G. F. Healy, Dublin, 1927), *A Leaf in the Wind* (Quota Press, Belfast, 1929), *The Vestal Fire* (Orwell Press, Dublin, 1941), *Over the Water* (Orwell Press, 1943) and *One Landscape Still and Other Poems* (Secker & Warburg, London, 1958) — a distinguished though not extensive body of work, one rendered even more exiguous by a self-critical severity which led him to discard, select and refine from volume to volume until, with the Secker collection, he arrived at an almost final text.

The contents of the present volume (*Poems*, Gallery, 2001) are based on that collection, while dropping eleven and adding eight, including six 'new' poems from MacDonogh's brief final period, 1957-61. The Secker book, though relatively slim, was in effect a collected poems, 'all that he wished to preserve' arranged according to his own idea of his work, an order (not necessarily chronological) followed here. Eight poems are collected here for the first time. 'Afterpeace', 'The Dream' and 'Marriage Song' first appeared in *The Dublin Magazine*, 'The Rust is on the Lilac Bloom' and 'Far from Ben Bulben' in *The Irish Times*; while the other three are reproduced from his own typescripts. He dedicated the Secker volume to his wife, Ellen May ('Maisie') Connell MacDonogh; in the same spirit, this reissue of his work is dedicated to his two daughters,

Derek Mahon

Caroline and Boyer. Boyer is an artist and lives in Co Waterford. Caroline, a writer who lives in France and teaches at Caen University, is our principal source of biographical information, and her as yet unpublished doctoral thesis, 'A Study of Patrick MacDonogh's Poetry', has been invaluable in elucidating background and theme. She concedes that *One Landscape Still* was an ambiguous title. MacDonogh was not saying, 'Ireland is the only place for me,' but something more like, 'Here we are, prisoners of our condition'.

That volume, long out of print and now a collector's item, is a decent period piece bound and wrapped in quiet greens, the dustjacket proclaiming it a 'Poetry Book Society Recommendation' and recommending 'other poets from our [Secker's] list' including Theodore Roethke, Burns Singer, D. J. Enright and Jonathan Griffin. The front flyleaf informs us that MacDonogh first made his appearance on their list in 1944, in the small anthology *Irish Poems of Today* selected by Geoffrey Taylor from contributions to *The Bell*. This, it continues, is 'the first collection of his poems to be published and they reflect the author's passionate love of his native land'. The given price was 12/6d net. But of course it was by no means his first collection to be published, though his first (and last) to be published in England. As for 'passionate love of his native land', the ambiguous title has misled the blurb-writer, for there's rather more to it than that: '*tormented* love', not unique to him, would be more like it — though torment is passion too. The book was reviewed in a respectful if subdued fashion by, among others, John Hewitt (*Threshold*) and John Montague (*Studies*). Hewitt provided a brisk summary of MacDonogh's progress from the early poems with their conventional properties of willows, roses, lilacs, Babylon, Nineveh, Troy and, 'touching a forelock to local circumstance', leprechauns. He remarked on a Dowsonian atmosphere and Yeatsian derivation, noted an absence of originality but recognized the 'literary good breeding'. Serious praise he reserved for later work, especially 'Escape to Love' and 'O, Come to the Land', where he found in MacDonogh 'a hard objectivity towards himself and his generation'; and he concluded by recommending him as 'an addition to our imaginative estate'. Montague acknowledged 'the much anthologized lyrics, graceful and plaintive as early Yeats', where 'romantic lyrical pain merges into dialect and folk poems', but noticed the 'brooding, obsessive nature' of the book, and the 'desolate divisions of the spirit' they describe. Both remark on the Yeatsian properties and cadences — though even Yeats, of course, borrowed from Nora Hopper and Frank O'Connor, to name but two; equally both Hewitt and Montague were aware of something new and different. Somewhat belatedly, MacDonogh had established himself as a distinctive voice.

He was born in Dublin, where his father was founder and headmaster of Avoca School, Blackrock, and educated there and at Trinity College, where he read for an arts degree, shone at athletics and subsequently took a PhD with a thesis on Allingham. After graduation he worked as a teacher and commercial artist before joining the staff of Arthur Guinness, Son and Co Ltd, where he later held a senior executive post. The background is important. One of five children, he grew up in an earnest and convivial Protestant middle-class environment of tennis parties and hockey sticks, subsequently playing hockey for Ireland: a privileged environment also characteristic of his active and linear professional career, especially the prime-of-life years when he and his family lived at Cintra, a pleasant Georgian country house near Kinsealy, north Co Dublin. Rod and gun, field and stream, featured at weekends. During his last years, when ill health obliged him to take early retirement, MacDonogh lived in 'reduced circumstances' at Malahide and Portmarnock. Both he and his wife, a well-known mezzo-soprano, broadcast frequently on Radio Éireann, she specializing in Schubert, he in sporting and literary matters. Hill walker, fly-fisherman, golfer, he knew the country intimately from Wicklow to Mayo, from Antrim to Cork; but the customary landscapes of his poetry are those of north and south Co Dublin, and of Co Meath. After a certain point they are even more specifically those of the Kinsealy woodlands and the Malahide estuary. His friends included Lord Moyne, 'Con' Leventhal and Seamus Kelly ('Quidnunc' of *The Irish Times*); in England, Betjeman and Laurie Lee, the author of *Cider with Rosie*. He drove fast cars, Sunbeam Talbot and Jaguar, co-founded the Galway Oyster Festival, took a hand in John Huston's Youghal production of *Moby-Dick*, and made frequent appearances in literary pubs like the Pearl Bar and the Red Bank. Brian Fallon, in *An Age of Innocence: Irish Culture 1930-1960*, tells us this 'sensitive, much-loved man' was one of the *Dublin*

Derek Mahon

Magazine inner circle. He contributed also, as his acknowledgements indicate, to the books pages of large-circulation newspapers like *The Observer*, and to New York magazines including *Harper's* and *The American Mercury*.

Flirtation was notable less for the poems than for the black-and-white cover drawing (his own) in what Brian Fallon calls 'the then fashionable Harry Clarke style', the style also of Cecil ffrench-Salkeld's decorative murals in Davy Byrne's (Dublin) pub: an art-deco 1920s-Arcadian idiom depicting harlequinesque *fêtes galantes*. (Celtic motifs would appear later.) We associate these properties with the whimsical, adolescent nostalgia of Laforgue and *Le Grand Meaulnes*; and indeed there was, and remained, something lost-domainish about MacDonogh's sensibility — an inflection audible even now in the work of William Trevor and Jennifer Johnston. These early poems are juvenilia, Keatsian pastiche; though later developments suggest that 'The Eve of St Agnes' remained a useful and even bracing model. It's not until *A Leaf in the Wind* that he begins to be interesting, with 'Helen' and 'A Drunk Man' (later 'The Drunkard') which made it into the Secker volume. Not included in that volume is the unusual and rather rambling 'A Belfast Shipping Clerk Goes to His Work', where a young MacDonogh figure, sent by Guinness's to the northern capital, with its 'gantries looming through the mist', thinks fondly of summers in Wicklow, 'the quiet crackling of the gorse' and 'the shining altar of the sea'.

The Vestal Fire is a heroic epithalamion in thirteen sections, some long, some short. A devoted lover of 'companionable women', almost a Muse poet in the Gravesian sense, he embraced sexual love as the highest form of human understanding, and these fourteen pages, intensely erotic yet idealistic — even 'Petrarchan', as he says elsewhere — are his first sustained attempt to measure his own experience of this not uncommon revelation. It's a love poem, or series of love poems, in search of absolute sincerity and commitment, almost of self-definition — 'my constant light' — where the winsome, wanly dancing nymph-like figure of the *Flirtation* cover girl is found to be a grown-up woman and treated accordingly. An excited and slightly incoherent work, over-long, overly discursive, overly cerebral, it's also overly anxious to arrive at the right sort of conclusions. But the short passages he retained and which are included here ('Curtain' and 'You, Too, at Midnight Suddenly

Awaking') are very fine; and the exercise, noble in itself, allowed him to approach a subject more fully developed later — that of essential solitude. Here already, in this solemnly happy poem with its echoes of Spenser and Donne ('This night is ours'), an austere, quasi-religious disposition makes itself heard, one oddly nostalgic for a spiritual regimen it rejects too violently. The positive, 'life-loving' aspirations the poem so vigorously espouses co-exist with an exile among 'waking thoughts' under an 'actual cold observant sky'. It's the old mind-body problem, with 'dancing spring' cursed by a need 'to discipline my thought with naked line'.

Over the Water, published only two years later, is the culmination of his early work and remains a remarkable achievement by any standards. Here, collected for the first time, are the classic anthology pieces, the popular lyrics and several intriguing, much more 'modern' poems like 'Dodona's Oaks were Still' and the title piece itself. He is no longer writing tentative poems; nearly all will survive later inspection, and most are included here. How to explain this sudden burst of creative confidence and exactitude? An emotional settling, perhaps, with wife and family, and a new political awareness after long silence during the 1930s — an awareness not quite explicit in the manner of Auden and MacNeice, but implicit in the situations of his 'characters', released from tedium and galvanized into fruitful tension and flow by the wartime atmosphere both in Ireland and England. Brian Inglis, the author of *West Briton* (1962), records that, on the outbreak of the second world war, he and his Malahide set joined the British armed forces as a matter of course — though he resolved in his own mind that he would resign his RAF commission should Britain re-invade 'Éire'. MacDonogh, older but from a not dissimilar social group, must have had similarly complex feelings about the whole business, especially in the light of his friendship with the English poet Phoebe Hesketh, the 'war widow' in the poem of that title. But the wartime mood affected him in another way too, confirming a cultural identification with the Gael and issuing in the 'folk' poems for which he became chiefly known, 'She Walked Unaware' and 'The Widow of Drynam'.

He writes elsewhere of the Irish poetic genius as 'at once spiritual and sensuous', qualities we associate with, say, Clarke's 'The Straying Student' or Padraic Fallon's 'Mary Hynes', and which he too

Derek Mahon

combines here. These dramatic monologues, rural in setting, their speakers respectively a lovelorn youth and a proud old woman, are beautifully crafted and in some ways characteristic utterances, artifacts even, from the much maligned Yeats and De Valera era of traditional sanctity and comeliness which produced so much of the finest Irish art and literature. A centuries-old tradition of *aisling* and *cailleach* lives on in both, together with an unregenerate eroticism and radical defiance. Here are Synge's 'wild words', the garrulous narration, dramatic self-awareness and aristocratic peasant pride, the wandering lines and 'planted' off-rhymes, the concrete imagery and emotional realism of Ó Rathaille and Eibhlín Dhubh Ní Chonaill. If 'Be Still as You are Beautiful' seems to recommend, shamelessly, that the recipient 'look good and say nothing', the heroic and vital note in 'The Widow of Drynam', as so often in Gaelic poetry, is struck by a woman, in the voice of an Ireland most of us have forgotten or never knew: for one not really familiar with what Jennifer Johnston calls 'my own unspoken language', his recreation, in a modern setting, of the intonations of the Gaelic 18th century is the more remarkable.

Amorous, introspective, philosophical and contemporary-history poems merge into one another with their wonderful titles: 'Soon with the Lilac Fades Another Spring', 'This Morning I Wakened Among Loud Cries of Seagulls'. A love poem will present itself in folk guise, a 'war' poem will contain a love story; everything discursive carries a specific gravity of intense emotional experience, mixing memory and desire. A generalized piece like 'The Bone-Bright Tree', for instance, a codger's lament for 'courteous acumen', 'astringency' and 'strict articulation', invoking the stoical suicide of Petronius, *arbiter elegantiarum*, records one of a series of psychological crises relating, in part, to a vaguely guilt-ridden detachment he seems to have considered endemic to the Protestant situation. This anxiety is present even in the much-quoted Swiftian epigram 'No Mean City', a bleak glimpse of Dublin social life in the not so distant past. Dogged by a morbid sense of isolation, despite job and family, he tried to escape this, in life, through manic activity of various kinds — and, in the work, by embodying the rupture between subject and object, perceiver and perceived, text and context, in highly wrought formal structures. As if this isolation were not enough, Caroline, in her thesis, alludes to that Meredithian theme, 'the deep and prolonged struggle between man and wife', quotes Coleridge on 'the unfathomable hell within', and finds here, as in his crisp abstractions, the true strength and modernity of the work.

One of the last in whom a 'Revival' texture and aesthetic are evident, he risked inclusion among the 'twilighters' and 'antiquarians' to whom his friend Beckett gave such a hard time in the 1934 essay 'Recent Irish Poetry'. The adopted personalities and archaic coloration of the folk poems might seem to incriminate him, together with F. R. Higgins and early Clarke, in 'the flight from self-awareness' and even a yearning for 'the wan bliss on the rim'; but the pathos of these poems springs from a very personal romanticism. The son in 'Drynam' has gone to 'the war', perhaps an older war; but with 'Over the Water' and 'War Widow' we are definitely in the 1940s. These belong to a whole genre of wartime love-and-separation poetry, fiction and film, a genre to which MacNeice and Elizabeth Bowen were only two of the most vivid contributors. 'War Widow' is addressed to Phoebe Hesketh, with whom MacDonogh conducted a fruitful friendship then and later; while the magnificent 'Over the Water', one of his finest achievements, inscribes their relationship in another of his dramatic monologues, though dramatic in a more complex fashion than hitherto. As in 'Drynam', an adopted personality speaks. A soldier, in London during the Blitz, thinks of his lover in Ireland and wishes her beside him: a displacement of the poet, in Ireland, thinking of his lover in England and wishing himself there. A frequent visitor, he knew the London atmosphere, and picks up on the 'Apocalyptic' mood of the time: for example, despite obvious differences, he greatly admired the work of Dylan Thomas. There is a comparable exhilaration here, though the subtext is one of loss, failure, unfulfilment: his final theme, if one redeemed by his gift for clarity of design and aphoristic closure.

Conceived as a birthright, the theme is symbolized in the 'bone-bright tree' (compare and contrast Joyce's 'heaventree of stars'); as a moonlit hieroglyphic landscape void of human agency but alive with creatures, owl and pigeon, mouse and fox, like Leopardi's night-time glade of dancing hares. What is figured is a crisis of sensibility, an examination not of conscience but of consciousness. A morbid unspontaneity — the 'original sin', so to speak, in the

Derek Mahon

Protestant soul — is scrutinized with self-conscious unspontaneity. He doesn't seek, much less achieve, the perhaps rather forced emotional triumphalism of 'A Prayer for My Daughter' and 'Among School Children'. His theme is implenitude; his wistful love of organic growth and generative archetype goes unrequited. The waves break regardless; the trees are mute. This is what happens in 'Dunleary Harbour' and 'Dodona's Oaks were Still'. The first of these, another of his strongest pieces, asks the old question, 'Was it spirit or flesh first committed, first suffered the wrong?' — and adapts a Bowen phrase to commemorate a vitality, his own and that of his social group, now evidently a thing of the past: 'the death of the innocent heart, the end of surprise'. The suburban trees of Dunleary (*sic*) take on, characteristically, a mythic and mystical significance in 'Dodona's Oaks'. According to Graves, the oracular oaks of Dodona in Epirus were the object of a Diana moon cult, involving mistletoe, therefore sacred to the Muse; but, in the eremitic solitude imagined by the narrator — a St Kevin-at-Glendalough scene — the druidic boughs prove unforthcoming, are silent in wind and limb.

Silent too is the sleeping house in that fine dejection ode, 'Escape to Love', as he wakes to dawn consciousness — 'felicitous space', in Bachelard's phrase, where, taking the fun out of birdsong and sunny window, the mental sky darkens and a premonition of death stirs 'like a mouse in the gut'. (The book about bones and mice in 20th-century poetry has yet to be written.) This is a short story, a sketch for a novel, a spiritual autobiography and diagnosis. On 'the first bright Sunday in March' he walks abroad through 'poisoned lands' and 'sun-dazed' fields, remembering with pain his inhibited mother, her 'frosty duty', 'chilly nurture' and 'acrimonious care': 'Mother of Rimbaud, weep for what you have done!' He contemplates with 'rueful self-knowledge' a limited literary achievement, his spiritual apostasy in 'a long indolent act of sacrilege' and — 'political orphan too' — his suspension between two kinds of sectarianism and estrangement from society generally; then, in a strange and violent conclusion, sacrifices himself to save a hunted hare. (The book about hares in Irish poetry is also long overdue.) There is something both Orphic and Christian about this gratuitous gesture; though its failure, in narrative terms, is of a piece with the existential failure the poem documents. At least we are not dealing here with a flight from

Wind and Limb

self-awareness: *au contraire*, 'Escape' is MacDonogh's most serious and resourceful effort to establish personal and cultural authenticity. The fairy-tale enchanted castle of earlier work diminishes finally, in 'Far from Ben Bulben' and 'Make Believe', to bone structure, the skull beneath the skin: to his 'proper dark', a bungalow at Portmarnock. Nothing wrong with that, many might envy him; but Caroline finds 'resignation' in the last poems — which she also describes, more positively, as 'succinct' and 'testamentary'. Though sound in wind and limb and evincing, she says, 'a kind of romantic and austere dignity', MacDonogh fell prey to psychiatric problems and spent increasing periods in mental hospitals. One of these coincided with the arrival of the Secker proofs, which he had no opportunity to correct; so that volume, his life's work, is full of misprints. Handwritten corrections appear, fortunately, in copies of the published book and are, of course, incorporated here. Besides the three previously unpublished typescripts, an old Guinness ledger survives where, carefully inscribed in fountain-pen blue ink, he sketches a perfunctory fragment of autobiography dwindling to diary entries and disconsolate reflections on the Cold War: 'If this misery was caused by the pressure of these or similar enormous anxieties it would at least have some dignity and honour about it . . . but as it really springs instead from an incorrigible ignorance of the value of money and from the impotent creative desire of one more emasculated soul I find it merely mean and despicable.' If, with the re-invasion of Ireland and other vulnerable societies by 'global capital', and the resulting devastation, the work of the Revival has to be done again, MacDonogh and others may yet come into their own.

This edition retains his order of contents. The rationale may seem inscrutable, but it's his own mature configuration, his own 'bone-bright tree': he placed the lines in a certain sequence, and the poems too — perhaps on the principle of 'radial time'. We are not trying to construct a contemporary, but granting a dead man the 'ineluctable modality' of his historical moment. Nor is this mere antiquarianism; for the poems live. Their knotty cerebrations and serious striving, the half-dozen masterpieces conceived, as it were, in thunderstorms, together with other 'glories infrequent, authentic, vouchsafed though unsought', constitute his own version of 'failing better'. 'To be an artist is to fail as no other dare fail,' says

Derek Mahon

Beckett in the *Dialogues*: 'that failure is his world and the shrink from it desertion, art and craft, good housekeeping.' The idea of failure, much underrated, thrives between freedom and necessity, between gravity and grace, in an 'endless quarrel between earth and sky'. The lonely impulse of delight negotiates with bone structure:

> One landscape still! —
> Memorial acres, old demented trees
> About a crumbling house, a stony hill,
> A solitary lake — forever these
> Restrict the image and impose their will.

Occupying, says Brian Fallon, 'a middle ground between traditionalism and modernism, as also between the consciously "Irish" note of Higgins and the more cosmopolitan tone of MacNeice, MacDonogh produced a compact and resilient body of work with a distinctive character'. Obsessed with youth and novelty, we sometimes patronize previous generations, imagining them to have been more naive than they were; for everything has been done or thought before in one form or another, though our historical provincialism tends to ignore the fact. We patronize, too, their difficult achievements — limited, like ours, but available to us if we're interested. They too thought themselves too smart for their own good; they too thought themselves cursed by wised-up meta-consciousness: indeed, it was one of their favourite themes. MacDonogh needs to be looked at again. Retrieval can resolve much, even in an age of humoristic deconstruction, and the ecstasy and frustration of an occluded talent can have the power of shaming a fluent posterity accustomed to much greater exposure. A good part of his example, paradoxically, will lie in his built-in 'obsolescence'; also in the amateurish, extra-curricular, unfinished air which, innocent of calculation and bright with idiosyncrasies (prosodic slippages, late jokes best overlooked, an addiction to 'w' sounds), confirms the authenticity of the enterprise. But *caveat emptor*: too often, revisiting the past with sophisticated hindsight and superior technical means, we lose the original aura, the poignant sense of imperfect, lost reality; we cease to 'walk unaware'. So much the worse for us if we can no longer praise without irony, as MacDonogh does in a prose piece, 'Out of the Night' (*The Dublin*

Magazine, 1958), those things, real or imagined, to whose dispersal his own work stands as such courageous testimony: 'religious faith, love between man and woman, nobility of conduct, unexplained gaiety of heart, order and beauty in the natural world'.

Sad Wings

Aside from Lawrence E. Harvey's *Samuel Beckett: Poet and Critic* (1970) there has been little critical discussion of Beckett's verse. Though seldom anthologized it is widely known, and some of it by heart, since the best of it speaks, or rather whispers, like his quietest dramatic pieces, to the inner ear; perhaps because the poems I mean are dramatic pieces in their own right. If not as familiar as the novels and plays, they have their own distinction. Like the prose, with which they have so much else in common, they are instantly engaging and, like the finest verse, mysteriously persistent in the mind and even the nerves; they have an almost physical presence. Graphic and vivid, they are also intensely musical: theatrical too, and continuous with the work for stage and radio. 'Whoroscope', for instance, considered a youthful exercise (and it's certainly that), is also a dramatic monologue of a kind to which Beckett would return in *Krapp's Last Tape, Not I* and *Ohio Impromptu*, while the minimalist 'Dieppe' is, among other things, a stage direction in the geometrical mode of *Footfalls, Ghost Trio* and . . . *but the clouds . . .* The early poems anticipate the manner of the novel trilogy: 'suck is not suck that alters', alluding to Shakespeare's Sonnet 116 ('Love is not love . . .'), prefigures the geriatric romance of Molly and Macmann in *Malone Dies*. Joycean in their comical obscurantism and finneganese locutions ('Not a syllogism out of him'; 'My squinty doaty!'), mixing the learned and the demotic, they are Joycean too in their direct appeal to the ear.

Beckett spoke, in his critical work, of a 'rupture', a disjunction between subject and object, between the perceiving sensibility and the unreality of reality. He belonged, with Thomas MacGreevy and Denis Devlin, to the 1930s generation of Irish poets, and shared their fractured modernist aesthetic if not their religious convictions: 'a low-down highbrow low-church Protestant', for him poetry was the only prayer, 'the only way out of the tongue-tied profanity',

Sad Wings

as he put it in 'Humanistic Quietism', his review of MacGreevy. MacGreevy was an important influence on Beckett the poet, notably in the peripatetic 'Echo's Bones' sequence, early work owing much to MacGreevy's 'cab poem' (Beckett's phrase) 'Crón Tráth na nDéithe' — roughly, twilight of the gods. Both thought highly of Eliot. (James Knowlson, in *Damned to Fame*, likens Beckett's early manner to that of 'Prufrock' and 'Rhapsody on a Windy Night'.)

'Enueg', 'Sanies', 'Serena': odd titles. We need to know, as the 'Notes' to the Calder *Collected Poems* tell us, that the enueg (*ennui*) was a Provençal lament, the serena their evening poem. A sanies is a morbid discharge; and while Beckett achieved some of his happiest effects with the morbid, not to say the incurable, it is nonetheless striking how often, flying in the face of their hilarious gloom (they 'enjoy ill-health'), the poems evince traditional graces like 'Meath shining through a chink in the hills'. It helps to be introduced to the strange and archaic words that Beckett is so fond of, to know that 'Whoroscope' is spoken by Descartes; that *Dortmunder* is a German beer, Malacoda a deceitful demon in Dante. Although grounded in 'real life' (a youthful infatuation, the death of his father), 'Alba' and 'Da Tagte Es' are chock-a-block with literary allusion. 'Da Tagte Es' derives from a medieval German poem; the alba is the aubade, and so on. But there is a principle at work whereby the less obviously obscure the source and the less erudite the scholarly apparatus, the more lyrical and memorable the poem and the more closely it approximates to that condition identified by Beckett himself, in his 'Homage to Jack B. Yeats', as 'high solitary art uniquely self-pervaded, one with its well-head in a hiddenmost of spirit, not to be clarified in any other light'.

'A Beckett poem,' says Anthony Cronin in *The Last Modernist*, thinking of the early work, 'is an almost indecipherable tangle of recondite references and allusions' — but this ceases to be so after a certain point. With the French poems and the shorter lyrics we can leave behind Augustine and Descartes, Dante and Goethe, confident in the knowledge that it is Beckett's own voice we are hearing now — except in the sometimes surprising translations. Beckett himself formed a low opinion of his youthful verse (the fiction too), which he described as 'showing off', yet he kept it in print. One reason, suggests Cronin, may have been that he began as a poet and 'in a manner commoner in France than in England, continued to think of himself as such, even after he had virtually abandoned poetry for prose'. The history of 'Whoroscope' is well known. Nancy Cunard of the Hours Press advertised a prize for a poem on the subject of time ('for or against'), which was given to the twenty-four-year-old Beckett. The title relates to Descartes' refusal to have his horoscope cast, since this would predetermine the day of his death. This prize-winning exercise in modernist pastiche is little more than a bit of fun. The point of it can be teased out, in a way, with the help of the Eliot-like 'Notes'; but it is not to be taken seriously, nor was it meant to be. Of interest, though, are the Joycean rodomontade ('Them were the days I sat in the hot-cupboard throwing Jesuits out of the skylight') and the curious pre-echoes of many a later and more laconic soliloquy: 'Who's that? Hals? Let him wait'; 'What's that? How long?'; then, with a sudden flash of lyricism, he 'who has climbed the bitter steps' (Descartes was a late riser, but Christina of Sweden required him to be in attendance at five in the morning) asks to be spared by his foes for a natural death as unpredictable as his birth-date is secret:

and grant me my second
starless inscrutable hour.

The literally rambling 'Enueg', 'Sanies' and 'Serena' series from *Echo's Bones* (1935), interspersed with shorter poems, cycle ('zeep'), trudge and drift around Dublin, London and Paris, noting such things as an old man 'scuttling along between a crutch and a stick', tulips 'shining on Guinness's barges' in the Liffey, the 'mackerel' (*maquereaux*) at billiards in the American Bar, rue Mouffetard, thunder in Regent's Park, the Crystal Palace glimpsed from Primrose Hill. The touristic contingency of these peregrinations ('Gnome' invokes 'the years of wandering') bespeaks, in Montale's phrase, solitary inanition, an apparently 'wasted' youth; and the cold eye cast on most people and things, even natural phenomena ('the tattered sky like an ink of pestilence', 'a black west throttled by clouds'), sees only the anxiety and confusion of the period: compare, for example, David Gascoyne. But the random method, or lack of method, throws up rare moments of wit ('smoke more fruit') and oddly luminous intervals ('my breath held in the midst of thickets'; even 'all things full of gods'), so tone is unreliable and

Sad Wings

intention, if any, unclear — in his own words, 'the work of a very young man with nothing to say and the itch to make'.

Of the shorter poems in *Echo's Bones* one at least, 'Alba', is in a different, more affective register — perhaps because, in its slightly incoherent way, it is a love poem, or a sketch for one, frustrated by inhibition and a wished-for renunciation of the flesh in the form of a picturesque 'Buddhist' reverie: 'rain on the bamboos flower of smoke alley of willows'. 'Cascando' ('Cascadingly', a Beckettian musical tempo), written in youth for a young American woman who quickly dropped the acquaintance ('is it not better abort than be barren'), reads like the work of an adolescent, not of a grown man: 'the hours after you are gone are so leaden', 'if you do not love me I shall not be loved' and so on. But all this neurotic work, this 'work' on his neuroses, cleared his head for plainer, truer things both in English and French. These are the 'existential lyrics' (his own phrase though used in another connection): 'Dieppe', the immediately post-war 'Saint-Lô'. The existential lyric shares certain features, not least its brevity, with the Imagist poem, though it's free of the Imagist preciosity, partaking rather of the 'Spartan maieutics' Beckett commended in Pound. One of those poems that make immediate contact, 'Dieppe' does so less for its verbal than for its visual, even filmic character:

> *again the last ebb*
> *the dead shingle*
> *the turning then the steps*
> *towards the lights of old.*

The last line, originally *'vers les vieilles lumières'*, then 'towards the lighted town', before finding its final shape, seems provisional. The English version is not as sharp as the French. We lose the stage-directional quality of 'demi-tour', the 'steps' are ambiguous (footfalls or civic amenities?) and the last line seems finally untranslatable. But even in English the idea is there, the situation instantly recognizable. It's a stage direction, yes, but also so much more; for ebb and shingle recall the 'melancholy, long, withdrawing roar' of 'Dover Beach', of all such beaches, and the retreat of metaphysical certitude, while steps and lights point to aspirations for ever disappointed, for ever renewed. The beach will be known to Molloy,

Derek Mahon

he of the sucking-stones, and to Winnie in *Happy Days* (1961). Erskine's twenty-four-page 'short statement' in *Watt* (1953) remembers 'on the dark shingle the turning for the last time again to the lights of the little town', but the moment had already been caught. 'Dieppe' points to the later, more exiguous poetic mode. Written in French before the second world war and translated into English by the author, it suggests not festivity or consolation, but the tedium of time-honoured illuminations — including, perhaps, the shoreline cogito of the human figure itself. (There is no 'I', but it appears to be singular.) The French poems in general share this new transparency: 'vive morte ma seule saison', 'je suis ce cours de sable', and the strange 'je voudrais que mon amour meure', translated by the author as 'I would like my love to die':

> I would like my love to die
> and the rain to be raining on the graveyard
> and on me walking the streets
> mourning her who thought she loved me.

The exigencies of the existential lyric, and those of translation, are perhaps responsible for Beckett's revision, as in 'Dieppe', of the last line here, originally 'pleurant celle qui crut m'aimer', then 'mourning the first and last to love me'.

This revisionism, this come-and-go, is itself a visual enactment. Beckett sometimes seems to anticipate the camera and the production team. There's a self-consciously filmic quality in 'je voudrais' as there is in 'Dieppe', and it may or may not be fanciful to guess that the graveyard, besides deriving from Yeats ('He Wishes His Beloved Were Dead') and Joyce ('She Weeps Over Rahoon'), owes something to Carol Reed's *The Third Man* (1949), with which it's roughly contemporaneous. (One might take the filmic question further and locate one more source for *Godot* in the two prisoners on the run in Renoir's pre-war *La Grande Illusion*, 1937.) The soppy-tough note is there to be deplored if we want to take him literally, but 'je voudrais' is really saying something else: 'I'd like to do a screenplay.' Beckett had once written to Eisenstein, asking to be taken on, but had no response; though he did write a screenplay later for Buster Keaton (*Film*, 1965).

Saint-Lô (Manche) stands on the river Vire: some twenty miles from the Channel coast, it was wrecked by intensive bombardment in June 1944. Beckett, as interpreter and storekeeper, spent some months on the staff of the Irish Hospital there the following year. 'Saint-Lô', which first appeared in *The Irish Times* in June, 1946, moves abruptly from the shimmering river to the devastation, from a mild and agreeable two lines to an apocalyptic sphere contained in the word 'havoc' as the poem's music moves from Schubert to, say, Messiaen or Ligeti. Everyone likes 'Saint-Lô'. Lawrence Harvey speaks of its 'brief and unadorned perfection':

Vire will wind in other shadows
unborn through the bright ways tremble
and the old mind ghost-forsaken
sink into its havoc.

This intimate 20th-century *virelai* turns on the French *virer* (to turn), derived in turn from the Latin *vibrare* (to shake but also to gleam), and all this is in 'wind', 'bright' and 'tremble'. The oddly shocking 'havoc' of the last line is a private imprecation, the only way out of the tongue-tied profanity: that 'other shadows' will rise from the ruins affords no consolation — except in so far as such a desolate scene might give, as he put it in a Radio Éireann broadcast at the time, 'an inkling of the terms in which our condition is to be thought again'. By contrast, 'Tailpiece' ('who may tell the tale . . .') and 'Song' ('Age is when to a man . . .'), the first originating in the fragmentary but intriguing 'Addenda' to *Watt*, the second in the radio play *Words and Music*, are almost quaint in their fluent lyricism, an unexpected quality they share with certain passages in the plays. 'Song', an old man's love-lament for a lost 'face in the ashes', is noticeably poignant — as is the best of Beckett, prose and verse. The simpler he is, the better he is, and we can watch the lines clearing as we proceed. 'Song', for example, reads like an elegy for his cousin Peggy Sinclair with whom he had complex relations as a young man. Peggy's father was Jewish, the family lived in Germany; she died of tuberculosis in 1933. If anything here suggests Paul Celan's 'Deathfugue' ('your ashen hair Shulamith'), so be it. Ashes and embers recur in the plays.

The mental-movie trope is the active principle in much of the seemingly casual 'Mirlitonnades' ('Doggerels'; 'Whistles'; 'Burbles') where, as in the silent Keaton *Film,* a sombre figure is constantly observed. The face in shadow, sets and movements *noir* and enigmatic (head, light bulb, window, floor), the figure receives silent or whispered intimations we apprehend only as mime. There is black humour (an 'incontinent' yields up his forfeit soul an hour before the appointed time); and there are shining moments, as when the lonely figure, emerging from its 'hermitage', sees the calm *after* the storm, or suns itself on a bench in St Andrew's (Church of Scotland) graveyard in Tangier. ('Personally,' says the narrator of *First Love,* 'I have no bone to pick with graveyards.') The same or a similar figure (let us think of it as 'Sam') features in two poems of the 1970s, 'Roundelay' and 'Something There', engaged in his two most representative actions, walking on a beach and waiting for a sign. 'Roundelay' is a reprise, forty years on, of 'Dieppe', and 'Something There' a remake ('the eye / opens wide') of the Keaton *Film.* The faint interruption of Sam's solipsism ('something there / somewhere outside / the head') seems to indicate a world of normative reality, something besides the now customary dark communings, and for a moment there is, what, hope? But the eye closes once more and, as it were, goes back to sleep. Not such an untroubled sleep this time, perhaps, since the interruption is not unique: 'so the odd time / out there / somewhere out there . . .' It has happened before; it will happen again.

Samuel Beckett once told the present writer how much he was enjoying old age, the loss of memory and vocabulary ('I've been looking forward to it all my life'), and the loss or stripping away of a once photographic memory and a once sumptuous speech ('chastisement', 'pestilence', 'sphincter', 'declension', 'asphodels') provides the rationale for a related piece, in fact his final question or statement. Watt, remembering *1 Corinthians 13,* had hoped 'to see Mr Knott face to face', catching only a few glimpses of him 'as it were in a glass' while toying runically with simple words. Beckett is still doing it at the end with 'What is the Word'. This started life in French as 'comment dire'; but 'what is the word' is much more suggestive than 'comment dire', since 'what' is perhaps the answer, as Cronin points out: 'The uncertainty which had been given expression in *Watt,* the first work of his maturity, is echoed in his last, for this was Samuel Beckett's last piece of writing.'

Speaking of Bram van Velde in the third of the brilliant and

Sad Wings

mischievous *Dialogues with Georges Duthuit*, Beckett proposes 'an art unresentful of its insuperable indigence' such as, he claims, never before existed — though his true preference was for livelier artists like Kandinsky and Klee: 'Let us, for once, be foolish enough not to turn tail. All have turned wisely tail, before the ultimate penury'; and he implicitly associates his own practice with the stance he claims to admire in the Dutch artist van Velde: 'There are many ways in which the thing I am trying in vain to say may be tried in vain to be said.' One of the earliest formulations is the incident, in *Watt*, of the 'piano chooners', one blind, who stand in a sunlit music room exchanging doom-laden remarks about Mr Knott's instrument. For Watt the scene takes on a 'purely plastic content' and becomes 'an example of light commenting bodies, and stillness motion, and silence sound, and comment comment'. Another is the 'soul landscape' described in the 'Addenda' to the same work. 'Sky', 'waste' and Watt are 'of a dark colour': 'The source of the feeble light diffused over this scene is unknown. Beneath Watt the waste rose and fell. All was silent.' Then there is Lucky's 'think' in *Waiting for Godot* where 'the skull in Connemara', 'the tennis' and 'Cunard' combine to suggest a Proustian glimpse of childhood, a summer afternoon in the West of Ireland during long-ago school holidays. What these formulations have in common is a highly pictorial quality. We remember Beckett's interest in the art of Jack B. Yeats (the dark waste, the skull) and, in the incident of the piano chooners, the musical dimensions of the plays. The chooners are a play in themselves, or as good as a play (light commenting bodies). The poems, like the novels and plays, aside from their visual properties, are 'really' musical compositions. Except for Jack Yeats's older brother, the Yeats of *The Tower*, there are few if any discernible literary affinities after the early modernist phase.

'Imagination at wits' end spreads its sad wings' (*Ill Seen Ill Said*): categories expand and fuse in the search for residual human resources. The poems are chamber music, plays or films, sequences in the novels and plays are 'poetry' of an easily recognizable kind, like the well-known 'All the dead voices' exchange in *Godot* and the slowly accumulating wealth of lyrical passages in the later prose from, say, *Texts for Nothing* onward: 'Ruins true refuge long last towards which so many false time out of mind' (*Lessness*). These prose 'poems', with a famous economy of means, achieve an

Derek Mahon

off-beat and sometimes surprisingly beautiful poetic intensity. Important titles in this progression would include *From an Abandoned Work, Imagination Dead Imagine, For to End Yet Again* and shorter 'fizzles' like 'Still', 'Afar a Bird' and 'One Evening' ('the old sunlit face'). *Ill Seen Ill Said* and *Stirrings Still* are among his finest contributions to the genre — the last contemporaneous with 'What is the Word' and of special interest since it was his last work in prose. Beckett's later prose is a new kind of poetry, in English at least. Take the statement of the theme in 'Still' (1975): 'Bright at last close of a dark day the sun shines out at last and goes down' — a brief cascade of monosyllables like a series of musical notes. The poems and prose are synergistic. Obscure symbolic shapes, like the head bowed in darkness, appear and reappear in both and in the plays: 'Skull alone in a dark place pent bowed on a board to begin.' And finally *Stirrings Still* (1989): 'One night as he sat at his table head on hands he saw himself rise and go.' Not head *in* hands but head *on* hands: every gesture signifies. Poet, dramatist, *seanchaí*, raconteur: just as it would be misleading to suggest that Lucky's 'think' is a sort of comic mime of the history of Western philosophy, so too it would be futile to try to 'place' Beckett; for his verse, like his prose, is finally *sui generis*. Not inexpressive, as its author might have wished, but expressive of a rare vision, like the 'brief scattered lights' in *Malone Dies*: 'They were things that scarcely were, on the confines of silence and dark, and soon ceased.'

An Open Secret

John Betjeman's daughter Candida, born in Dublin in 1942, records that her father's 'attempts to improve Anglo-Irish relations' during the second world war were 'effected with a light touch'. It was, in fact, his famous light touch, later a popular feature of his TV programmes, that chiefly recommended him for the job of wartime press attaché to the UK Representative in Dublin, a position he occupied from January 1941 to September 1943. Considered by his superiors at the British Ministry of Information to be 'the sort of chap who could get on with the Irish', he didn't even need to be diplomatic; he had only to be himself. A naturally whimsical, witty, mischievous man, he could be expected to take to Dublin like a duck to water; and so it proved. He was a poet too, and knew Ireland already from previous visits to various scions of the Ascendancy (or the 'Descendancy' as they now called themselves) he had known since his Oxford days. He rented a house at Clondalkin, then in open country, where his wife Penelope could ride. The UK Representative's office was at 50 Upper Mount Street. Betjeman's room there was rather dark, so he painted it a campy 'boudoir pink' and hung it with John Piper paintings of bombed London churches. A devout Anglican, he took a great interest not only in the Church of Ireland but also, ecumenically, in the Catholic Church, corresponding on occasion with Archbishop McQuaid. He frequented Government and diplomatic circles, knew many fellow writers and journalists, and spent time with the Palace Bar crowd which included Patrick Kavanagh, Myles na gCopaleen and the *Irish Times* people. He forged some useful cultural links, helping to place work by Kavanagh and others in London periodicals, fixing them up with the BBC and initiating a Jack Yeats show at the National Gallery in London. He took Kavanagh for drives in the country, and Kavanagh wrote a rather perfunctory poem, 'Candida', for her first birthday. Endowed with

Derek Mahon

a 'whim of iron', Betjeman learned enough Irish to write short letters in the language on British Government stationery and sing 'Róisín Dubh' (sixteen verses by heart) with tears streaming down his face. He contributed to *The Dublin Magazine*, opened art exhibitions, took part in a Tourist Board architectural survey and imported films for the Irish Film Society in the diplomatic bag. He later joked that he was a 'spy', whatever the word may be thought to mean. It's hard to imagine him snooping around dockyards or photographing confidential papers. Perhaps he's best described as a British 'agent' — which he was, as press attaché, by definition. He was *literally* a British agent: how could he not be, and why not? But he was one with a difference. Elizabeth Bowen, also reporting to London, thought Betjeman 'a silly ass', but the silly-ass act disguised a real seriousness. No one was taken in, and no one really minded much: like most Dublin secrets, it was an open secret that he was a secret agent. Like Bowen, Betjeman urged British respect for Irish neutrality — a neutrality on the side of the Allies. 'He looked upon it as his duty,' said *The Irish Times* on his departure, 'not only to interpret England to the Irish, but also to interpret Ireland sympathetically to the English, and if any English visitor went away with an unsympathetic view of Ireland it was not the fault of Mr Betjeman.' Besides, it wasn't the Irish he kept an eye on so much as the Germans, who had their own polite if rather gloomy (mostly non-Nazi) representatives at a house in nearby Northumberland Road. His opposite number Karl Peterson, whom Betjeman thought 'a nice chap', married and settled in Ireland after the war.

Betjeman's Irish poetic career had begun on a previous visit with 'Sir John Piers' (1938), a cycle of five poems first published as a very slim volume from the offices of the *Westmeath Examiner*, which tells the true story of a rakish baronet of the Regency period outcast from society for his seduction of a friend's wife. Next came a *faux-naif* panegyric, in the metre and rhyme scheme of 'The Bells of Shandon', on 'An Impoverished Irish Peer':

> On his ten-ton schooner
> Upon Lough Gowna
> And the silver birches
>   Along the land

An Open Secret

> *Where the little pebbles*
> *Do sing like trebles*
> *And the water bubbles*
> *Upon the strand . . .*

A deceptive naivety was part of his stock-in-trade. It enabled him to be unashamedly old-fashioned and sentimental without appearing simple-minded, and gave his nostalgia the voice of an earlier time. A snob, like many poets, he could write with ferocity about aspects of modern England he disliked, but he never said a bad word about Ireland — not in public at any rate. As the poet Máire Mhac an tSaoi, a Dublin friend of the Betjemans, observed: 'His Irish poems are full of instinctive sympathy, and in most of them he is not, you notice, being satirical.' Did he condescend? A little, perhaps, but no more than he condescended to provincial England, and his condescension, obviously a referred period feature, provokes not annoyance but amusement. He was devoted to Cornwall, another 'Celtic' place remote from metropolitan life, and Ireland could be seen as a greater Cornwall. He presented himself as a pre-modern poet and a figure of fun, but his own version of modernism was to make subversive fun of 'poetry' even as he wrote it. It's noticeable how much he had in common with his old Highgate schoolmaster T. S. Eliot (the Anglicanism and love of historic London), and with his own more modern contemporaries like Auden and MacNeice. All, including Eliot, excelled at light verse; all were proficient in a great variety of verse forms. 'In Memory of Basil, Marquess of Dufferin and Ava', commemorating an Oxford friend who died fighting the Japanese in Burma, is in classical hexameters ('Friend of my youth you are dead, and a long peal pours from the steeple'); 'Longfellow's Visit to Venice', 'to be read in a quiet New England accent' ('Here for centuries have artists come to see the vistas quaint'), employs a metre reminiscent of *Hiawatha*.

When Laurence Olivier came over to film the Agincourt scenes for *Henry V* in May, 1943, since the English skies were full of planes, it was Betjeman who arranged for the use of the Powerscourt estate at Enniskerry, Co Wicklow. A man who liked to mix with titled folk, he knew Lord and Lady Powerscourt (the poet Sheila Wingfield) and was on visiting terms with 'Insany' (Lord Dunsany) and Edward and Christine Longford of the Gate Theatre; also Lord Hemphill of

Derek Mahon

Tulira, Co Galway, a house which features prominently in George Moore's *Hail and Farewell*. Prone to excitable crushes, he took a great fancy to Emily, Lady Hemphill, *née* Sears, a Bostonian heiress in origin, who became his Muse for a while. There are two Emily poems, 'Ireland with Emily' and 'The Irish Unionist's Farewell to Greta Hellstrom in 1922'. The first, inspired by a bicycle ride he took with Emily in Connemara, describes a Sunday morning in June:

> *Bells are booming down the bohreens,*
> *White the mist along the grass;*
> *Now the Julias, Maeves and Maureens*
> *Move between the fields to Mass...*

He imagines the whole country at prayer — Roscommon, Westmeath, Kildare — and picks out for special notice 'ruins in demesnes deserted', bogs and townlands. A long tracking shot zooms in on the Burren, Co Clare:

> *Stony seaboard, far and foreign,*
> *Stony hills poured over space,*
> *Stony outcrop of the Burren,*
> *Stones in every fertile place...*

There's nothing difficult about Betjeman's work; it all bubbles along quite transparently and carries the reader with it. His subtle registers demand close scrutiny however, and there are mysteries, for instance the circumstances surrounding 'The Irish Unionist's Farewell'. This was written not in 1922 but in 1944, after his return to England. He is himself the 'Irish Unionist', thinking back to the historic moment of separation (Ireland from England) for which the poignant scene described here is a metaphor. And who was Greta Hellstrom? There was evidently no Greta Hellstrom (no 'Swedish beauty') as such, but he saw Emily more than once in the seaside town of Dungarvan, Co Waterford, while both were staying in the neighbourhood, she at Helvick Lodge, Ring. His biographer Bevis Hillier lists other candidates too, but it seems clear that the poem is at one remove from biographical fact — a sort of short story or one-act play based, perhaps, on a private joke. As a film critic he had disliked the star system but admitted, 'If I met Greta Garbo I would faint':

> Golden haired and golden hearted
> I would ever have you be
> As you were when last we parted
> Smiling slow and sad at me.
> Oh, the fighting down of passion!
> Oh, the century-seeming pain —
> Parting in this off-hand fashion
> In Dungarvan in the rain.

He returned to Irish themes in the post-war years. A new friend, Elizabeth Cavendish, with whom he stayed at Lismore Castle, provided the unlikely surname in 'A Lament for Moira McCavendish'. He is on a train which stopped, presumably, at Mallow. Lismore Castle belonged (still does) to the Cavendishes, Dukes of Devonshire; James II, Fred Astaire and various Kennedys, among others, stayed there. Betjeman turns everything into a sentimental Oirish song. The castle becomes a 'wee cabin', Elizabeth a 'colleen' (Moira); the metre he chooses is one favoured by Thomas Moore in the *Irish Melodies*:

> The roll of the railway made musing creative.
> I thought of the colleen I soon was to see
> With her wiry black hair and grey eyes of the native,
> Sweet Moira McCavendish, acushla machree...

Why a 'lament'? Reading between the lines, it looks as if his train was not met ('The McCavendish ass-cart was nowhere in sight': the Rolls didn't show up) and he had to make his own way to Lismore, some miles distant. Around this trivial incident he weaves a keen of grief for 'Moira' as if she were dead, and calls upon the whole countryside to share in his 'desolation'. Betjeman liked desolation and neglect, old churches and winding roads, especially in Ireland. He sings his laments to Irish airs he has picked up, be they taken from Moore, 'traditional' or both. 'His mansion's a ruin, his woods are cut down' ('The Small Towns of Ireland') is a commonplace of 17th-century Gaelic poetry: 'Cill Chais', for example, one of his favourite poems.

Derek Mahon

Hazlitt famously remarked that Moore 'converts the wild Harp of Erin into a Musical Snuff-box', and no doubt something similar might be said of Betjeman, not that he would have minded: an antiquarian, he probably liked musical snuff-boxes. He certainly felt an affinity with the author of the *Melodies* who is buried not in Ireland but in Wiltshire where he had a country house. 'Ireland's Own' is subtitled 'The Burial of Thomas Moore'. The English poet reflects on the paradox of an Irish national poet buried in England, whose soul belongs to Ireland. Just to complicate matters further the traditional metre is not only that of Moore's 'The Meeting of the Waters' but also 'The Ould Orange Flute' (and 'Sweet Betsy from Pike'):

> *I can but account you neglected and poor,*
>   *Dear bard of my boyhood, mellifluous Moore,*
> *That far from the land which of all you loved best*
>   *In a village of England your bones should have rest.*
>
> *The critics may scorn you and Hazlitt may carp*
>   *At the 'Musical Snuff-box' you made of the Harp:*
> *The Regency drawing rooms that thrilled with your song*
>   *Are not the true world to which now you belong.*

Penelope, like the then Taoiseach, was a great one for romantic rural simplicity. Before leaving Ireland, says Hillier, she and her husband called on De Valera, at his request, to say goodbye. 'I hope you won't let the Irish roads deteriorate,' said Penelope, always forthright to the point of tactlessness. 'I mean, I hope you won't have them metalled and tarmacked.'

The Strings are False

MacNeice takes the title for his autobiography from *Julius Caesar*, Act IV, Scene iii. Lucius, Brutus's servant, is asleep when Caesar's ghost visits Brutus in his tent before Philippi. After the ghost's departure Lucius, dreaming, cries out, 'The strings, my lord, are false' (out of tune), and Brutus says, 'He thinks he still is at his instrument.' Strings, in the present context, recall the bardic harp in the Irish-themed radio plays, Coleridge's 'Eolian' harp ('Music slumbering on her instrument') and perhaps Musset's 'Nuit de Mai', quoted by André in Chapter II: *'Poète, prends ton luth.'* He was evidently keen on Shakespeare's Roman plays, for Antony and Cleopatra suggested the line 'We are dying, Egypt, dying' in 'The Sunlight on the Garden' (1937), a song of regret for his first wife Mary Ezra ('Mariette') written after their divorce. Riddled with characteristic 1930s middle-class guilt ('And not expecting pardon'), the poem comments too on the historical situation. The young couple have been living in a fools' paradise, it seems, and now 'the earth compels'. If the deaths of Antony and Cleopatra are made to signify the deciduous nature of privilege, perhaps the wars following Julius's death might be read, in MacNeice's shorthand, as the anti-fascist struggles of the period, culminating in the second world war; or perhaps this is too literal an interpretation. In any case the time is out of joint, the music of the spheres isn't getting through.

Philippi, though, was a turning point, and *The Strings are False* was begun at a turning point in MacNeice's life. There were two American trips between his London University job and his appointment to the BBC in 1941. The first trip lasted four weeks, March-April 1939, and the second ten months, January-November 1940. The first was planned around a lecture tour of colleges in the New York, Boston and Philadelphia areas; the second began with a semester of poetry teaching at Cornell University in upstate New York and extended to include an emergency operation for peritonitis, a recuperative summer in Connecticut and a working holiday in New York City itself, where he spent part of the time at the famous Auden house in Brooklyn Heights. Keen on New York and the writer Eleanor Clark, not named by MacNeice, he considered remaining in the States as Auden was to do, but changed his mind. His biographer tells us he drafted Chapters IV-IX at Cornell in February-March, and Chapters I-III on his second homeward trip from New York to Liverpool in the Cunarder *Samaria*, now full of Canadian airmen and British merchant seamen (survivors of the torpedoed *Jervis Bay*) taken on at Halifax, Nova Scotia. The book begins at sea, describing 'the voyage and his two visits to America, starting his narrative with the end towards which subsequent chapters would move until the circle was complete' (Stallworthy, *Louis MacNeice*, 1995); so it spans more than half a lifetime, 1907-40. Set aside and unfinished at his death in 1963, it was retrieved and edited for posthumous publication by his friend and executor E. R. (Eric) Dodds in 1965. Reissued in 1996, it was reissued once again in MacNeice's centenary year, when attention was once more focused on this singular and exciting poet.

Using the title 'Landscapes of Childhood and Youth', Dodds included as an Appendix some further autobiographical pages by MacNeice written in 1957: 'In the beginning was the Irish rain ... I pressed my nose against the streaming nursery window for a glimpse of the funeral procession on its way to the cemetery the other side of the hawthorn hedge.' Born in Belfast, 'between the mountain and the gantries', he grew up ten miles from the city in Carrickfergus, Co Antrim, on the north shore of Belfast Lough, where his father was the Church of Ireland rector. His ancestors, Sligo farmers, converted somewhere along the road and took part in Protestant proselytizing missions in Connemara. Having thus provoked local displeasure, grandfather MacNeice left with his family and moved to Dublin. Louis' father, later a bishop, 'kept something in him solitary and wild' ('The Strand') and remembered the West with nostalgia for the rest of his life — as did Louis' mother, from a similar background. Louis and his sister Elizabeth inherited this romance and came to regard the West as Tír na nÓg, a land of lost content: 'The very name Connemara seemed too rich for any ordinary place.' As a child he thought of it as 'a country of windswept open spaces and mountains blazing with whins and seas that were never quiet, with drowned palaces beneath them, and seals and eagles and turf-smoke and cottagers who were always laughing... But I was not to visit Achill or Connemara until I had left school. So for many years I lived on a nostalgia for somewhere I had never been.' When his schooling took him to Marlborough and Oxford, and his university work to Birmingham and London, Ireland itself increasingly played the windswept role, becoming a warm, slightly mad alternative to the demands of English life. He was under no illusions about the country, voiced periodic exasperation with its sectarianism, censorship and introversion, but kept up his Irish friendships and paid frequent visits to both North and South, his timing generally determined by rugby fixtures.

His contemporary John Hilton, in another Appendix, ('Louis MacNeice at Marlborough and Oxford'), describes the young poet as 'a non-stop variety show'. Though privately melancholic (his mother died when he was seven), MacNeice for that very reason valued gaiety, warmth, 'the drunkenness of things being various', and considered his birthright to include a hereditary 'Gaelic' anarchy. Described by an English girl, not unfavourably perhaps, as 'Sinn Féin-looking', he had played the wild Irish boy at his Dorset prep school (Sherborne) but later grew into an elegant, even dandified young man of sophisticated taste and easy manners, if unsure of his exact place in the world. 'I am going back,' he writes, 'to a past which is not there (that England — or Europe for that matter — will never be the same again is already a cliché), returning somewhere I belong but have not, as it now is, been. The world for me has become inverted; America is the known and England the unknown ...' 'I will look back,' he decides, 'and return later to pick up the present, or rather to pick up the future.' This back-to-the-future design resembles, on a larger scale, the viral 'spirals' Michael Longley notes in the genetic code of MacNeice's verse (Louis MacNeice, *Selected Poems*, Introduction). The picture of childhood is brilliantly fresh: the gloomy house, that 'nursery', white sails out on the lough, long grass on top of a wall, combed by the wind, mean streets of Ulster, its amazing light. Sexuality stirs on a Scottish holiday when, pre-puberty, he notices a girl in riding-breeches: 'Her walking about in breeches was a challenge; I would chase her through the pine trees and catch her, then I would show her. Show her what? I really didn't know.'

Derek Mahon

'Waking up in the night train from Stranraer to Euston I said to myself "I am in England" but could not believe it.' At Sherborne, he and his mates discover the *Morte d'Arthur* and form a Malory gang, which gives you some idea. At Marlborough he gets to know Graham Shepard ('The Casualty'), John Betjeman ('a triumphant misfit') and the aesthete Anthony Blunt ('He considered it very low to talk politics'). In his last school year he reads a book on Greek philosophy and is 'swept away by Heraclitus, by the thesis that everything is flux and fire'. At Oxford he reads Honour Mods and Greats, but finds that 'homosexuality and "intelligence", heterosexuality and brawn, were almost inexorably paired. This left me out in the cold and I took to drink.' He meets Mariette, 'a nursery-rhyme shepherdess', and they get engaged, though already there are ominous signs: 'How can I marry, I thought to myself sometimes, someone who does not like the wind? . . . I enjoyed metaphysics very much and hoped for a world-view, whereas Mariette only hoped for a house of her own.' She gets the house, but his metaphysics remain divided between Plato and Aristotle ('Nobody mentioned Democritus'). He graduates and takes up a lectureship in Greek at Birmingham under Dodds, a fellow Ulsterman, later Regius Professor at Oxford. Louis and Mariette share an idyll, living for five sheltered years in a converted stables while Europe prepares for war. 'Four or five times a week we went to the cinema, going solely for entertainment and never for value': four or five times a week! An American graduate student, 'Tsalic' (Charles Katzman), comes to stay and Mariette, 'lonely in her mind', goes off with him. MacNeice quits Birmingham, visits republican Spain (a long chapter) and, rewinding to Chapter II, catches up with Mariette and Tsalic, now chicken farming in New Jersey and subsisting on government loans. He is in Ireland when Britain declares war on Germany.

After Mariette's departure the momentum increases. Suddenly he's all over the place, his life in flux, a whirl of flashing minutes. Distracted by thoughts of Eleanor Clark, met in 1939, he revisits the States in 1940 to spend the Easter semester at Cornell, and here he rewinds to the beginning, at sea and on his way back to the future in unknown wartime Britain. High points of the narrative: rowdy at Oxford; Birmingham in the thirties; Spanish interlude; neutral Ireland; neutral America; aboard the *Samaria*. The American

The Strings are False

chapters are particularly vivid, thanks in part to his cool, dispassionate eye: 'The skyscrapers are not so much functional, a saving of good space, as concrete fantasies of power; thus half the offices in the Empire State Building have never been rented.' A sad visit to Atlantic City, which might as well be Southend: 'It was a Jewish holiday, and besides the season was over; very few people were about, the fun-shows and booths were idle. On the grey sand were long rows of empty garish deck chairs and Negroes with ponies and one or two gulls walking far out near the waves.' The Brooklyn household, 'still being painted and without much furniture or carpets, but a warren of the arts, Auden writing in one room, a girl novelist in another, a composer composing and a singer hitting a high note, and Gypsy Rose Lee, the striptease queen, coming round for meals like a whirlwind of laughter and sex'. He has an eye for festive things: at a football game they play 'the famous Cornell tune "High above Cayuga's Waters" while a Syracuse representative walks before the crowd on stilts covered in long, long pants, chewing gum with would-be nonchalance'. And he philosophizes constantly: 'I . . . have lived a life of episodes, isolating incidents or people or aspects of people in the hope of finding something self-contained, having despaired of a self-contained world.' Which was greatly to his poetic advantage. Watch out for the dreams: he was good at dreams.

Terence Brown (*Louis MacNeice: Sceptical Vision*, 1975) was one of the first to point out that there's much more to the poet than the well-known 'surface brilliance'. Brown traces the philosophical development, which spirals back to Heraclitus, river in spate, the living moment and what Brown calls 'the value of incarnate existence'. Incarnate existence is what this unfinished autobiography is about. A young man's book, it has the implicit quest structure of someone trying to find his place (he found it later) on a planet torn by war and spinning meaninglessly in space: 'You might just pick up a star here and there in a rift.' It has too the incidental effect of making at least partly known to us a complex personality acquaintances found hard to fathom. We glimpse the wild man there, the moonstruck artist behind the urbane exterior. Straight with himself and others, witty and dedicated, he was also, in Hilton's phrase, a 'tough aesthete', and needed to be. Bereft in childhood by his mother's death and his father's 'conspiracy with God', he had an

Derek Mahon

orphaned imagination; like Mariette he too, however sociable, was lonely in his mind. He gets the look and sound of the 20th century, the fun and fright: for all its glitz and showbiz it was a tough time. He was very much a poet of those years, of cinema and politics, of jazz and genocide. He took everything to heart, and he seems to have talked less as the years went by. He read verse, says Hilton, 'with a vibrant, plangent, scrannel, sometimes harsh, almost raucous, sometimes warmly rolling voice'. The virile, liquorish Anglo-Irish baritone never quite lost its Ulster intonation, or is this my wishful thinking? He was morose, yes; but you knew that, even if you got on the wrong side of him, he wouldn't clobber you like some. The lip might curl, the gnashers flash, but that was just his manner: the thin glance was a speculative and not unfriendly one. He seemed, like his later work, grim and sardonic, scored by long experience, though there was a wistful nobility too. If the world he loved so much had let him down, the long head rose above it — as his best work now rises above that of his contemporaries.

MacNeice, 'the War' and the BBC

One of the best books about London during the second world war is Charles Ritchie's *The Siren Years* (1974). Ritchie, a young Canadian diplomat, conducted a close and lasting friendship with Elizabeth Bowen, who dedicated to him one of her best books. *The Heat of the Day*, a psychological thriller about treason, was published in 1949; it was Bowen's only war novel. Now, one of the intriguing things about *The Heat of the Day* is its subversion of conventional values. A representative of Britain's Secret Service plants himself arrogantly in a London living room 'like a German in Paris' — this from an author who was herself a sort of spy, reporting to Whitehall on conditions in her own country, Ireland. Ritchie, in his memoirs, records his and Bowen's uneasiness in wartime London: both 'foreigners', one Anglo-Irish, one Anglo-Canadian, and both inclined to ironical and subversive thoughts. I believe MacNeice was a similar case. There was an initial indecisiveness in 1939-40 as he shifted around between England, Ireland and America. No doubt his private life had a lot to do with this; but a certain ambiguity persisted. Not that he was pro-Hitler; *au contraire*. Indeed, there is a sense in which he was more anti-Hitler than the English, and this because he was Irish. In an early poem, 'Turf-stacks', written in Co Mayo, he speaks of

> *The little sardine men crammed in a monster toy*
> *Who tilt their aggregate beast against our crumbling Troy.*

Elsewhere, in his 'Epitaph for Liberal Poets', he denounces 'the tight-lipped technocratic conquistadores'; and both these types, the sardine men and the conquistadores, are, it seems to me, persons of Anglo-Saxon origin, creatures of office routine and the exigencies of industrial civilization. Ironically, MacNeice himself would become a creature of office routine and something of a technocrat in his role of radio producer; and the tensions thus established would prove fruitful in his later work. The sardine men and the conquistadores, who have now taken over, posed even then a threat to everything MacNeice held dear — 'the drunkenness of things being various' as he puts it in 'Snow'; those things which, in 'Train to Dublin', are 'rich and breathing gold', and which he celebrated in love poems and in the magnificent elegy for Graham Shepard, with whom MacNeice had been to school at Marlborough. When he writes, in 'An Eclogue for Christmas',

> *We shall go down like palaeolithic man*
> *Before some new Ice Age or Genghiz Khan*

the values whose loss he imagines are those celebrated in 'Snow' and 'Train to Dublin', in the anarchy of 'Bagpipe Music', and in 'Prayer before Birth'. We need to look seriously at a poem like 'Brother Fire', dated 1942, about the morning after a London air-raid, a spectacle he 'celebrates' with wild, anarchic irony:

> *O delicate walker, babbler, dialectician Fire,*
> *O enemy and image of ourselves,*
> *Did we not on those mornings after the All Clear,*
> *When you were looting shops in elemental joy*
> *And singing as you swarmed up city block and spire,*
> *Echo your thoughts in ours? 'Destroy! Destroy!'*

Bowen too was fascinated by the air-raids, perhaps because a bomb half-wrecked her house; as Auden observed, 'all poets love explosions'. 'Brother Fire' is one of MacNeice's key wartime poems.

He describes, in *The Strings are False*, a walking tour in the West of Ireland in August and September 1939: 'The Closing Album' was written at this time. He was in Galway when he heard of the outbreak of war and 'a young man in sports clothes said: "Eire of course will stay neutral, but I hope the English knock hell out of Hitler."' He took a dim view of Irish neutrality on the simple grounds that everyone should be pitching in to defeat fascism. He seems not to have been impressed by De Valera's neutral policy. There is, in fact, a MacNeice poem entitled 'Neutrality', dated 1942, which reads very bitterly: 'Off your own shores,' he says, 'the mackerel are fat on the flesh of your kin.' He is thinking of the many seamen lost through the action of U-boats on the North Atlantic convoys, lives which might have been saved by Irish participation in the conflict. That word 'kin' raises a number of questions — though it's well known that thousands of Irishmen, mostly from the South, served the Allied cause.

MacNeice had, as it happens, particular reason to be bitter. His friend Graham Shepard, temporarily with the Royal Navy, was torpedoed and drowned in 1942, an event which gave rise to one of MacNeice's finest poems, 'The Casualty'. I've spoken of 'the drunkenness of things being various', the sense of dazzle and fun that always appealed to MacNeice, and identified it, a little complacently perhaps, with his sense of himself as Irish; so it's interesting to note that, except for some of the love poems (he met his second wife, Hedli, during the war), 'The Casualty' represents the consummation, in MacNeice's verse, of this particular quality; for Shepard was, of all things, an Englishman. He appears in *The Strings are False* as 'an inky little boy who didn't quite fit into the Marlborough pattern. In appearance and manner he was a stray from some other place or era, a surprising blend of precocious worldly-wisdom and a faunal innocence. His feeling for fantasy geared with mine. He lived by right of himself, untidy and often unwashed, and he gabbled so that people found him hard to follow. He spent much of his time thinking about dances in Surrey and bathing parties in Cornwall. A sort of Cockney leprechaun, he had an enthusiasm not encouraged at Marlborough.' He was, in other words, a kind of Irishman. MacNeice contrasts him with their rather cold contemporary Anthony Blunt.

The London of 1941, when MacNeice began his broadcasting career, has been well described by many writers — by Cyril Connolly, Stephen Spender, Elizabeth Bowen, and by Robert Hewison, whose book *Under Siege: Literary Life in London 1939-45* is something of a minor classic. Literary life in London centred on Soho, a short walk from the BBC, and MacNeice commuted regularly from one to the other. Pubs were important. The Highlander was frequented by film technicians and so came to be used by writers like Dylan Thomas who were working on films for the Ministry of Information. Others favoured the Yorkminster, known as the French Pub because it was French owned and catered to

Derek Mahon

French refugees. 'The back bar of the Café Royal,' says Hewison, 'was appreciated for its supply of Irish whiskey, whose availability was, paradoxically, a consequence of Ireland's neutrality and the restrictions on Scotch whisky production.' 'For servicemen on leave' (Hewison again) 'the pubs were an exotic outlet for enthusiasm stifled by the military machine; to civilians working in dull jobs, or even interesting ones at the BBC, Soho represented an escape into a world that defied the increasing limitations of wartime controls; the emphasis was on individuality and personality, on the outrageous as opposed to the routine,' and he quotes MacNeice's poem 'Alcohol':

> *On golden seas of drink, so the Greek poet said,*
> *Rich and poor are alike. Looking around in war*
> *We watch the many who have returned to the dead*
> *Ordering time-and-again the same-as-before:*
>
> *Those Haves who cannot bear making a choice,*
> *Those Have-nots who are bored with having nothing to choose,*
> *Call for their drinks in the same tone of voice,*
> *Find a factitious popular front in booze.*

There is nihilism here, if we look at the dark side; on the bright side there is democracy, as the phrase 'popular front' indicates. MacNeice would later abandon Soho for the BBC's own pub, the George in Mortimer Street, farther west, as also did Dylan Thomas and others who survived the siren years. Despite the pubbability, MacNeice always stood a little apart from those with whom he had been grouped, notes Hewison, and never abandoned the role of commentator.

There was no patriotic war poetry from MacNeice; his characteristic mode was ironical and anarchic, while that of Dylan Thomas was rhapsodic and surreal. But the war provided them both with answers to some of their problems, and the war for them, like the peace which succeeded it, was very much a matter of the BBC. Thomas found a new way to earn a precarious living, and wrote the one great masterpiece of radio drama, his 'play for voices', *Under Milk Wood*, finished and transmitted the year he died. The Beeb — more precisely, the Features Department — provided MacNeice, a 'gregarious solitary' as he has been called, with a sense of community. It was and remains a semi-state body, a private corporation nominally independent of government. Features Dept, set up during the war to act as a propaganda unit, was headed by an immensely sympathetic and imaginative man, Laurence Gilliam, who liked to give writers their head and made a point of frustrating authority. During and after the war, the department, situated in Broadcasting House, employed at different times MacNeice, Thomas, W. R. Rodgers, Dan Davin, H. A. L. Craig and R. D. Smith, husband of the novelist Olivia Manning. Ireland was strongly represented. In *Autumn Journal* (1939) MacNeice had expressed a need for community, and this was now gratified. 'For MacNeice,' says Barbara Coulton, 'Features was a new world. He had been dissatisfied with academic life; now war had interrupted everyone's lives, setting people unsuspectingly on new courses, if they survived.' 'Gilliam,' says Coulton, 'was experienced in journalism, and had a particular enthusiasm for radio documentaries; he was a man of wide-ranging interests and inspiring integrity. He was also a *bon viveur*, unpunctual, and a tower of strength to his subordinates.' MacNeice lists Gilliam and his subordinates in *Autumn Sequel* (1953), a poem unlike the earlier *Autumn Journal* in being written in *terza rima*. There's something slightly mechanical about it, and it has never enjoyed the same success as the *Journal*. The characters, practically all men, appear under pseudonyms. Thus Gilliam is Herriot, Dylan Thomas is Gwilym and so on. After a while the BBC crowd begin to merge into one, becoming a composite figure, anecdotal, pint in hand, hard-working, hard-drinking, devoted to rugby and cricket. The poem is over a hundred pages in length. Inevitably there are *longueurs*; but it has its moments and is an important document for the student of MacNeice, recording the texture and activity of his life in the 1940s and 1950s. In Canto 4 he describes his initiation into Features, his agreement to 'join this new crusade', and his agreement to stay on after the war.

In the space of twenty years MacNeice wrote and produced over a hundred scripts. The first, *Word from America*, went out on 15 February 1941; *Britain to America* went out on the 26 July 1942. He had been greatly impressed by the American Ed Murrow's reports from wartime London and started out by trying something similar. His first radio play, *Christopher Columbus*, was scheduled for 12 October 1942, the 450th anniversary of Columbus' landfall

Derek Mahon

in the New World. Other programmes dealt with Belfast, with Norway, Russia and Greece. Another play, *The Dark Tower*, went out in January 1946, his version of the *Agamemnon* later the same year; and so on. Other post-war programmes included features on Indian and Ghanaian independence and three more plays: *The Administrator*, *The Mad Islands* and *Persons from Porlock*.

There was a close relationship between MacNeice's poetry and radio work. It is a broadcasting cliché that, although there are millions of listeners out there, each one listens alone, as one reads a book. Radio is an intimate medium, and intimate techniques work best. MacNeice, like Dylan Thomas, understood this instinctively. A play about the death of Graham Shepard uses the device of a drowning man's recall of his past life, voices alternating with the sound of the waves. It has been pointed out that radio drama works best when the characters' voices are contained in an echoing hollow — a cave, a tunnel, a living room. His last play, *Persons from Porlock*, makes use of the cave. The narrator, an artist related to the cave painters of Lascaux, is trapped in a tunnel where he tries to swim against the stream, images clearly borrowed from the 'caves of ice' and 'sacred river' of Coleridge's 'Kubla Khan'; the persons from Porlock represent the same kind of distraction from artistic creation that they represented for Coleridge. It must be said that during the 1950s, when he was busiest at Features, there was a certain falling-off in the poetry itself, although this was to be rectified towards the end. After *Autumn Sequel* his verse grows disillusioned, even frightened, as if he doubted the value of the enterprise.

'Visitations' and the later, complex 'Memoranda to Horace', where he finds 'life restricted to standing room only', demonstrate similarly distressing symptoms. There's an early and very good poem called 'The Death Wish', and I hope it isn't posthumously impertinent to suggest that this was a symptom with which MacNeice was uncomfortably acquainted, I mean from an early age. Whatever about that, his attitude to radio work underwent a subtle change during the later 1950s. This was connected with important changes within the BBC itself, where administrative persons and other, more disciplined departments looked with increasing disfavour on Features, which began to be seen as something of a spoilt child. Time-and-motion experts were called in and presented everyone with a questionnaire. When the sardine man came to collect MacNeice's he found that the poet, who liked to sit with his feet on his desk and gaze out the window, had left several blank spaces. What, inquired the sardine man, were you doing in the blank spaces? 'Thinking,' replied MacNeice laconically. As Coulton points out, a poem like that addressed 'To Posterity' acquires special significance in the light of these circumstances:

> When books have all seized up like the books in graveyards
> And reading and even speaking have been replaced
> By other, less difficult, media, we wonder if you
> Will find in flowers and fruit the same colour and taste
> They held for us for whom they were framed in words,
> And will your grass be green, your sky be blue,
> Or will your birds be always wingless birds?

One day in the George he sat morosely putting back into Greek Callimachus' short elegy for Heraclitus (William Cory's translation): 'They told me, Heraclitus, they told me you were dead...' But he stuck at it, producing in the autumn of 1959 his own play about the Battle of Clontarf, *They Met on Good Friday*, with Patrick Magee regal as Brian Boru; also *The Mad Islands* (1961), based on the voyage of Maelduin, with Denys Hawthorne as Maelduin. MacNeice at this time was absorbed in the Irish sagas, which provided material for a short sequence of poems entitled 'Dark Age Glosses'; the relationship between poetry and radio continued. It was now seriously threatened, however, by two things: the rise of Drama Department as a separate unit (and it had already established itself with Donald McWhinnie's prize-winning production of Beckett's *All That Fall*) and the new hegemony of television. During the summer of 1963 MacNeice, always meticulous in these matters, accompanied technicians to an underground cave in Yorkshire to check the sound for *Persons from Porlock*, and developed pneumonia; he died in September in a London hospital, and is buried in Co Down. Alec Reid and Terence Brown, perhaps taking their cue from the Heraclitus story, chose as an epigraph to *Time Was Away* the final couplet of Cory's translation:

> Still are thy pleasant voices, thy nightingales, awake;
> For Death, he taketh all away, but them he cannot take.

Derek Mahon

   I prefer to think that these lines, these pleasant voices, refer not to the radio work which, though excellent, is by its nature ephemeral, but to the poems MacNeice left us, their intimate whispers still echoing somewhere in the ether.

Human Resources

Everyone likes MacNeice. I met him twice, if you can call it meeting — and found him, as I'd expected, saturnine. Both times he was in rugby mode. Calling one afternoon at the flat in Regent's Park he shared with the actress Mary Wimbush, we found him watching a match on TV and saying little. Constrained by his rugby-watching silence, I said little myself. What did I expect, poetry talk? (A big fan, I'd just read his latest collection *Solstices*, which I thought disappointing: this must have been 1961.) We watched some rugby and then it was time to go. I got the impression that, even without the rugby, he would have been uncommunicative. The curtains were half closed and I saw only a grave grey head and a sombre equine face; though literally long in the tooth, he had presence. I was virtually ignored but didn't mind, aware that, while to me he was the great poet, to him I was nobody in particular. Grand houses in Regent's Park were not my usual ambience. I was much struck by this one, by the elegant Mary Wimbush, and by the voices. Louis was nasal Oxford, a sonorous growl, Mary pure BBC circa 1960; those there of my own age had already adopted 'Mockney' and a shared idiom of *branché*, cool and *ciao*.

Some months later I was sitting with other students in a well-known Dublin pub — Neary's of Chatham Street — when I noticed two older men at a nearby table, one talkative, one taciturn. The taciturn one was MacNeice. With the bumptiousness of youth we went over and introduced ourselves; he didn't remember me of course. He wore some kind of an anorak, looked unkempt, and acknowledged us with a polite snarl and a sidelong flash of the horsey teeth. The talkative one, Bill Webb, books editor of the *Guardian*, chuckled at our intrusion. He was a lively man in tweeds, with a short pepper-and-salt beard, who had put himself in charge of the truculent Louis. Both were on the whiskey, the effect being to make Webb witty and MacNeice morose. We talked to

Derek Mahon

Webb and I tried in vain to get a response out of MacNeice, preferably some poetry talk. Perhaps, frustrated by his reluctance, I got a bit truculent too. (What a pain in the neck I must have been.) They'd been to an international at Lansdowne Road, and MacNeice's report appeared the next week in the *New Statesman* for which he wrote occasionally, its circulation greater then than now. He mentioned Dublin pubs and remarked on their 'aggressive' (bad mannered) students. We had been put in our place.

Not exactly Keats and Coleridge, is it? But it's seldom a good idea to meet your admired authors; you will often be disappointed. (Not always: Keats wasn't, for one.) Not meaning any harm, they may take no notice of you or, meaning a little harm, they may put you down. Besides, they are generally older, wearier and less forthcoming than you might wish, and words of wisdom will be few. Such was my experience of MacNeice. I was just some Belfast whippersnapper; he didn't want to be bothered (why should he?) and he was tired of words, of which he had written a great many. Tired too, perhaps, of life itself: it's there in the last poems. 'He practised,' says his friend John Hilton in an appendix to *The Strings are False*, 'a certain spiritual economy that I take to have been necessary to the protection of his inner world. He was afraid — as in the 'Prayer before Birth' — of being spilled.' That was in his early years, and it seems to have remained true to the end.

MacNeice was as prolific in correspondence as in verse, radio work and critical prose. He was one of those people who write all the time and at length — a dying breed in the email era, but he preceded the email era. The first letters in the Faber selection, to his father and sister, are dated 1914, when he was seven; the last, to his daughter the artist Corinna and to Charles Monteith of Faber, 20 and 26 August 1963. He died a week later. Before returning in November 1940 during the Battle of the Atlantic, he had written from New York to Eric Dodds in Oxford that, in the event of his death, 'if any mug wants to publish my letters', he didn't want those to his father or stepmother included as 'they nearly always contain some falsity. I also regret most of my undergraduate letters (esp. to Anthony Blunt) which are nearly always v. affected & forced but I suppose they might be amusing to social historians . . . (How mortuary-egotistical all this sounds)'. He survived the voyage, failed the RN selection board (eyesight) and instead joined the

Human Resources

BBC, to which he remained under contract for twenty years.

The Faber selection includes many letters to his two wives, Mary and Hedli, to Dodds and Mrs Dodds, to the young American author Eleanor Clark, his Faber editors Eliot and Monteith, Laurence Gilliam and W. R. Rodgers of the BBC, and the magazine editors Geoffrey Grigson and John Lehmann. This was his milieu. Notable absentees include Auden, who didn't keep letters, and radio cronies like Jack Dillon and R. D. Smith whom he saw almost daily. There are three great sequences — to Dodds, to Clark and to Hedli. The Clark sequence starts on 21 April 1939, aboard the *Queen Mary* as he returns from his first American lecture tour, having met and 'fallen in love' with her almost immediately at a New York party. Eleven pages in the Faber edition, it was quickly followed by a dozen more in the same vein: 'We were probably quite right not to sleep together just now because that makes it (a) much more delicate but (b) much fuller of possibilities . . . All the same, I feel very Western Wind about it.' He was in America again a year later ('Meeting Point'), still madly in love despite several involvements in the interim; but now a mutually critical note intrudes.

Clark was a remarkable figure in her own right: a Vassar graduate, a *New Yorker* contributor and a glamorous radical in the fashion of the time, briefly married to one of Trotsky's secretaries in Mexico. She rebukes MacNeice for snobbery and self-absorption; he defends himself at length: 'I thought you might accuse me of inhumanity (which I'll explain about in a moment) but what do you mean I have an awful lack of curiosity about the world? I was curious about the world and suffering from it before you were born . . .' He, and she too it seems, were great analysts of the emotions, he a skilled rhetorician; but behind the vociferous give-and-take a fairly obvious explanation suggests itself. They weren't really compatible for anything more than a sort of cocktail romance; the physical dimension is absent. He was infatuated, but it was all in the head really. Clark, wary of him as far as one can tell, seems to have had the measure of the situation. When he returns to wartime London the romance begins to fade, and then he tells her he's re-married (to the singer Hedli Anderson). His hopes of getting to America again to make some war-related programmes there were dashed, in any case, by a spat with the Admiralty. Aboard the destroyer *Chelsea* on assignment, he and Jack Dillon got themselves

Derek Mahon

into hot water by overdoing it a bit in the wardroom one fine night. The captain took a dim view and complained to the Beeb, obliging MacNeice to defend their behaviour like a bad boy: 'After the singing stopped, it's still possible that now — owing to the small size and acoustic qualities of the wardroom — the conversation and laughter between myself, Dillon and some of the officers may have been more penetrating than we realized . . . The picture of us asleep at 7.15 am with half-empty glasses still in our hands strikes me as highly coloured.'

The Hedli sequence starts on 10 August 1947 when he writes to her from Delhi, where he had been sent, with the redoubtable Dillon and a BBC van, to cover the Independence celebrations — and, as it turned out, the 'communal trouble' attending Partition. This Indian trip took them to most of the larger cities, to Kashmir and as far south as Cape Comorin. 'Darling,' he writes, 'would you mind keeping these letters all together somewhere as they will remind me of things & so far I haven't had time to keep a diary etc.' These Hedli letters *are* his Indian diary, and tremendously lively they are too, the functioning chaos of the subcontinent chiming with his own aesthetic of exuberant dazzle and variety, 'whatever it is that jigs and dances'. Strange figures pop up amid the elephants and monkeys, like the head of the Cow Protection Campaign. A religious or an economic campaign? 'My dear young man, you cannot separate things like that. Everything is one. Religious, economic, they are the same thing.' And he meets the popular lady poet and nationalist Sarojini Naidu, she who is credited with the remark that it cost the movement a fortune to keep Gandhi in poverty. The letters don't go in much for critical commentary, of others' work or his own (all that is available elsewhere), but they are recognizably from the hand that wrote *Autumn Journal* and *Autumn Sequel*, and in the same voice with its distinctive 'acoustic qualities' — gossipy, brisk, attentive to curious detail, alive to the passing moment.

It was Philip Larkin who said, in an obituary notice, that MacNeice could have written the words of 'These Foolish Things'. To many people he's still a poet of London and New York in the 1930s, worldly, suave and satirical. His poetry of the time was a cinematic one of city lights and cocktail bars, his philosophy one of shining surfaces, 'the sunlight on the garden', the 'dazzle on the sea'. The

Irish light in his head was a metaphor for the variety of human experience and personality. His pleasure in things became, in his social poetry, a pleasure in people. His work enacts a struggle between darkness and light. The darkness derived from a psychiatric disorder in his mother which proved incurable, from a sheltered childhood in 'darkest Ulster', and an ambiguous fear of solitude: at school in England his fellows 'could never breathe my darkness'. The light, by contrast, was prismatic. Variety being the spice of life, he set himself to champion variety and oppose homogeneity; his poetic *joie de vivre* had its source in a breaking wave. Summoning, in Michael Longley's phrase, 'all available human resources against anarchy and despair', his vivid apprehension of the physical world marks him out from his English contemporaries, whose effects are generally more abstract. One thinks of Auden's theoretical cast of mind, Spender's idealism, Day Lewis's rhetoric. MacNeice too was no slouch at these things: an Oxford graduate in Greats, he knew his way around academic philosophy. He makes frequent fun of the subject but there is a strong philosophical undertow in even (or especially) his most sparkling work. Versed in the smoke and mirrors, he used, in his poetry, real smoke and mirrors as erotic props. He and Betjeman were probably among the first, in Britain at least, to make frequent use of brand names. A lover of 'Bijoux and long-eared dogs and silken legs', of limousine and crêpe-de-chine, scent-spray and 'milk-white telephone', he embraced the prescribed glamour — though that was less than half the story.

The centenary *Collected Poems*, ed. Peter McDonald, replacing Dodds' 1979 edition, provides a more comprehensive view. It's remarkable what a vigorous, glittering talent MacNeice had then, how versatile and inclusive he could be. The often close connection between poetic energy and the larger political drama was strong in one who, while resisting political commitment, famously said, 'I would have a poet able-bodied, fond of talking, a reader of the newspapers, capable of pity and laughter, informed in economics, appreciative of women, involved in personal relationships, actively interested in politics . . .' Highly appreciative of women, he was usually (if not always happily) in love, a condition conducive to poetry but also a consolation and resource against the frightfulness of the public sphere. Like his poetic contemporaries he was lucky to flourish in the 1930s and 1940s, hugely 'interesting times' as in the

Derek Mahon

Chinese curse; for him too it was his finest hour, the moment when it all came together, even as it seemed to be blowing apart: apocalyptic nightmare, humane despair, erotic intensity and romantic hope. His poems of that time, the love life bubbling away while the bombs began to fall, have clarity, assurance and a raw consciousness of the historical moment. War and separation: he gets over the failed affair with Eleanor Clark; Graham Shepard is lost at sea; he marries a second time (Hedli Anderson) and publishes *Springboard* (1944), a high-wire volume, dizzy and Dionysian. He never wrote quite as well again. Harry Clifton puts it like this: 'The war passed, and with it the world-historical dimension, the depth of field behind the love poems of the previous decade.' Post-war Britain offered exhaustion, not exhilaration, and all the poetry shrank. It was time for irony and pop music.

He was vastly prolific. Barbara Coulton lists over a hundred radio features, not to speak of the plays and other prose works. As for the poems, he published far too many for his own good. *Out of the Picture* (1937) can't have added much to his early appeal, or *Ten Burnt Offerings* (1952) to his later reputation. *Autumn Sequel* (1954) was judged, perhaps unfairly, a tedious failure, and the later volumes contain too many pieces with titles like 'Indoor Sports' and 'Country Week-End'. 'This middle stretch of life is bad for poets,' he wrote, though he picked himself up towards the end; some years before the end in fact. *Visitations* (1957) and *Solstices* (1961), in contrast to the jazzy pre-war volumes and the spectacular wartime ones, are quiet, undemanding and gloomily introspective, as if conscious of diminished expectation, 'youth and poetry departed'; but they face up to disenchantment and 'failure' with touching honesty. After the Age of Anxiety the anxiety of age. These two volumes represent, in their own modest fashion, a valuable contribution to the literature of the climacteric. Still in his forties and fifties, he was already writing like a grumpy old man. Of his last volume *The Burning Perch* (1963), he notes that 'fear and resentment seem here to be serving me in the same way as Yeats in his old age claimed to have been served by "lust and rage"'. 'Highly coloured' occasions increased in frequency and duration and lowered his resistance to the pneumonia that carried him off at the age of fifty-six. Like many another he disliked the new pop culture, the beginnings of the post-modern world, its raucous self-regard satirized and deplored in 'Budgie' ('The mirror jerks in the weightless cage') and 'Memoranda to Horace'. His late work is a withdrawal ('To opt out now seems better than capitulate'), an admission of his defeat by 'the too well-lighted and over-advertised' idols of the age, but he managed the final stretch better than Auden, for example. Were the issue not muddied by the usual Anglo-Irish claims and counter-claims, he might even now be recognized as ultimately the more rewarding poet, indeed one of the most rewarding of the 20th century.

Olivia Manning

We call it Romania now, but it used to be called Rumania, and that's where Olivia went in 1939 when she married R. D. (Reggie) Smith. Reggie was a lecturer with the British Council in Bucharest and, as war struck Rumania and then Greece, the Smiths (the 'Pringles' as they appear in her Balkan and Levant trilogies) moved on to Egypt and Palestine, where Reggie ran a radio station. He worked thereafter for the BBC in London, while she wrote up their experiences in Bucharest and Athens, Cairo and Jerusalem. She published other things besides, but she's now remembered chiefly for the six-novel series she called *The Fortunes of War*. She was lucky, really, to find herself in the Rumanian capital when war broke out. It gave her a huge advantage as a writer, for there was no other English novelist to cover the same ground. She had it all to herself, and she made the most of it. Her wartime Bucharest is both a world of its own and a unique documentary record. Circumstances conspired to give her an exotic location, a gallery of unusual types, political upheaval, revolution and invasion. 'I write from experience,' she said, 'I have no fantasy' — but this is too modest. I assumed for a long time that *The Rain Forest* (1974), set on an island in the Indian Ocean, was based on a visit to somewhere like the Maldives; but not a bit of it. She imagined the whole thing. She describes the Eighth Army's war in the desert with great conviction though she wasn't there. She knew people who were, and had read her Tolstoy. Anthony Burgess, in fact, compared her to Tolstoy, which might have been nice if it weren't so excessive; but, meaning no harm, he also called her 'the most considerable of our women novelists', a phrase to which she took exception for obvious reasons — though her biographer, Eve Patten, speaking of Manning's 'extended postwar narrative of reproach', emphasizes her 'woman's perspective'. She was of her time and generation, keen on romantic places and characters. A prime example of this, and perhaps her most memorable creation, is 'Yaki'

Olivia Manning

(Prince Yakimov), seldom far from centre stage in the Balkan trilogy. A middle-aged remittance man, son of a White Russian father and an Irish mother, he is nonetheless an Englishman by education and long residence, and speaks the outmoded slang of the 1920s. Living beyond his means in London, Paris and Berlin, he has drifted around Europe, sponging in his gentle way until credit is exhausted, then moving on. As usual, Yaki in Bucharest finds friends, raises funds, and moves into a grand hotel, the centre of activity. He associates with journalists and impoverished toffs like himself. Harriet, Olivia's proxy, can't bring herself to approve of him in Bucharest, although later, in Athens, she realizes he has somehow become an old friend. Dreamily amoral, Yaki takes what he can get, including confidential papers belonging to Guy Pringle. Finding himself in the northern town of Cluj, where the Germans have established a foothold, he blithely presents himself at the house of the newly imported Gauleiter, an old acquaintance from Weimar days, and half-wittedly trades Guy's secret information for a good dinner. The incident, hilarious and horrifying both, is totally convincing. Yaki's appalling innocence, the Gauleiter's childish depravity — everything comes together perfectly.

In *The Great Fortune* (1960) and *The Spoilt City* (1962) Guy is taken up with his work as a lecturer, leaving Harriet free to explore the life of Bucharest. Here, as elsewhere, atmospheres and qualities of light are deftly evoked, though even in Egypt later she stops short of the full-blown aestheticism we find in, say, Lawrence Durrell's *Alexandria Quartet*. The seasons in Bucharest are vividly rendered, but the winter she describes has a special interest, partly because of its Ruritanian, fairy-tale quality, with icicles hanging 'like swords' from palace gates, but also for a very different reason. Guy is a big-hearted Marxist, Harriet more conservative, but she has a charitable eye for 'the destitute peasant families, their bread-winners conscripted, driven by winter into the capital . . . Each morning a cart went round to collect the bodies dug from the snow. Many of these were found in bunches, frozen inseparably, so they were thrown as they were found, together, into the communal grave.'

She was a traditional, not an experimental novelist, and probably thought *The Alexandria Quartet* overdone. She was once rather fierce to Beckett, it seems, mistakenly accusing him of being anti-life; but the difference in aim and method between the two is so vast that there is simply no comparison to be made. She was a traditional novelist in her transparency and linearity; the important thing wasn't the nature of narrative discourse, which she took for granted, but the nature of the world to be narrated. So when she observes a solitary — as it were Beckettian — figure, an Egyptian peasant, from a passing car, she puts herself in his shoes for a moment, though only for a moment; 'She saw a peasant, head bound up in a scarf, mooning along the pavement. The scarf indicated that he had toothache or a cold, but she knew he was not thinking of his ailments. Instead he was telling himself one of the fantasies that compensate the poor for their poverty. A shopkeeper had once told her that a rich American lady had fallen in love with a guide at the pyramids and gone to live with him in his one-roomed village hut. Harriet had laughed at the story, but the shopkeeper believed it because belief itself made life tolerable. She knew the peasant in the scarf, grinning, head wagging, was imagining just such a romance for himself.'

A notoriously 'difficult' character, though never misanthropic as such, she came increasingly to view mankind with misgiving — or rather her initial misgivings, fostered by childhood insecurity, youthful hardship, and a cast of a thousand phonies, took on an almost philosophical consistency. This is the great strength of *The Rain Forest*. Briefly, it's the story of an English couple, Hugh and Kristy Foster, who go out to spend a year or so on a fictitious island in the Indian Ocean, where Hugh is to be a government PR man. The island, Al-Bustan, is a gorgeous place, abounding in exotic flora and fauna. The name means, in Arabic, the Garden; and if we choose to think of the Garden of Eden, well, why not? Here too the theme is the spoliation of natural innocence. This innocence has its darker side: ignorance, the unknown, symbolized by the impenetrable rain forest at one end of the island. If we take Al-Bustan to be the world we've inherited, the line-up of opposing factions in the community represents the perennial confrontation of good and evil. The author may not have seen it in quite that light, but the white denizens of the luxurious Praslin Hotel receive no sympathy, not even when the place is wrecked by an earthquake: 'These people were the enemy, the devourers. They made a ruthless demand on life; for them the world was being squandered, its resources used up, its wildlife decimated, its seas polluted, the sea life destroyed and the seabirds in their thousands killed by their accursed oil tankers.'

A book she greatly admired was Malcolm Lowry's *Under the Volcano*, which ends with the legend, seen in a Mexican park: '¿*Le gusta este jardín que es suyo? ¡Evite que sus hijos lo destruyan!*' — 'Do you like this garden of yours? Don't let your children destroy it!' *The Rain Forest* carries a similar warning. Everyone, it seems, from the drugged hippies with their sickly infant to the ferociously acquisitive white South Africans, is mindlessly wasting or using up the earth's resources; and a recurrent motif, the weeping turtles daily transported from the beach to the canning factory, signals the mute grief of the natural world.

Olivia was crazy about animals, especially cats. Harriet takes in a stray kitten in Bucharest, and in Al-Bustan Kristy befriends a lemur who comes to the Fosters' table each night for food. She saw the plight of animals as the plight of the world itself. One character in *The Rain Forest*, a scientist, speculates on the likelihood of a new and undiscovered virus: 'When one species has overbred itself, as we have, nature strikes back with a decimating force. We keep parrying the blows, but one day a blow will come from an unexpected quarter. It *could* come from this area of forest.' There's an old chap in the book called Simpson, an Englishman who has spent most of his life in India. He hasn't been home for ages and doesn't know what it's like. He and Kristy become as friendly as the generation gap permits, and he confides in her his disappointment with life:

> 'It's no fun getting old, like a worn-out car. You think you've learnt the game, then you find all the young ones are playing a different game.'
> 'Not so different, really,' replied Kristy. 'The trouble is, life seems so temporary now. There is to be no future for us.'
> Simpson stared at her in astonishment. 'Why do you say that?'
> 'Surely you know the world is being used up. Even England is becoming an over-populated, polluted slum.'
> 'You don't say!'
> He took a step away from her and looked as though he thought her a little mad. She went in through the bead curtain feeling that, at his age, he might as well retain his innocence.

Dying to Get Home

Camus visited the American continent twice, the United States in 1946, South America in 1949. One result was *Journaux de Voyage*, first published in 1978, and *American Journals* (tr. Hugh Levick, 1995) is a translation of that book — the first, I take it, in English; so this is a significant addition to the Camus canon. Significant, but in some respects disappointing. Camus' text is a mere 120 pages of generous print, and much of it was written at sea. Moreover, he seems to have disliked, and is therefore unsympathetic towards, or uninterested in, many aspects of the United States; and he was ill, with 'bronchitis at least', during much of the South American trip, with the result that his responses are often bad-tempered and perfunctory. Although he was, as they say, at the height of his fame (*La Peste* appeared, to great acclaim, in 1947), there is an almost pathological morbidity evident in these pages, some talk of suicide, and a certain surly scepticism towards the outside world. Much is omitted that might have made absorbing reading. His difficulty with the immigration people in New York, for example. Camus describes himself as having been 'treated as suspect', and leaves the rest to our imagination, including his own reaction. (He'd once been a Communist Party member.) He gives lectures, but doesn't tell us where or about what. There is no mention of his friendship with Patricia Blake, the young woman who was his constant companion in New York. His first and most publicized lecture, on familiar themes, was in fact delivered at Columbia University; and there were out-of-town trips to Vassar and elsewhere.

First impression of New York: 'A hideous, inhuman city, though I know that one changes one's mind.' Everyone, he notices, 'looks like they've stepped out of a B-film'. He himself, although he naturally doesn't say so, looked as if he had stepped out of a film too, one of those skilful private-eye movies of the period; with his good looks and Bogartian intensity he drew the attention of women

Dying to Get Home

wherever he went. On Broadway at night he was amazed by the lights: 'I am just coming out of five years of night, and this orgy of violent lights gives me for the first time the impression of a new continent. An enormous, fifty-foot-high Camel billboard: a GI with his mouth wide open blows enormous puffs of *real* smoke. So much bad taste hardly seems imaginable.' But he relents, as he knew he would: 'Yes, there is an American tragic, but I still don't know what it's made from.' He picks up a few clues in Harlem, where he visits the jazz clubs, for black America meets with his approval. There are sublime moments: birdsong and evening star in Washington, a magnificent first glimpse of the Quebec countryside on a trip to Canada. But, very much a man of his time, what intrigues him and inspires him is to be found in New York: 'Sometimes, from beyond the skyscrapers, the cry of a tug-boat finds you in your insomnia, and you remember this desert of iron and cement is an island.' Or the man in the Holland Tunnel: 'All day long on a raised footbridge he counts the cars which pass endlessly in a deafening din the whole length of the violently lit tunnel which is too long for him to be able to see either one of the exits: hero of a modern novel.'

Three years later, the world-famous author of *La Peste* set out apprehensively on an official cultural mission to Brazil, Uruguay, Chile and Argentina. Again, the sea: 'I've always been calm at sea, and for a moment this infinite solitude is good for me, although today I have the impression that this sea is made of all the tears in the world.' Staring from the stern of the ship at night, he contemplates suicide in an abstract sort of way, but settles instead for Vigny in his bare cabin: 'Either this stripped-down solitude or the storm of love; nothing else in the world interests me.' He and the other passengers disembark briefly at Dakar, where he smells 'my Africa', then on to Rio, taking in some spectacular sunsets on the way, though 'nature abhors miracles that last too long'. As for Rio, the now-famous author is the victim of pretentious officials and phoney socialites of every kind. His 'common touch' comes to the rescue, though, and he makes friends with a black theatre group. On being asked what he would most like to do he says he would like to see a football match, thus touching a national chord. The suspicion grows that, wherever he goes, Camus — though not a native-born Frenchman — is dying to get home. Despite his friendships with the Argentine poet Victoria Ocampo and the exiled Spanish intellectual José Bergamin, he can't quite take these foreign lands entirely seriously; at one point, in remote Iguape (Brazil), he observes that 'at this exact moment it is midnight in Paris'; yet the Iguape experience contributed to his own creative work. It was there that he watched the ceremony involving the 'growing stone', and the experience later surfaced in the short story of that title included in *Exile and the Kingdom* (1957). After the American trip Camus never left Europe again; but one day in Amsterdam was enough to give rise to his best book, *La Chute* (1956).

'We live not by justice but by grace' (Thoreau). Camus talked a lot about justice but, in the Algerian context, preferred his mother. Justice is a cold concept in any case. A 'judge-penitent' like the narrator in *The Fall* (tr. Justin O'Brien, 1957), he stopped preaching in this last novel, found a more introspective mode and revealed himself as a poet in prose, with an elegant purity of style that some found annoying; hence, in part, the French tendency to belittle him as middlebrow. He himself had been aware of the danger in *The Plague* (tr. Stuart Gilbert, 1947), where I think he caricatures himself in the town clerk and aspiring writer Joseph Grand, a perfectionist who is having 'no end of trouble' with the opening sentence of a projected book, noticing in it 'a facility of tone approximating, remotely perhaps but recognizably, to the common-place'. Any shadow of justice in *The Fall* is of a cosmic kind and far removed from its vengeful connotations in the political sphere, post-war France for example. Instead we have the poetry of Holland, 'a dream of gold and smoke', the sea 'steaming like wet washing', the doves above Amsterdam. His star has faded because we're no longer engaged by the issues of his time, but the poetry remains. France has produced many novelists since, but none to compare with those of his generation. These things go in cycles and have to do with more than literary merit.

Prospects of the Sea

It's now nearly sixty years since the death of Dylan Thomas. He's by no means a forgotten figure of course, and certainly not in Wales; but so recurrent and strangely dismissive have been the attacks on his reputation we might be forgiven for forgetting to take him entirely seriously. Those who feel that poetry has lost touch with some vital function could do worse than read him again. As it happens, contemporary criticism has recognized what we knew instinctively all along — that he was the real thing (despite his own disclaimers), the true vatic voice if rather overdone from time to time. We listened entranced to those recordings first time round, though the real work took place on the page. Graves long ago recorded his own response to those famously sonorous Welsh BBC tones: 'He could put on the *hwyl*, albeit in English as spoken in Langham Place; and, when I listened to him broadcasting, I had to keep a tight hold of myself to avoid being seduced.' Poetic prodigies are monstrous and ill-omened, he tells us, while conceding that 'the poems show every sign of an alert and sober intelligence'. Graves's poetic scheme, as summarized in 'To Juan at the Winter Solstice', approves both 'learned bard' and 'gifted child'. Graves himself was the learned bard; Thomas, though quite well-read (at any rate he read what he needed to read), we may take as a gifted child — in his own famous formulation, 'the Rimbaud of Cwmdonkin Drive', for ever high on all the vowels of the rainbow. As for 'monstrous and ill-omened', this is surely unfair to one who started out with such courage and so few advantages. Those few were very real however: a happy childhood; a good education at Swansea Grammar School where his father was English master; confidence, wit, a puckish charm and native genius. One might also add that, by going from school straight into local theatre and journalism, he instinctively protected his secret, explosive talent from academic discipline and constraint — an advantage he shared with Hardy and Yeats, to name but two. (He thought Yeats the 'best', while Hardy was his 'favourite'.) This remained the pattern. An actor and journalist himself, he preferred actors and journalists to academics who, with some exceptions, scared him stiff. The real thing, he chose like Yeats 'excited reverie' over 'earnest company' and critical theory.

Many still treasure the naive amplitude of the old Dent *Collected Poems* (1952), with its portrait by Augustus John, and cherish a handful of poems there made widely available for the first time: 'The Force that through the Green Fuse Drives the Flower', 'A Refusal to Mourn the Death, by Fire, of a Child in London', 'The Hunchback in the Park', 'Fern Hill' and the one everyone knows, 'Do Not Go Gentle into that Good Night'. Some of the earliest poems, written in his teens, speak still to the adolescent in all of us: 'Before I Knocked', 'Where Once the Waters of Your Face' — body poems, hymns to genetic turmoil. 'The greatest description I know of our earthiness,' he wrote to Pamela Hansford Johnson, 'is to be found in John Donne's *Devotions*, where he describes man as earth of the earth, his body earth, his hair a wild shrub growing out of the land. All thoughts and actions emanate from the body ... Every idea, intuitive or intellectual, can be imagined and translated in terms of the body, its flesh, skin, blood, sinews, veins, glands, organs, cells or senses.' A 'receiving station for creaturely intimations', in Seamus Heaney's phrase, he was not only keen to bed this refined young woman but also in psychosexual revolt against the provincial industrialism of South Wales and, by extension, 'modern civilization' — which he nonetheless enjoyed in the form of comics, thrillers and popular science.

The short stories, echoing Lawrence, take a dim view of the industrial landscape. 'Just Like Little Dogs', in thirties *noir* mode, finds our hero 'listening to the noises from the muffled town, a goods train shunting, a siren in the docks, the hoarse trams in the streets far behind, one bark of a dog, unplaceable sounds, iron being beaten, the distant creaking of wood, doors slamming where there were no houses, an engine coughing like a sheep on a hill'; and this, from 'One Warm Saturday': 'The light from the one weak lamp in a rusty circle fell across the brick-heaps and the broken wood and the dust that had been houses once, where the small and hardly known and never-to-be-forgotten people of the dirty town had lived and loved and died and, always, lost.' An environment

Prospects of the Sea

from which, in 'Where Tawe Flows', the protagonist dreams of escape: 'It was understood that he would soon be leaving for London to make a career in Chelsea as a freelance journalist; he was penniless and hoped, in a vague way, to live on women.' He did indeed make a career in Chelsea as a freelance journalist; also as a screenwriter in Wardour Street and as a brilliant broadcaster in Langham Place, where he impressed and worked with people like MacNeice. The speaker in 'Return Journey' describes his younger self as 'a bombastic adolescent provincial Bohemian, a gabbling, ambitious, mock-tough, pretentious young man', anxious to be gone.

'I'm not a countryman,' he told Vernon Watkins. 'I stand for, if anything, the aspidistra, the provincial drive, the morning café, the evening pub, hotel and cinema, bookshop and tube station.' But another of his early advantages was, precisely, a strong rural connection through his parents' Welsh-speaking country background. He lived at different times in many different places (many of the 'right' places, you might say): Fitzrovia, Chelsea, Oxford, Sussex, Dorset and Cornwall, not counting brief forays to Donegal and Tuscany, a writers' conference in Prague and film work in Tehran where, in need of cash as always, he researched a promotional feature for the Anglo-Iranian Oil Company. But in a sense, if he left Swansea he never really left Wales — not rural Carmarthenshire certainly, where an uncle and aunt, Jack and Ann Jones, had their old farm Fern Hill, the scene of his idyllic childhood holidays; but more particularly the seaside, coastal Wales of the Gower Peninsula, New Quay and Laugharne (pron. Larne), where he and Caitlin finally settled. Dylan's day in misty-castled Laugharne, reports the stormy but crucial Caitlin in *Leftover Life to Kill* (1957), consisted of an ostensibly very simple, even 'moronic' routine: mornings in the pub; late lunch and then, 'blown up with muck and somnolence, up to his humble shed nesting high above the estuary, and bang into intensive scribbling' — a tidal rhythm celebrated in the ebbing-and-flowing structure of the 'Author's Prologue' specially written for *Collected Poems*.

The poems fall roughly into groups, cycles even: the adolescent, 'surrealist' and wartime poems; poems of love and marriage; birthday poems and elegies; and finally the tantalizing, unfinished sequence first projected under the title 'In Country Heaven'. The adolescent and 'surrealist' poems were, astonishingly, written or at least drafted

Derek Mahon

between the ages of seventeen and twenty. Bursting with testosterone and oestrogen, some frankly onanistic, they shocked and intrigued his first readers in equal measure. The usual euphemism was 'visceral'. The unborn speak; much of the action takes place in the womb; genitals are everywhere in 'obscure' paraphrase, sexual frustration and confusion never far away (but that's life) in poems like 'I See the Boys of Summer' and the still extraordinary, renegade-Christian 'Before I Knocked', a defining moment in the poetry of the time, the 'Jesus poem' about incarnation, spirit and flesh:

> *As yet ungotten, I did suffer;*
> *The rack of dreams my lily bones*
> *Did twist into a living cipher,*
> *And flesh was snipped to cross the lines*
> *Of gallow crosses on the liver*
> *And brambles in the wringing brains.*

Registers and motifs of this kind would be picked up by other poets and artists within a few years when the neo-Romantic, 'New Apocalypse' movement got going. The inchoate meanings of the early poems can be, and have been, extensively figured out. What is at issue here is the creative principle itself. 'Light Breaks Where No Sun Shines', for instance, develops the implications of Donne's medieval, indeed immemorial 'stardust' picture of the human physique, an idea known to Giordano Bruno and ancient Egypt. Relatedly, the beautiful 'Where Once the Waters of Your Face' clings to a natural magic under threat of extinction:

> *Dry as a tomb, your coloured lids*
> *Shall not be latched while magic glides*
> *Sage on the earth and sky;*
> *There shall be corals in your beds,*
> *There shall be serpents in your tides,*
> *Till all our sea-faiths die.*

Some of the difficulties facing a new reader derive from the difficulties facing this new and highly original writer in his early days, and a number of these poems — 'Should Lanterns Shine', 'I Have Longed to Move Away', 'Once It Was the Colour of Saying', even perhaps the strange, daunting and haunting 'Altarwise by Owl-Light' sequence — are concerned with the perplexities of the creative act itself, perplexities ultimately resolved, in the simplest and most moving terms, with 'In My Craft or Sullen Art' — where, in Berkeley's phrase, 'the obvious but amazing truth 'tis no witchcraft to see' (that ideas are fictions) reveals itself to the moonstruck poet who realizes he writes not for glory:

> *But for the lovers, their arms*
> *Round the griefs of the ages,*
> *Who pay no praise or wages*
> *Nor heed my craft or art.*

His 'maturity' is usually dated to 'After the Funeral' (1939), the first of the great elegies, this one for his aunt Ann Jones of Fern Hill; for this was the death of childhood, and the poem is almost the first in which he gets out of himself and confronts (as he had already done in prose) the external world of personality and society, here the provincial constraint of Ann's 'fist of a face' and her 'room with a stuffed fox and a stale fern'. Soon enough, though, he rises to the occasion and, harking back to an older Wales, the 'exuberant bardsmanship' he honoured in Dafydd ap Gwilym, declares himself 'Ann's bard on a raised hearth', and breathes new life into fox and fern. (Thomas loved 'ferned and foxy woods'; elsewhere we have 'fox light' and, vividly, 'a torch of foxes foams'.) But 'After the Funeral' introduces a new theme, one destined to be of the first importance, the inadequacy of language to the fact of death, a subject already present in certain of the early poems but now seized upon and expanded to tremendous effect during the second world war and specifically during the London Blitz. His initial response to the war was one of horror and derision ('Dylan-shooting begins; girls hot and stupid for soldiers flock knickerless on the cliff'); but it was the making of him. Strikingly unfit for active service, he turned seriously to radio work and documentary film — inspired, like so many, by the communal wartime spirit, besides the need to earn in a grim, spivvy economy.

'A Refusal to Mourn', though refusing the usual consolations, is an intensely religious poem, in the vein of Welsh pulpit declamation so often evident in Thomas's work. The Biblical last line, which

Derek Mahon

once aroused much critical puzzlement, is explicable in terms of *Revelation 20-21*: the first death is the natural one, the second the Day of Judgement which the innocent child will be spared. The real problems lie elsewhere, in the main body of the poem, where the details are by no means clear. A naive first reader, like oneself at sixteen, will be thrown initially by the exiguous punctuation, a standard feature of the poems and one quite easily if impertinently clarified by punctuating the verse for oneself so that, fitted out with hyphens and commas to be immediately readable, the 'Refusal' would begin:

> *Never until the mankind-making,*
> *Bird-, beast- and flower-*
> *Fathering and all-humbling darkness*
> *Tells with silence the last light breaking*
> *And the still hour*
> *Is come, of the sea tumbling in harness . . .*

When a house fills with smoke in 'A Child's Christmas in Wales', the fire brigade is called; also Ernie Jenkins because he 'likes fires'. The Blitz, frightful in itself, provoked a remarkable range of artistic response: Elizabeth Bowen's best fiction, Eliot's 'Little Gidding' and MacNeice's *Springboard* volume; a renewed interest in music; the graphics of Paul Nash and Henry Moore. There's much to be said, indeed, for putting Thomas in the cultural context of the period. 'Ceremony After a Fire Raid' is organ music, 'Fern Hill' a picture by Marc Chagall. The poetic 'New Apocalypse' and the neo-Romantic movement in art responded to the same impulses; the countryside, largely overlooked by the urbane Marxists of the thirties ('the idiocy of rural life') was rediscovered. This coincided with Thomas's own rediscovery of Wales and issued in some of his finest work.

The love-and-marriage poems have been curiously neglected, perhaps because he published few 'love poems' as the term is generally understood, though his whole work is a love poem really. 'Love in the Asylum' has been virtually ignored, and 'The Hunchback in the Park', one of his greatest triumphs, admired for its simplicity and circumstantial detail though it too is a love poem — to the creative dream, the imagined girl, the Muse herself, 'a woman figure without fault' who watches over the darkness. 'Into Her Lying Down Head'

Prospects of the Sea

and 'A Winter's Tale', also oddly neglected, perhaps for reasons of tact, are love poems too, Caitlin poems, and form a curious pair, like Dylan and Caitlin themselves. Photographs by Bill Brandt and Rollie McKenna show her to have been a singularly gorgeous young woman (the Macnamaras of Co Clare were known for their star quality); but her married life wasn't easy. What began as love in a cottage ended up as love in a mist.

While Dylan was away carousing in Soho, and later in Greenwich Village, she raised three children in their fairly isolated Boat House, beset by solitude and financial problems. 'Into Her Lying Down Head' is about marital infidelities, real or imagined, and isolation (though Laugharne, like St Ives and Kinsale, is now on the tourist map); while 'A Winter's Tale', more love story than lyric in structure, resolves all difficulties, all needs, in a fairy-tale nature eroticism owing much, significantly, to traditional biomorphic Celtic imagery: the 'carved mouths in the rock are wind swept strings', blackbirds 'like priests in the cloaked hedge row', thickets 'antlered like deer'. This fine and substantial poem of 135 lines has been largely disregarded too, perhaps for its too obviously picturesque and sentimental touches, perhaps for its calm mystery, its uncharacteristic quietude, its absence of verbal fun and games. Those of us in favour of mature sexuality will find it celebrated here:

> Burning in the bride bed of love, in the whirl-
> Pool at the wanting centre, in the folds
> Of paradise, in the spun bud of the world.
> And she rose with him flowering in her melting snow.

The more autobiographical birthday poems of these years contain many fine things, even if some have the air of diary entries, extensive notes to himself in preparation for something larger. Except for 'Lament', with its Nogood Boyo slap-and-tickle, they aren't really about himself at all, the self-regarding exercises some have taken them for, but objective sketches of Laugharne and environs as seen from the 'house on stilts' and the writing shed, of tidal activity and bird life; 'finches fly', herons 'spire and spear'. Conscious of approaching middle age (it's been suggested that he died 'of middle age', though some thought he was just getting into his stride) and a need to enlarge his scope, he concentrated his considerable resources

Derek Mahon

on a new, ambitious post-war project; and then his revered father died. Heaney has written movingly about the 'almost sobbing counterpoint' of 'Do Not Go Gentle': 'This is a son comforting a father; yet it is also, conceivably, the neophyte in him addressing the legend, the green fuse addressing the burnt-out case'; and he invokes, in relation to Dylan, the myth of Orpheus, one who also charmed the birds from the trees yet came to grief in the end. The Orphean voice is there certainly; so too, increasingly, is the Dionysian. This had the legendary tragic outcome ('a bad end, thank God'), as in 'the road to ruin I must run'; but also a festive potential which empowered the last poems and the improvisational, lightweight but historically interesting 'play for voices', *Under Milk Wood*, with its finneganese night music, its comic polyphony and now quaint period detail. He knew, it goes without saying, his visionary Vaughan and his baroque Milton, while relishing the eccentricities of parochial life. The earliest stories — 'The Burning Baby', 'The School for Witches' — are Gothic, counter-Reformation imaginings which surface again, transfigured, in the natural magic of the last poems. His historical reach was a long one.

Thomas had a knack for titles when he chose: *The Map of Love* (1939), *Deaths and Entrances* (1946). After the war he started planning the long poem or sequence, perhaps a volume, to be entitled 'In Country Heaven'. He himself understood the dynamics of such enterprises. 'Grandiose schemes are built in order that they may be dropped,' he said, going on to add that, with luck, shorter poems of greater weight and depth might emerge 'than all the unwritten greatness'; and that's exactly what happened in this instance. The project imagined a world blown to bits by nuclear disaster, with the lost human race looking down from above and remembering life on earth: 'places, fears, love, exultation, misery, animal joy, ignorance and mysteries, all *we* know and do not know'. It will become, he hopes, 'an affirmation of the beautiful and terrible worth of the earth, a praise of what is and could be on this lump in the skies'. Of this 'grandiose' project three substantial poems survive: in order of composition, 'In Country Sleep', 'Over Sir John's Hill' and 'In the White Giant's Thigh'. Though perhaps less popular than some of the more immediately dramatic lyrics, these represent his crowning achievement. A trilogy complete in itself, the sequence moves from a vision of peace and refuge (a prayer for his daughter Aeronwy

Prospects of the Sea

asleep in Laugharne) to the menacing external world (whatever is predatory and destructive: there were now nuclear weapons not far away), and concludes in an ecstasy of rhapsodic resolution and celebration. Laugharne represented for this nature visionary, said Vernon Watkins, 'the last refuge of life and sanity in a nightmare world, the last irregular protest against the regularity and symmetry of madness'. The theme was that of a sacramental universe, the unity of creation. All plants and animals ('thick as thieves'), birds, beasts and flowers, the lake that 'harps to a hail stone', 'the rain telling its beads' figured in this ecological conception (*'Sanctum sanctorum* the animal eye of the wood'), as did the precious human singularity comically recorded, as if for a too solemn posterity, in *Under Milk Wood.*

Reality withdraws from technology, even from the microphone. 'Over Sir John's Hill', the most anxious and contrived of the three, also set in Laugharne, is continuous with the Blitz poems as the Cold War was immediately continuous with the defeat of Germany and Japan. It was a short step from the East End 'slum of fire' to the destruction of Dresden, the atomic era and the photogenic obliteration of Hiroshima and Nagasaki, a geopolitical script spectrally implicit in Thomas's amateur ornithology ('the birds watch *me,*' he said). His friends the priestly heron and crane are here but the nuclear 'hawk on fire', in its 'hoisted cloud', is what he focuses on as it threatens the 'small birds of the bay' with their 'breast of whistles'. A lover of *Paradise Lost,* as of all lost Edens, he sometimes seems to have lived imaginatively in the 17th century, still fighting a private war between the medieval and modern worlds — whence perhaps the religious intensity, even when consciously satirical, everywhere in the work from 'Before I Knocked' to 'In the White Giant's Thigh', that feminized reworking of Shakespeare's 73rd Sonnet ('Bare ruin'd choirs where late the sweet birds sang'). Feminist critics have praised the 'White Giant's Thigh' for its affirmation of female sexuality, quoting Julia Kristeva on 'biological thought'. The 'big girls', the Gwyneths and Rhiannons of the early prose, come into their own here as 'daughters of darkness' in the archaic night, though curiously we're not in Wales but in Dorset, near Caitlin's mother's house. The white giant is the butch fertility figure cut into the 'high chalk hill' of Cerne Abbas, where the poet walks after dark in the 'gigantic glade' as if in a graveyard — though

Derek Mahon

it *is* a sort of Wales since the figure was thought to date from pre-Roman, Celtic times. Much of the incidental detail of the women's buried lives is 'Welsh' too in 'Fern Hill' mode:

> *The dust of their kettles and clocks swings to and fro*
> *Where the hay rides now or the bracken kitchens rust*
> *As the arc of the billhooks that flashed the hedges low*
> *And cut the birds' boughs that the minstrel sap ran red.*
> *They from houses where the harvest kneels, hold me hard,*
> *Who heard the tall bell sail down the Sundays of the dead*
> *And the rain wring out its tongues on the faded yard.*

The anglocentric hostility this 'dog among the fairies' once provoked has largely evaporated. The legend, inaugurated by John Malcom Brinnin's *Dylan Thomas in America* (1956) and consolidated by Constantine FitzGibbon's *The Life of Dylan Thomas* (1965), lives on. The hectic alcoholism and premature death at the age of thirty-nine, precipitated by the exhaustion of punishing lecture tours, crippling anxieties, and the notorious morphine overdose, ensure that the legend survives along with the work, helped in great measure by the pop-cultural influence of the Beats, the hero-worship of self-styled Bob Dylan and even the death from heroin of Sid Vicious, who also spent serious time at the Chelsea Hotel on West 23rd Street, New York — a haven, in those days, for musicians, artists and writers. There's a certain logic in this. Thomas, the hero of many a solitary teenage room and himself a subversive folk-rock Dionysian celebrity before the concept was co-opted and institutionalized, struck an immediate chord with the young. A proto-feminist and radical pacifist, he talked the talk and walked the walk. Still, it's hard to know who to compare him with in international terms, if such comparisons need be made. Hart Crane perhaps, the Rimbaud of Cleveland, Ohio, with whom he shared a high-strung metaphorical density and an aspiration to overarching schemes. But I'd like to propose another, unlikely and in most ways antithetical figure (Dylan was anything but diplomatic), a fellow contributor to Marguerite Caetani's once renowned magazine *Botteghe Oscure*. I mean the later Saint-John Perse, also a student of Rimbaud, wind, hail, rain and snow; of birds, sea light and oceanic forces, the prospects of the sea. When the French poet writes that birds, 'conceived by a first inflection and destined for long resonance, move like words to a cosmic rhythm, inscribing themselves instinctively in the great vagrant poem of the evolving earth', he's on the same planet as Dylan Thomas. Disoriented, impenitent, 'dying of strangers', Thomas left us a faith in unfashionable notions like inspiration and genius; also an exhilarating poetry not of diminished but of enhanced expectation — in his own words, a contribution to reality: 'The world is never the same once a good poem has been added to it. A good poem helps to change the shape and significance of the universe.'

Whale and Pelican

Robert Lowell had great respect for critics, especially the poet-critics who were his chosen luminaries in youth, but his own practice was deliberately at variance with theirs. Though he spent much time in Academe, he was not academic by nature. He describes himself as 'anxious not to do the standard analytical essay', preferring to be 'much sloppier and more intuitive'. This is all to the good, and the amphibious conversational style of the prose memoirs is very much his own. We wouldn't really want to read his analysis of *The Good Soldier*. He knows this, and gives us instead an unforgettable picture of the author lecturing at a writers' conference in Colorado: 'Once I watched an audience of hundreds walk out on [Ford] as he exquisitely, ludicrously and inaudibly imitated the elaborate, periphrastic style of Henry James; they could neither hear nor sympathize.' The deliberately 'sloppy' manner allows, also, for a raciness of idiom, as if poetry were a kind of sport, which it often is. On Frost: 'There was music in his voice, in the spin on his language.' On Ransom: 'His mouth was large and always in slow perceptible motion, quivering with tedium, tighter-drawn to repel ignorant rudeness or giving an encouraging grimace.' The essays on modern American poetry run the gamut from Frost to Plath. They are personal essays. Lowell knew most of his subjects, and is remarkably shrewd: 'Eliot's fierceness was restrained, his dullness was never more than the possum's feigned death.' Unfashionably, but in my own view laudably, he seems to prefer Crane to Williams, while acknowledging Williams. His piece on Jarrell is an obituary tribute, and brings out the best in Lowell, as consistently generous in print as he was mischievous in conversation. [Jarrell] 'seemed to make no distinction between what he would say in our hearing and what he would say behind our backs; if anything, absence made him more discreet.' Of Plath: 'What is most heroic in her is not her force, but the desperate practicality of her control.'

Whale and Pelican

Though not a scholar, Lowell nevertheless writes precociously on the *Iliad* and illuminatingly on the *Metamorphoses*. 'The trouble with criticism is that it makes points,' he observes in 'Poets and the Theatre'. This is one of his best pieces. 'I have always felt splenetic about the stage, known very little about it and shivered at the suggestion that I write for it. Two years ago, however, I was translating Racine's *Phèdre* and found I was more interested in the drama than the poetry. I now feel double-faced looking on plays as some barbarian Gaul or Goth might have first looked on Rome, his shaggy head full of moral disgust, plunder and adaptation.' That 'moral disgust' reminds us that Lowell was born into the New England puritan tradition, with which he conducted a lifelong love-hate relationship. Of Cotton Mather, the Salem witch-hunter, he writes: 'His soft, bookish hands are indelibly stained with blood — a black image to set against our white busts of Washington and Lincoln; his face is not on a postage stamp.' Of Thoreau: 'He had the shy, brief, ascetic life of Pascal, Herbert and Hopkins.' Of his grandfather, the poet and diplomat James Russell Lowell: 'I envy his strenuous grace, and fear affinities with the cold, gone-out fire.' Of Longfellow: 'Tennyson without gin.' Of Emily Dickinson: 'She brought to poetry not only spoken language but her own self-speaking language, she made the language of her contemporaries obsolete — if anyone had heard her.' Inevitably, the most valuable items are those on his own practice, and the autobiographical pieces that end the book. Replying to comments on his poem 'Skunk Hour' he complains 'not that I am misunderstood, but that I am over-understood. I am seen through.' That being the case, he comes clean. The poem has its sources in other poems, by St John of the Cross (we knew *that*), by Elizabeth Bishop and Annette von Droste-Hülshoff — this last a considerable revelation. (She provided the unusual stanza form too.) The 'dark night' of the poem he describes as an existential night — what the mystics call a dark night of the soul. A generation of reductive critics has charged him with pretentiousness in this connection, yet the documentary evidence is here to show that he did experience such things. Hitherto unpublished, 'Near the Unbalanced Aquarium' is a twenty-page account of his 1954 incarceration in the Payne-Whitney Clinic, New York, for an attack of 'pathological enthusiasm', comparable to Lowry's *Lunar Caustic* but more devastating because so utterly matter-of-fact: 'Down the corridor, almost a city block away, I heard the elevator shut.' He receives massive injections, records his own social 'cunning' and picks on a fellow patient, making him cry. He directs imaginary traffic in the ward, sings the *Rex Tremendae Majestatis* to the tune of 'Yankee Doodle' in the shower, is deprived of pyjama cord and matches, and sits gaping through Scrabble games, 'unable to form the simplest word'. He remembers his father, 'a gentle, faithful and dim man', wonders why he was 'agin him' and concludes, 'I hope there will be peace'.

Saskia Hamilton, in her introduction to the *Letters*, speaks of his love of 'line, form, quality', all evident in the poetry, while the letters have 'the immediacy of the first rhythm, and the first thought, that occurred to him — the very thing he revised away in his poems'. Some of the best are to Elizabeth Bishop: 'My great fault is rhetorical melodrama . . . I wish I weren't gravely impractical by nature and habit.' (One is tempted to add, and by choice?) Sloppy, shabby, bearish, stupid, dim — this is how he describes himself in the down-time between manic episodes and in the more extended relief of his later lithium-induced equilibrium. It became a persona, almost a promotional device, whereas he was as sharp as an open razor and wicked with it. The apotropaic 'swimming' hands so often described, mimetic of infinite nuance, sketched also a grave and aleatoric irresponsibility. He knew he was symptomatic of something scary in the American psyche, and used the knowledge creatively, even to the extent of 'rhetorical melodrama'. He calls this his 'great fault'; but the evidence of his later work, after *Near the Ocean*, suggests that his greatest faults were, sadly, faith in his own domineering mystique, a morose arrogance, and the related belief that everything he wrote was of equal interest and importance. Interest and importance surfaced only sporadically in the later work, *Notebook* and the rest, which show a great falling-off into blather and slither; blame it on the medication. Slither is there too in the later letters, especially in those to his ex-wife Elizabeth Hardwick, which are full of excuses and evasions. (Auden had harsh things to say about 'men who leave behind them a trail of weeping women'.) 'My eyes have seen what my hand did,' wrote Lowell in his last book, *Day by Day* — but did he, by that stage, really know what he was doing? More to the point is a line from 'Eye and Tooth': 'I am tired. Everyone's tired of my turmoil.' It's a measure of his significance as symptom and prophet that this timely thought contained a larger, geopolitical truth.

Since the feminist era it's become common to prefer Bishop to Lowell, and one can see why. Though light-headed, unlike Bishop he had little lightness of touch. The 'Quaker Graveyard', a wondrous compendium of quotes (Thoreau etc.), shifts tons of shipping, blubber and trauma, and the displacement is or was overwhelming; but besides the heavy stuff we long for the relief of lightness too. To be fair, he sometimes provides it ('Our Lady of Walsingham'). So too in a quiet piece like 'Skunk Hour', significantly dedicated to Bishop. Here is the lightness we miss in so much of his work, and it's no surprise that younger generations prefer her warmth and wit to his forceful monumentality (power mania if you like), riding for preference not his 'blue-lung'd combers' lumbering to the kill, but her playful froth. She was gay in both senses, 'awful but cheerful' — most of the time. 'Why was I a human being?' she asks in 'The Country Mouse'. Her animals, like those of Marianne Moore, are various shapes and sizes, some light, some heavy. 'The Moose' for example (the Muse?), a 'grand, otherworldly' female, mysterious, towering and, amusingly, 'awful plain', is decidedly heavy, but the poem moves at a light, dreamy pace and hammers nothing home. Raindrops in 'The End of March' are 'heavy with light'. Not the same thing as light verse, though she does that too, her lighter poetry is a flock of birds to Lowell's mighty whale, as if from a famous scene in *Moby-Dick*: in her case pelicans, puffins and 'white herons got up as angels', picturesque species anyhow, wind under their wings. Or not. Some of her birds — sandpiper, rooster — tend not to fly, or fly only to fight ('Roosters').

I noticed last year that, at some point in the distant past, I had cheerfully and ineptly plagiarized her beautiful line about sand, 'Mixed with quartz grains, rose and amethyst'. I changed it at once, but the shock made me look more closely at 'Sandpiper', where she describes the bird as 'a student of Blake' ('To see the world in a grain of sand'). We're all looking more closely now, and noticing the importance of everything small and light. Italo Calvino, in his posthumous *Six Memos for the Next Millennium*, recommends lightness to future authors, together with quickness and other desirable things, as liberating agents, and cites *De Rerum Natura*. Lucretius' first concern, Calvino says, is to 'prevent the weight of

Derek Mahon

matter from crushing us'. Atomization is the thing, so everything including ourselves can make unpredictable deviations. Lucretius looks at dust particles in a shaft of sunlight in a dark room, and at sea shells, all similar but each one different, cast up by waves on the 'imbibing sand'. (But to invoke Lucretius is to be too heavy.) To Bishop's sandpiper the world is a mist, then 'minute and vast and clear'. A watercolourist, she too saw clearly, certainly where machinery and armaments were concerned. 'Roosters', first published in 1941 when America was again gearing up for war, takes place in a 'gun-metal blue dark' and quickly turns into a fairly explicit anti-war poem; but the roosters' 'uncontrolled, traditional cries' eventually fade to vague 'wandering lines in marble': lightness, deviations, ancient history. We know about the artistic temperament, its 'irresponsibility'. Lowell, gravely irresponsible, insists on his responsibility; Bishop, irresponsible on principle, responds to things intuitively. They impinge not on her conscience but on her nerves. Her ethics lie in the precision with which she registers phenomena and events. It's a question of tact and taste, of a genuine responsibility to the real world:

> *Happy the people in the swimming-pool and on the yacht,*
> *Happy the man in that airplane, likely as not —*
> *And out there where the coral reef is a shelf*
> *The water runs at it, leaps, throws itself*
> *Lightly, lightly, whitening in the air:*
> *An acre of cold white spray is there*
> *Dancing happily by itself.*
>   ('Pleasure Seas')

Paws

'The sort of thing that gives me pause (paws) is whether I do more than like you very, very much.' Growing girls used to be warned about the danger of being 'interfered' with. Larkin, more than once, used the word in the larger sense of 'saying love but meaning interference' ('He Hears that his Beloved has become Engaged', 1953). The same thought crops up several times in *Letters to Monica* (2010) — his long-time friend and confidante Monica Jones, a lecturer in English at Leicester University. He writes from Belfast (his second job) in 1951, 'It seems to me that *bending someone else to your will* is the very stuff of sex . . . And what's more, both sides *would sooner have it that way than not at all*. I wouldn't.' Seven years later, from Hull, where he lived for the rest of his life: 'I seem entirely lacking in that *desire to impose oneself* that is such a feature of masculine behaviour . . . Bothering people. Inflicting oneself on people.' Was he being quite sincere, or was this recurrent theme a self-serving device to avoid the subject of marriage? A famously reclusive bachelor, he insists throughout on his incurable 'selfishness' — cherishes it indeed. He and Monica slept together as occasion offered, and shared holidays; but always there is this reserve, a fear of getting too deeply involved. He *was* deeply involved though, and toward the end they finally lived together. Monica survived him in more senses than one, and after her own death in 2001 there came to light more than a thousand items from his side of the correspondence.

Anthony Thwaite notes in his introduction that their 'friendship and correspondence began with books and reading'. He sent her his novel *Jill*, and proofs of *A Girl in Winter*, and it went from there. Gripes, gossip and hypochondria followed, together with 'affectionate whimsy' about the world of Beatrix Potter. She is a rabbit ('Dearest Bun'), he a seal, and his humorous sketches of them in these roles adorn the text. Gripes include living conditions here and there till he had his own house; the shortcomings of colleagues, and the rise and rise of 'K' (Kingsley Amis), described as 'really not interested in much more than showing off'. Amis and his first wife Hilly are 'DIRTY RICH CHILDREN' who 'REFUSE TO SUFFER'. Music is a favourite topic. Larkin and Monica were keen radio listeners and seem to have spent half their evenings tuned-in to the old BBC Third Programme. Bach always hits the spot: 'as exciting as jazz'. He talks about favourite authors: Hardy, Samuel Butler, D. H. Lawrence who 'has always meant so much more to me than any other writer'; campily, Wilde, 'Saki', Rolfe, Iris Murdoch, Stevie Smith; and a book he loved, strangely, Connolly's *The Rock Pool*. (Perhaps he saw himself as Naylor in another life.) Name-checked contemporaries include G. S. ('George') Fraser, who gets it in the neck (he was Monica's head of department at Leicester), Robert Conquest, Donald Davie and D. J. Enright. She sends him (1950) a Christmas present that gives great and lasting pleasure: *The Wind in the Willows* illustrated by Arthur Rackham. He sends her poems for her comments, some still in the throes of composition, and some we haven't seen before, like this:

> *Ring a ring a roses*
> *A coronary thrombosis*
> *A seizure! A seizure!*
> *All fall down.*

He complains of writer's block (1951): 'It may be that I am not trying to write about what *really* interests me, like not being able to write about what really interests me for instance.'

His general remarks about poetry are sometimes obvious enough ('The most fascinating effects are got by playing off the rhythm and language of speech against [those] of poetry'), sometimes trade secrets ('I often feel poems have to have some falsity in them, like yeast, or they won't "rise"': this from Larkin!). 'Often one spends weeks trying to write a poem out of the conscious mind that never comes to anything — these are the sort of "ideal" poems that one feels ought to be written, but don't because (I fancy) they lack the vital spark of *self-interest*. A "real" poem is a pleasure to write.' 'I could never feel that Chaucer was as real as the *Daily Mail*, & so I was never an academic.' American poetry is largely 'tripe'; 'All modern thinking and practice is *wrong*.' Again and again he returns to the seemingly unquestioned facts of 'ordinary' life: 'How much more interesting & worth writing about Betjeman's subjects are than most other modern poets — I mean, whether so-and-so achieves some metaphysical inner unity is not really so interesting to us as the over-building of rural Middlesex.' The art he likes is 19th-century English art as found in provincial galleries, and 'the only good life is to live in some sodding seedy city & work & keep yr gob shut & be unhappy'. But this is self-caricature. He is perfectly capable of rapture. At Christmas 1953 he writes of 'the sharp stars & dropping rime & curled-up animals & fires ageing into ash & the wind going quietly along the lanes as it's accustomed to do & meeting no one'. Again, 'I had the most thrilling experience of seeing, from the coast between Cushendun & Fair Head ... the Mull of Kintyre, Scotland, a great paw of rock couchant in the still evening water, absurdly near.' Another paw.

Larkin's aren't the kind of poems that need explaining (like Betjeman's you just read them), but the letters fill out the persona. He wouldn't have liked the Poundian word 'persona', so let's say personality. His low-key but oddly forceful personality is one of the things that come out most vividly in the work, and is a sort of poetic statement in itself. The letters are part of the poetry in that sense. 'Such attics cleared of me! Such absences!' Somehow he always lived in upper rooms before buying the house in Hull. An evocative drawing here of his Belfast flat includes a skylight ('!'), which seems an important prop for a student of clouds. His, and Monica's, devotion to the radio (he liked a *big* radio) gets an airing in 'Broadcast' (1961). He knows she's at the concert, which ends with the usual ovation:

> *Leaving me desperate to pick out*
> *Your hands, tiny in all that air, applauding.*

Unfortunately it wasn't Monica at the concert but Maeve Brennan, which annoyed Monica when she saw the poem in *The Listener*. 'Talking in Bed' (1960) *was* about Monica, and she hadn't liked that either:

Derek Mahon

It becomes still more difficult to find
Words both true and kind,
Or not untrue and not unkind.

He two-timed her for years with Maeve, a fellow librarian and not to be confused with her namesake the Irish-American writer. When he speaks of marriage with its 'constant lack of solitude', that's only part of the story; and he *could* be a little unkind: 'Abandon yr harsh didactic voice & use only the soft musical one . . . You're getting a habit of *boring* your face up or round into the features of the listener — *don't* do it! It's most trying.' They clearly got on each others' nerves at times, but she must have been frustrated by his evident detachment, and exasperated by the difficulty of getting him to talk.

Which brings us back to the poetry and the bleak social vision he there dramatized. Born of personal experience (family and so on), this was real enough but admitted that yeast-like 'falsity': he exaggerates for effect, and it works, making the poems trenchant and hilarious. Not all the poems though. We quote, for fun, 'Vers de Société' and the like, but it's the more sonorous register of 'Church Going' and 'An Arundel Tomb' we prize above all. Perhaps like his beloved Hardy he was a religious poet deprived of religion (perhaps most poets are) and shared Hardy's philosophic fatalism while 'hoping it might be so'. He wouldn't have put it that way — but never trust the teller, trust the tale. The poems sing almost despite, almost to spite him. There is even, dare one say, a buried *sacramental* substance in the work: 'Water', 'Sad Steps'. And all the time he thought, or many of his fans thought, he was your average disenchanted modern bloke.

Airy-fairy notions of this kind find no place in these letters to the woman he liked best, and this is a measure of his solitude — this, and the fact that he wrote so many. He, and Monica too, preferred the fountain pen to the telephone. One agreeable feature is the inclusion, as footnotes, of passages from her side of the correspondence, where she shows herself able for him if finally baffled by his self-sufficiency. 'An auto-erotic writer case incapable of love', in his own estimation, 'for anyone but himself', he was no misogynist, though, and could obviously be very loving, as much here demonstrates. Also naughty: 'Yes, I liked the red suspender belt.' He liked her open-work stockings too, and her 'French rig': 'You shd know by now what an old fetishist I am.' As for those growing girls, in due course they found their way into the work, notably the pastiche school story *Trouble at Willow Gables*. When a clique of willowy sixth-formers sent him a fan letter ('Where were they when I needed them?') he predicted that massed schoolgirl choirs would one day sing 'They fuck you up' in the Albert Hall. (It may yet happen.) Good to know that he liked Belfast: 'I felt overwhelmingly at Easter that, although nowhere is really "home" to me, Belfast probably means more to me, packs a stronger emotional punch, than anywhere else, even Oxford.'

The Sadness Lurks So Deep

When you stop to look back and see all those days dreaming of a future. And say then, that was my life.
— J. P. Donleavy, *The Beastly Beatitudes of Balthazar B.*

Sebastian Dangerfield, George Smith, Samuel S and Balthazar B: Donleavy's protagonists, like Beckett's, are all the same man. The saddest man, the loneliest man, the randiest man, the nicest man, a singular man at any rate: the proportions change from book to book, but the mixture is always the same. Donleavy Man is a fairy-tale character: a cat with nine lives; a dog with two tails or with no tail at all. He is, most importantly, an American citizen — or, in the case of Balthazar, a secret American posing as a European aristocrat like someone in Henry James. The American thing is vital to a sympathetic appreciation of Donleavy. People often think of him as an Irish writer, but he isn't; he can't be. He belongs, with Scott Fitzgerald and Henry Miller, to the American expatriate tradition. The expatriate thing is important, too. It is, perhaps, no accident that his dullest novel, *A Singular Man*, is set in New York. It's only in foreign cities that the Donleavy magic works, since it's only there that the fairy tale can be told. So we have Dublin, London, Paris and Vienna — but above all Dublin, for the faded elegance that's in it. Here, in this fairy-tale setting (so generations of English and American Trinity people will tell you), the last scion of a non-existent dynasty, 'an aristocrat wherever I flee', can act out his dreams of *gloria mundi*: 'O where is the dignity? Old families and estates? Carriages and footmen? The vulgarity that has come to pass.' Donleavy Man, by his own admission, is a natural aristocrat, with the physique and (when the wind blows) the tailoring one would expect. What, aside from himself, does he believe in? What is he looking for? The simple things: 'to sow, please, one's desperate bag of wild oats in this country. Somewhere there must be a fissure

The Sadness Lurks So Deep

in this granite ground.' And: 'The wife would say, ah, your nibs, is the repast to your liking, would you be wanting now a little hot cup of the tea, another rasher of the bacon. And would he, climbing back up these stairs, ever be king? To say another rasher of bacon. Ever be husband to have a wife. Be father to have a son.' Love, then, and a pillow for the soul, 'where the seaweeds rise and fall at night in Balscaddoon Bay'. But there is no rest for the wicked, and Donleavy Man, 'the eternal tourist', can find at best a precarious syncretism of the dream and the reality. The humour is in the precariousness. One night of wine and dine (on tick) before the nagging wife comes home; one month of richness in a clean house before the dread Scully knocks on the door.

To every Quixote his Sancho Panza, and this sad knight has his. O'Keefe in *The Ginger Man* is Beefy in *The Beastly Beatitudes*. O'Keefe and Dangerfield merge to some extent in the person of Samuel S. *The Saddest Summer*, 120 pages in the Penguin edition, is a strange little book and arguably the best-sustained piece of work Donleavy has done. Sad Sam, a Harvard graduate on the brink of middle age, lives alone in a seedy boarding house in Vienna. Mostly broke, and without energy to move or improve his condition, he spends his time drinking coffee and seeing a psychiatrist. Suddenly, in the space of one day, he gets two chances to boost the morale. A friendly countess offers him an income for life and an American co-ed doing Europe suggests the bed. What would Dangerfield have said? What, God help us, would O'Keefe have said? Samuel S refuses both offers — the money because of the indignity, the tumble because of the impermanence that's in it: 'To screw her is to let her get away.' She goes in any case, and with Sam's death Donleavy seems to have killed the possibility of a straight, unwhimsical pathos; for *The Saddest Summer*, despite its title, differs from the Dublin books in being not about 'sadness' but despair, a different texture altogether. In this it resembles *A Singular Man*. Which is the real Donleavy: the dying fall of the fairy tale or the mordant terror of his more frankly existential heroes?

For the moment he seems to have settled for an even more rarefied version of the fairy tale. *The Beastly Beatitudes* covers much of the same ground as *The Ginger Man*. Balthazar, a paragon of sensibility and refinement, is born in Paris, goes to school in

Derek Mahon

England and proceeds, for no obvious reason, to Trinity College, Dublin, where, after months of loneliness, he meets and falls in love with a Miss Fitzdare, from Co Fermanagh. Meanwhile he has met Beefy again. Beefy, an old school friend, is now reading Divinity at Trinity and hoping to live up to the limerick. His chances of a career in the Church of Ireland, and Balthazar's in the natural sciences, are cut short when they're found entertaining women in Beefy's room after midnight. They're sent down and the Fitzdare withdraws her favour. So Balthazar goes to London, hearing later of her death in a riding accident. The etiolated lyricism faintly audible behind the crash of breaking glass and the roar of burst pipes in *The Ginger Man* comes through loud and clear in *The Beastly Beatitudes*. Shamelessly tearful and self-indulgent, it celebrates an insulated melancholy only the rich can afford: 'Reach up and gather all this world. Before dark or any other people should ever come. And find you sheltering. As all hearts are. Worried lonely. Your eyes quiet. By the waters cold. Where the sadness lurks so deep.' Or take 'the sad little secret untold in Beefy's stout heart', read in a diary he kept at school:

> *I want*
> *A mummy*
> *And a daddy*
> *Please*
> *Help me*
> *Somebody.*

Great stretches of Donleavy are thoroughly tiresome and inconsequential, and he is a past master of the unfunny. *The Ginger Man* could profitably be cut by a third, *The Beastly Beatitudes* by a half and *A Singular Man* by three-quarters. What would remain is a small but delightful body of comic writing, a handful of memorable characters and a picture of Dublin life in the forties comparable to Henry Miller's Paris. There is, of course, no comparison to be made with Joyce; Donleavy is simply not in that league. His literary devices are limited in number and scope, his situations predictable and his *faux-naïveté* naive almost to the point of childishness. But somehow he has struck an important vein in the imagination of many; and his vision of Ireland, offensive or

The Sadness Lurks So Deep

hilarious according to taste, is instantly recognizable. Not because it's a cliché but because, at its most acute, it was once empirically true. Chris, the laundry girl in *The Ginger Man*, speaks for herself: 'Seedy bodies, their drunken smirks. I hate them. To listen to their snide remarks and their tight sneaky little nasty jokes. I hate this country.' Is this ungenerous? You must ask Chris — or Dymphna, or Mary, or Breda. Still, Donleavy's relationship to the country makes profound personal involvement impossible so that his judgements, however glancingly perceptive, remain those of a tourist, or a visiting student. A subtle music escapes him. When Balthazar goes to buy a motor car the salesman has this to say: 'It would pull two hundred Protestant donkeys backwards from Glasnevin to Rathgar and they desperate to get to Belfast away from the Pope.'

Can a poet not invent his own language? Yes, but he mustn't pretend it's the real one. Donleavy is on safer ground inside the walls of Trinity; and here he does excel. In many brief, transitional passages he captures the fugitive quality of undergraduate life as it once was: 'All these days of hope. Sitting through the golden afternoons the window open of one's room. To hear the glad carefree voices passing below. The white pop of a tennis ball.' And the zaniness, as of the Nigerian student who passes notes in Commons reading 'Sure-Footed', 'Mr Motto' or 'Dandelion'. An imbecile, thinks Balthazar. One day it's 'Blue Danube', and that evening he sees a headline: 'Blue Danube Wins Thirty to One'. Finally, though, Donleavy Man isn't interested in other people. He seeks a rich repose in this life, with a sweet dream of the next; he is the child of a lost world dragged kicking and screaming into the 20th century. He has nowhere to grow but stony ground, and nothing to say but his own sorrow in the hope that someone will hear. Could he ever take to religion for the comfort that's in it? 'No hell is under Ireland. Of that they're surely right. They say instead, a dark daughter. The country at the end of the earth. The oldest place.'

Self-parodistic traces of the grand manner form the substance of one of his funniest books, *The Unexpurgated Code*, an upmarket survival guide. Typical items provide advice 'Upon Being Excluded from *Who's Who*', 'Upon Walking into Places As If You Own Them' and 'Upon Doing Surreptitious Damage at a Party', 'The Au Pair' and 'Blowing on Soup'; and, for the morbid, there is a description of how to die and what it feels like: 'As the blood stops flowing, the light in the brain dims out. However, a not unpleasant phosphorescence persists. This is the soul.' As we race towards eternity, cleaning women gather on doorsteps to watch us pass. One of the most indispensable passages, 'Upon Abandoning Ship', is full of good things. (Always sleep in your monogrammed pyjamas in case of emergency, and keep a small pouch of uncut diamonds to ensure a place in a lifeboat.) And for those just setting up in style, 'Your front entrance should be flanked by gate lodges and your drive laid with small stones of a blue-grey tint which bang up under a vehicle's mudguards.' If Donleavy errs it is in devoting too much space to temper-ruffling situations like being snubbed and putting down insolence. Still, there is much good humour too. 'Upon Nude Encounters with Servants', for example, recalls the old Donleavy magic: 'Where passions become ignited do not dally to make small talk when the deed is done. Normal formalities of address may only be abandoned during orgasm. Remember, there is a household to be run.' Nor is he without philosophical substance. Take his theory of time (*The Onion Eaters*, 1971): 'Ah now without the present you wouldn't have a future. And sure the present is busy making the past while the future is waiting. And there's no harm keeping the future waiting while it's not here yet. And when you get there what is it but you're in the present all over again. Will you have milk first or last in the tea.'

1971

Against the Snow

Calvino proposed six qualities for future consideration, of which three characterize the work of Samuel Menashe: lightness, quickness, exactitude. Calvino's purpose was to sketch new, or rather renewable, modes of artistic thought, and restore them to the centre of contemporary discourse. He places the sort of lightness he approves — 'weightless gravity' is his term for it — in opposition to an inherited heaviness, residue of the industrial age, and calls on the simile of 'bits' in the flow of information along circuits in the form of electronic impulses. Computer science takes him back to the atomism of Lucretius, and from there to metamorphic Ovid. Many leaping, soaring and flying figures from myth, folklore and early science fiction (Cyrano de Bergerac; the people of Swift's Laputa) populate these pages of Calvino, whose import is ultimately socio-political. He speaks of a plague afflicting language with 'a loss of cognition and immediacy', an automatism that 'levels out all expression into the most generic, anonymous and abstract formulae'. Literature, and perhaps literature alone, he says, can create 'the antibodies to fight this plague' — something that has long been understood. 'In the even more congested times that await us,' he says, 'literature must aim at the maximum concentration of poetry and thought.' Although not, I think, conscious of such a deliberate programme, Menashe, once a much neglected poet, a tiny beep in the great hullabaloo, contributed to the creation of these antibodies. A selection of his work is available from the Library of America, with an introduction by Christopher Ricks.

Menashe (1925-2011) was born in New York and spent most of his life there, downtown on Thompson Street, south of Houston, in an ascetic bachelor apartment which was once a 'cold-water flat'. This kind of Manhattan is often the scene of his poems, notes Donald Davie — who notes, also, the seashore, woods, pre-Revolutionary France, and 'an Israel of the soul'. He worked in the morning and commuted to Central Park in the afternoon, there to commune with the grass and trees. Though something of a recluse he was a gregarious recluse, a 'recluse about town'. He was also quite 'European'; he might have been French or Russian. His parents were Ukrainian Jews; in the years immediately following the second world war he spent four years on the GI Bill in Paris, where he wrote a doctoral thesis at the Sorbonne. He taught briefly at Bard College, but quit because 'I didn't believe in what I was doing'. He described himself as a 'private citizen', consistent with his independent, eremitic relation to the noisy poetry market. 'Quality in a quantitive age,' said Kathleen Raine, one of his earliest supporters, 'may easily pass unnoticed.' Other admirers included Robert Graves and Austin Clarke. Despite all this impressive sponsorship, it took him a long time to 'make his name', as he was always keen to explain — indeed it was one of his favourite topics of conversation, introduced (and presently dismissed) with resigned wonder. The reasons are obvious enough. His name looks hard to pronounce (Men*ash*). He published his first book in England, which didn't go down well back home (not playing the game); and, relatedly, he was artistically and spiritually at odds with an American orthodoxy that prescribes expansiveness, democracy and free verse. Samuel, in person, was no stranger to expansiveness, and would have considered himself a proper democratic American in most respects, though a hostile critic might call his art a narrow one. As for free verse, a careful sense of structure and rhythm, and the discreet use of rhyme, saved him from the anxious void where so much contemporary 'free' verse is trapped.

Those who know anything about him know that he was the author of extremely short poems, many a mere four lines: a poetry of and about particularity and articulation, like the parasol spokes of 'To Open'. Ricks calls them 'apothegms': 'His lines are there to be read between.' Often they have the numinous quality of hieroglyphics:

> *Reeds rise from water*
> *rippling under my eyes*
> *bulrushes tuft the shore*
> *at every instant I expect*
> *what is hidden everywhere.*

Against the Snow

Davie points out that he was not an epigrammatist: 'The poems have not been whittled down or chiselled clean of rhetoric; the rhetoric was never there.' Nor has he any interest in other short forms like the haiku. He is certainly a minimalist, like the Beckett of 'Saint-Lô' and 'Dieppe' — though, unlike Beckett, he is interested not in havoc but in epiphanic moments of happiness:

> *It is the sun that makes us smile*
> *It is the sun and spring has come*
> *Soon it will reach Norway*
> *Her wooden villages wet*
> *Laughter in each rivulet*
>   ('April')

These are all complete poems I'm quoting. Why so short? 'Some of those who approve of what I do have called my poems economical and concise,' he observed drily; and the editor who thought them 'too pure for contemporary taste' evidently saw the matter clearly if unimaginatively. He liked to quote Simone Weil — 'One must stick to the text of reality without adding or subtracting a syllable' — and his own mother who said, 'When one sees the tree in leaf one thinks the beauty of the tree is in its leaves, and then one sees the bare tree':

> *I am entrenched*
> *against the snow*
> *visor lowered*
> *to blunt its blow*
> *I am where I go*
>   ('Winter')

The poems are musical phrases dropped into silence like something by Satie or Cage. Unattributed programme notes for a recent Dublin conference on the subject of silence put it succinctly: 'Silence is a diminishing but renewable human resource. Creation occurs when silence is broken . . . [It] is at the heart of the creative act; it is what gives form and articulation to sound in music and to words in literature. [A person] with space for silent presence and reflection is less susceptible to conditioning and manipulation.' A market economy loves noise and fears its opposite; hence the ubiquity of pop music. We mustn't hear ourselves think or we might get ideas, some perhaps subversive. News must divert in both senses, entertain and distract. Rilke speaks of 'the uninterrupted news that grows out of silence'; so too does a-political Menashe. Davie points to what he calls a 'liturgical or devotional intention'. Blake, together with the Hebrew Bible, was one of his sacred texts: 'I believe the Prophets and Blake,' he writes. Jerusalem has an intense personal significance for him. Not the quotidian, journalistic Jerusalem of a contemporary Israeli like Amichai but a potent symbol of the imagination, that 'first emanation of divinity', as Yeats said of Blake, though rooted in the real: 'It is among stars that I wake'; 'There is no Jerusalem but this.'

'How shall we sing the Lord's song in a strange land?' (Psalm 13). He belonged to no obvious American tradition, but to a European romantic and existentialist one. His mother tongue was Yiddish, and I suspect he belonged, above all, to that Jewish mystical tradition of which Elie Wiesel remarked that there is indeed such a thing 'but we don't like to talk about it'. The long neglect came to an end before he died. No longer the most famously neglected American poet, he was in any case unresentful of his neglect — amused, rather, and perhaps exultant in his distinguished solitude: 'I did not revolt, I seceded. This is still a free country, one can still do so . . . In my hovel, I live outside the walls, the stronghold, of poet professors who, like the abbots of medieval monasteries, exchange visits, reading at each others' colleges, where they mould students in their own image.' Menashe in his 'hovel', though unconfrontationally, opposed a tiny light to the vast orthodoxy, confident in the knowledge of a unique vocation — 'The lost traveller's dream under the hill.' Calvino again: 'What many consider to be the vitality of the time — noisy, aggressive, revving, roaring — belongs to the realm of death, like a cemetery for rusty old cars.' Lightness succeeds heaviness. Menashe's light verse is not the same thing as humorous verse, though there is humour there too, always in the minimalist mode. No, we must use 'light' in Calvino's sense of weightless gravity. A butterfly, as we know, can contribute to climate change on the other side of the world.

A Given World

Anglophone readers approach contemporary French poetry with trepidation, suspecting (often rightly) that what they are being asked to read will prove to be puzzling, gratuitous, angular, abstract, inflated and doctrinaire, bearing little resemblance to poetry as it's understood in the rest of the world; but readers of Jaccottet need have no such fears. Unlike the closely interlocked cycles of Yves Bonnefoy, or the open-plan notations of André du Bouchet, Jaccottet's work is recognizably circumstantial, and empirical in its relation to 'reality'. Unlike many French poets, moreover, he is not greatly troubled by the disjunction between the signifying word and the thing signified; language is a given and suffices for his purpose, the lyrical apprehension of a given world. There is even, I think (though he himself might be startled by the idea), something 'English' in his mode of perception, something Keatsian. He refers more than once in his prose works to Keats's 'À l'automne' and is no stranger to 'negative capability'. The sort of note he strikes is not unlike that of David Gascoyne's *Poems 1938-42*, works of mystical attention like 'A Wartime Dawn' and 'The Gravel-Pit Field' — or, at a later date, of Kathleen Raine's 'On a Deserted Shore', for which he has expressed admiration. Significantly, he has attracted the interest of a number of English-language poets; though his direct *influence* is nowhere clearly discernible except perhaps in W. S. Merwin's *The Lice* (1969), where several pieces strike the Jaccottet note exactly. Take 'The Room':

> I think all this is somewhere in myself
> The cold room unlit before dawn
> Containing a stillness such as attends death
> And from a corner the sounds of a small bird trying
> From time to time to fly a few beats in the dark
> You would say it was dying it is immortal

Derek Mahon

Asked which French poet of recent times would be most likely to last, he named Éluard. Although closer to the phenomenology of Ponge, he recognized Éluard's lyrical genius and shares, indeed, a measure of common ground. '*Il y a une autre réalité,*' Éluard had said, '*mais elle est en celle-ci.*' ('There is another reality, but it resides in this one'); and this seeming paradox provides a key to Jaccottet's own thinking. He echoes Éluard with the phrase, '*l'autre monde présent peut-être dans celui-ci*' ('the other world present perhaps in this one'), and of a walk in wild country he observes, '*On dirait qu'on a changé de monde sans quitter celui-ci*' ('It's as if you changed worlds without leaving this one').

He began as an urban poet, a poet of post-war Paris; *L'Effraie* ('The Screech Owl', 1953) is full of alienation, existential fear and the onus of self-definition. The first poem in the volume, and therefore in the collected works, speaks already of death and the extinction of stars. Within a few pages he has described himself as 'a stranger in this life' and declared that he 'possesses nothing'. There are love poems too; but it's not until *L'Ignorant* ('Ignorance', 1957), completed after his marriage and removal to Grignan (Drôme), that he starts to come into his own; and for many readers this remains his outstanding collection. Several of his most admired poems are there — the title poem, 'Patience', 'The Voice' and 'The Tenant'; but *L'Ignorant*, impressive though it is, was also a clearing of space for something else. Having declared himself an 'ignorant' man, without 'possessions', he was ready to make his first significant advance. *Airs* (1967) is concerned with beginnings: '*À partir de rien, là est ma loi; tout le reste, fumée lointaine*' ('To start from nothing, that's my rule; everything else, distant smoke'). There is something of Beckett about this, the Beckett who spoke, in the *Dialogues*, of 'an art unresentful of its insuperable indigence' and declared that 'to be an artist is to fail as no other dare fail, failure is his world and the shrink from it desertion'; but Jaccottet meant to *start* from nothing, not to *end* there. He too speaks of '*le presque rien à dire*' ('the almost nothing to say'); but he finds Beckett too 'systematic' and, besides, Jaccottet is in love with the earth. Between flowery Grignan and Beckett's 'hole in the Marne mud' stretches a world of difference. 'Outside the cliques, unbothered with the fashion', in MacNeice's phrase, he has pursued a private vision consciously resistant to systematization. So much has been written as

A Given World

the demonstration of a theory, or in anticipation of certain kinds of critical exposition, rather than as primary artistic endeavour, that Jaccottet's resistance to the trend has acquired an exemplary, even a heroic quality. Like other minimalists he knows exiguity and exasperation; his '*Que reste-t-il?*' ('What remains?') places him in the tradition of solitary inquiry of which Diogenes, Montaigne and *L'Innommable* are but three examples: 'What remains to me is practically nothing, but it's like a narrow gate you have to go through'; and he proclaims his purpose as '*tirer de la limite même un chant*' ('to draw a song from the very limit'). A student of Rilke, he wishes to be '*attentif à ce qui, d'un autre monde, affleure dans le nôtre*' ('attentive to what, from another world, appears in our own') — the classic definition of a miracle; and he asks himself the Rilkean questions. Behind Jaccottet lie lines from the *Duino Elegies* — 'here is the time of the tellable, here is its home' (tr. J. B. Leishman) — though, in fairness to Jaccottet, he avoids '*la tentation de s'isoler en oraison, ce qui gêne quelquefois chez Rilke*', 'the temptation to lose oneself in prayer, so grating at times in Rilke'. One of the great poets of daybreak, in his role of 'first comer', early riser, he attends to the neglected things:

> At the end of the shadiest paths,
> among brambles, you will find an anemone
> bright and ordinary like the morning star.

He is a secular mystic. 'The natural object is always the adequate symbol,' said Pound, and Jaccottet's symbols are the elemental, pre-Socratic ones: tree, flower, sun, moon, road, hill, wind, water, bird, house, lamp. He is fascinated by light, especially what John le Carré calls 'the religious light between dawn and morning'; and by lamplit dusk, *l'heure bleue*, the ambiguous twilight of Magritte's *L'Empire des Lumières*. His characteristic posture is that of a man alone in a garden watching the sun rise, '*rebaptisé chaque matin par le jour*' ('rebaptized each morning by daybreak'), or seated at his desk by lamplight. 'I wonder,' mused Geoffrey Grigson in *The Private Art*, 'if deity and art don't originate in sparkle, glitter, crystal, refracted light, an abstracted portion of sun . . . the shine in the gravel after rain . . .' He is also an intensely visual poet. Nabokov, in *The Real Life of Sebastian Knight*, says of Clare

Derek Mahon

Bishop that 'she possessed that real sense of beauty which has less to do with art than with the constant readiness to discern the halo round a frying pan or the likeness between a weeping willow and a Skye terrier'; and so it is with Jaccottet. But the artist with whom he has the greatest affinity, I think, is Tal Coat, whose characteristic manner, developed in the 1950s, has been called 'lyrical abstraction': a natural scene or object is teased out until precise subject matter disappears and we are left with a few brushstrokes only, black on white, which qualify so to speak as ideograms — even as haiku, what Grigson calls 'a few words in space'. Jaccottet too developed a mode of lyrical abstraction based on Oriental precedents. *Airs* is a book of very short poems which, says the author, *'raconte de façon cachée une histoire d'amour'* ('contains a hidden love story'). The love story is there certainly, but the most striking thing about the poems is their technique — a few brushstrokes only, a few words in space, in contrast to the more traditional rhetoric of *L'Effraie* and *L'Ignorant*; and, few as the lines are, we have to read between them.

What do we miss in this poetry? Several things: vitality sometimes, humour, the demotic, the abrasive surfaces of the modern world. It's sparsely populated, and there's a certain thinness of texture, albeit deliberate. Sometimes it seems refined out of existence. There is (almost) no *sea*; for this is an inland poetry of river and hill, the country road, the lake in the woods. People? One often makes out a wifely presence but, except for actual brief appearances, as in 'Glimpses', she remains a shadowy figure. Most cheat with their own experience, he says, 'put it between parentheses, make it vanish'; yet he implicitly concedes value — perhaps, paradoxically, the greatest value — to the art of which he represents himself as a 'self-effacing' practitioner:

> *(Nothing at all, a footfall on the road,*
> *yet more mysterious than guide or god.)*

He speaks of *'la goutte d'eau pur'* ('the pure water-drop') of poetry, contrasting it with the complex stream of discourse favoured by critical theory as in *Tel Quel* ('As Is'), the lit-critical magazine which rejected literature, really, in favour of close textual analysis and the newly discovered disciplines of phenomenology and structuralism. 'Such nonsense to set up against such knowledge, ingenuity, doctrine! But perhaps poetry relies precisely on what is not argument. I, at least, rely on it.' The pure water-drop, visible in *Airs*, grows audible in *Pensées sous les nuages* ('Cloud Thoughts', 1983), a volume which moves from the photographic mode of 'Glimpses' to the celebratory music of 'To Henry Purcell'. Jaccottet's poems take place, characteristically, in the absence of most other noise; but in the tentative birdsong, running water and rustling leaves of his landscape one hears an enchantment, what used to be called the music of the spheres:

> *If ever they speak above us*
> *in the starry trees of their April.*

'Such knowledge, ingenuity, doctrine!' But, thanks in part to his example, primary endeavour has survived the years of critical theory, *Tel Quel* and the rest, and returned to the mainstream. Take for example the cycling, jazz-loving Jacques Réda whose *Hors les murs* (Gallimard, 1982, only yesterday really) explores, in pscychogeographical mode, an instantly recognizable public space. Its watchful *flânerie* derives from Baudelaire no doubt; its subject matter is the periphery of late 20th-century Paris, the suburbs whose names — Montreuil, Ivry, Sèvres, Vanves — provide many of the poems' titles:

> *De sorte que souvent la pente de l'ouvrage*
> *M'entraînait vers l'arrêt d'un bus ou Chez Roger,*
> *Troquet méditatif qui n'a guère changé.*
> *Le poème est un art que rien ne décourage.*
>
> *(So that often the slant of a creative urge*
> *Led down to a bus-stop or to Chez Roger,*
> *A thoughtful joint still much the same today.*
> *Poetry is an art nothing discourages.)*

Public transport is everywhere in, for example, the Faber anthology of *Twentieth-Century French Poems* (2002) edited by Stephen Romer — who reports a *retour au monde*, a return to the world. Lighted trains pass 'dining-rooms, wall-papers, bright kitchens',

Derek Mahon

and vanish into the dark as in Paul de Roux:

> *A remote train passes*
> *conveying the coldness of iron*
> *and the station with its icy winds*
> *where you dropped off a friend*
> *and where the empty platform*
> *is a whistling track*
> *to the hidden stars.*
>   (tr. Stephen Romer)

The journey continues.

An Unflinching Gaze

Not so long ago it was quite usual for poets of all nations to attach themselves to radical politics: South Americans, the Beats, French and Scottish poets, some marginal figures here and there. Now, as befits increasingly consumerist societies, this instinct has been replaced, with the aid of irony, by a complacent indulgence of market expectations. The commercial magazine paradigm — a bit of text embedded and paid for by pages of advertising — has evidently triumphed, even as journalism itself has been further debased by powerful and malign proprietors. Writers have been sedated with prizes and celebrity, cheap forms of advertising the corporate world awards itself: we have to learn to bite the hands that feed us. Readers have long been 'consumers' of literature and ideas, even of left-wing ideas. (Randall Jarrell gave us his own reaction to this as long ago as 1962 in his critical book *A Sad Heart at the Supermarket*.) The feminist movement has achieved many things but has always been too interested in the glass ceiling and not enough in the radical redesign of the whole building. The claims of ethnic identity, 'Gay Rights' and so on, important to some, have been sanctioned and used as safety valves for the reforming urge and distractions from the thought of greater change. A noisy silence has descended upon literature. It wasn't always so, and the salutary example of older generations is there to prove it. Take for example Anthony Cronin, whose *Collected Poems* (New Island, 2004), the fruit of more than fifty years' devotion to the craft, is one of the most radical such collections in recent years. It's also one of the most timely. I want to emphasize at once Cronin's importance as a poet first and foremost. This obvious fact has been a little blurred by other, more immediately visible, activities. He has conducted a distinguished literary career of a general nature as a novelist, critic, journalist and biographer, and is probably best known to the reading public as the author of *Dead as Doornails* (1975), that classic

Derek Mahon

memoir of the Behan and Kavanagh years, and (component parts of the same project) his lives of Flann O'Brien and Samuel Beckett. But it's Cronin the poet we're concerned with here, and a very considerable one he is too, often as striking and memorable as the big names he has written about so sensitively in his prose works. Has anyone ever noticed, for example, that his fourteen-page lament for the Royal Mail Ship *Titanic* (1961) is as remarkable, in its own fashion, as Kavanagh's *The Great Hunger*? Both are ambitious poems about 20th-century Ireland, though from different perspectives. The raw hurt in Kavanagh cries to heaven. Cronin is more philosophical, but behind his urbane and mordant narrative shines a ghostly wake of coffin ships. He too is writing about 'the Irish poor' but also about the nature of history, a theme central to his work then and since. Here, as elsewhere, we are in no doubt as to where his sympathies lie; but one of his most intriguing traits is his fascination with the British point of view. (Also the Ulster one — see him on William Conor's shipyard scene 'The Riveters'.)

He has spent substantial periods in England, where he cut a figure in the London literary world, and some of his best early work belongs to the Soho era when, like others in his position, he devised ill-paid radio features for the BBC while mixing with the great. I'm thinking of frequently anthologized pieces like 'Lines for a Painter' and 'Responsibilities' (about irresponsibility), both very much of their time yet curiously persistent in the mind. The second of these, particularly, has a strange period magic which is really not so 'period' on reflection since it describes one sort of immigrant life still known even today, as in the compulsive daily gaze at the 'grimy primrose' of 'the western sky of winter London'. It's a young man's poem about being 'light in the head, lugubrious, cynical, free' — a wonderful adjectival line-up — in Camden Town and the Finchley Road, 'Highgate and Hampstead in a fine October' — which puts me oddly in mind of Betjeman's 'Parliament Hill Fields'. It was during or shortly after his London time that his *Titanic* appeared in a once widely available *Penguin Book of Longer Contemporary Poems* (1966), where people of my own generation first came upon it, recognizing immediately that here was something unusual and far-reaching. But it takes us barely a quarter of the way into the *Collected Poems* and there is better yet to come.

The next high point is 'Letter to an Englishman' (1975), an eleven-page epistle in rhymed couplets from Kilkee, Co Clare, evidently one of the author's favourite counties, relating a succinct history of 20th-century Ireland. He will later describe himself as 'not one for description'. He favours, like Swift, a plain conversational style, the obvious and perfect mode for his own truth to experience, though lyricism keeps breaking in with sudden luminous images ('twig-breaking winter', 'inland sea-light') and thought-stopping phrases ('flowing fields of cloud', 'time waiting on a leaf in autumn woods'); and his visions of the *Titanic* are tremendously vivid. But his is finally a discursive art, a vehicle for anecdote, argument, and the inclusive historical overview at which he is so adept. Which brings me to 'The End of the Modern World' (1989), an extraordinary hundred-page sequence of fourteen-liners, some rhymed, some half-rhymed, some thrown off, which tackles without fear or shame most of the big themes too many contemporaries avoid. The title recalls Karl Kraus, the Austrian satirist and author of the epic anti-war play *The Last Days of Mankind* (1919) and indeed Cronin invokes Kraus. Baudelaire, Lenin, Freud and Angela Carter make frequent appearances too, for we are dealing here with nothing less than civilization and its discontents, a thousand years of psycho-sexual politics from the Dark Tower to the day 'technology brought Tahiti to the suburbs'. There are other large-scale recent achievements, notably 'The Minotaur' (1999), a contemporary revisiting of the Greek myth that out-Muirs the Scottish poet Edwin Muir, a translator of Kafka.

The dark thing in its lair,
Which belongs here, as do we,
As native as ourselves,
Breathing the summer air.

This, and much else, is very fine. But 'The End of the Modern World' is the key text and his finest achievement to date. Not in terms of length alone, though its sustained concentration stands in reproachful contrast to the work of many a slighter lyricist, but in its panoramic scope, the astonishing confidence with which it takes so much in its thematic stride, the range and depth of its knowledge and understanding, its grasp of how the world works, its candour and humanity. We say 'for love or money'. But love and money, the

Derek Mahon

'without which not', tend not to get their due in modern poetry, since we've become both ultra-ironical and strangely coy about such things. We seldom write openly about the money that runs our lives; and love, as distinct from sex, was something known to previous generations. Cronin, however, doesn't flinch. He looks love and money in the eye in 'a time of lost poetic' and, like Baudelaire, he sees the long heartbreaking connection. A combination of knightly quest saga, *fin-de-siècle* thriller and *noir* romance, it's also, uniquely and ingeniously, that paradoxical thing, an economic and political diagnosis of 20th-century Europe which is at the same time witty, sexy and 'a good read': a demanding page-turner, but a page-turner even so. The man knows everything, and dishes it out with a grave, tolerant chuckle. A house of lore, a lifetime in the making, it stands as a monument to the dubiously modern, even as the values on which it insists dissolve in the misty relativities of the post-modern. He is an old-fashioned liberal humanist in a harsh new era, and to be honoured as such. Above all, he is a lover of life, a friend to women and the young, and one of the great survivors. Despite his disabused — i.e. realistic — take on the world, he can't help being in love with it and its radiance of magic moments on windy cliff or in sunlit garden. Despite a brisk refusal of sentimentality, there is a delicate wholeheartedness throughout, and sometimes even an air of mystery, as in 'Shadows' (about the cars in old movies) and 'Ovid', where he picks out one detail from the *Metamorphoses*, that of a girl's hair 'simply tied back by a single ribbon'. He tells no lies. This is the real world; we live in history.

He wouldn't want to be considered a 'national poet' (we have several), but in a certain way he is, albeit a contrarian one. The comparison, *mutatis mutandis*, might be with Pablo Neruda of Chile, who also saw poetry and politics as part of the same activity. He too has known hard times. He too has spent thoughtful hours on the heights of Machu Picchu, though we call them the Cliffs of Moher. The final poem, the four-page 'Meditation on a Clare Clifftop' (Cronin has lots to say and always writes expansively), strikes a note of gratitude and serenity as he gazes down on 'gulls in spume-shot air' — 'America beneath me too,' he slily adds — and has a good look at our place in the scheme of things. He doesn't go as far as Yeats who got around to claiming that the universe was a creation of the human mind. He gives us, nonetheless, our due significance, a significance we share with whales and protozoa — and with the evening star, 'beneficent and pale' above the waves, which can't be bought, sold or extinguished.

Some call my own stuff 'chilly', and I'm happy with that if it means I'm one of those who try to avoid sentimentality and look for a more bracing note. Maybe the slight chill is a side effect of the contrarian impulse; perhaps it's just one more character defect. Be that as it may, Tony Cronin is an admirably *warm* contrarian. His plain speaking fulfils one demand of the poetic function as traditionally understood and currently sidestepped. Academic relativism makes no enemies, imagines no alternatives to consensus and disregards, for example, what some of us insist on calling American imperialism — 'full-spectrum dominance' in Pentagonese. Words lose their meanings or, like 'liberal', are made to mean their opposites. Useful phrases come to mean different things — 'time-serving', for instance, now seldom heard but vaguely thought to mean something like 'clock-watching', when what it really means is truckling to received opinion, the 'wisdom' of the age: name your own candidates. The so-called 'real world', the global capitalist model, is taken as a given, a fact of life; few writers seem to question it or the crazed version of reality it imposes. Self-censorship is everywhere. A fascistic devotion to technology delivers the totalitarian dream — what Hal Crowther, writing in *Granta* (2011), calls 'a submissive population of consumers and employees, tightly wired and monitored and purged of rogue individuals'. We need to look again at the shameful abandonment of 'elitism'. These rogue individuals are the true elite. Join us in our 'serene despair' (Umberto Saba).

Gin and Cloud

'The remains of Miss Emily Norton Kervick were committed to the grave one cold day in March of 1927. On that morning — the third — a Mass for the Dead had been offered for the repose of her soul, and she was buried without delay in Griffenwrath cemetery.' Even so did Aidan Higgins, in 1960, make his ceremonious debut with a fine short story entitled 'Killachter Meadow' about the last days of, yes, a Big House near Celbridge, Co Kildare, a theme taken up at greater length and to memorable effect in his first novel *Langrishe, Go Down* (1966), an outstanding work of the time and a modern classic. It won the James Tait Black Memorial Prize, quite a thing then, and established its author as Ireland's finest contemporary prose stylist. Traditionally, as with Elizabeth Bowen and J. G. Farrell, the Big House novel concerns an 'Anglo-Irish' family, urgent political events bearing on the immediate situation, and preferably a good old blaze in the final pages. *Langrishe, Go Down* is at an angle to this. The family, once Protestant and now Catholic, have grand but distant connections, political events (the rise of fascism in Europe) seem far away, and instead of incendiarism there is entropy.

Set in the 1930s, in De Valera's Ireland, the novel traces the decline of the once prosperous Langrishes of Springfield House, now reduced to a Chekhovian trio of shabby-genteel sisters. Helen, the eldest and least irresponsible, has consulted their Dublin solicitor about the financial situation and been advised that they will have to sell the house. The others, silly Lily and lazy Imogen, take the news glumly, without knowing what to do about it, Lily being preoccupied with the hens and Imogen, the youngest, with thoughts of a past fling. Bitter and desolate, Helen dies soon after and the book comes to an end; but in a long flashback that forms the central narrative we hear the six-year-old story of Imogen and Otto Beck, a visiting German research student: 'She had a little touch of

Gin and Cloud

colour on her cheeks. An old love had put it there. The memory of past obscenities gave her that rose glow on sallow cheeks when she was old.'

The lovers are beautifully realized. Imogen is a good-natured, ironical, sensual woman not in her first youth, imaginative and discontented. Otto, the same age, is a hard, cold, pedantic, domineering character, impressive, annoying and dangerous: 'He runs his tongue over his dry lips like a fox licking its chops.' An outlandish, 'legendary' figure ('that face among the leaves') with green eyes and red hair, he wears corduroys and dirty tennis shoes without socks: 'Vengeful manner, cruel lover; I wouldn't mind being his trollop.' He lives rent-free in the back lodge, made available to him by Major Langrishe, the women's father, since deceased. Perched in a tree-top, he observes Imogen at her flighty 'air baths' in the woods. Together they spend 'gin days' and summer nights — till the rows begin. His manners are brusque, his views peremptory and severe; he speaks of 'culturally inferior' nations: 'Oh, he was hard on people.'

An important feature of the novel, and one largely responsible for the stately pace at which the narrative moves, is the leisurely and minute contemplation of the Kildare countryside where it takes place. Helen and Imogen, from snobbery and indolence, are not greatly interested in their surroundings, but 'foxy' Otto, naturalist and opportunist, has made himself familiar with the fauna; he takes trout and rabbits and keeps a weather eye on the clouds. The sexton in the local graveyard discourses to morbid Helen on mortality and the swift passage of the centuries, recalling the grand folk thereabouts as far back as Bartholomew Vanhomrigh, 'the Dutchman, Vanessy's da'. The Celbridge of Higgins's youth is vividly recalled in all its practical detail.

Otto is writing a thesis in Celtic Studies. He can tell you about the night sky and the Munich whores with equal detachment; to his foxy eye, life is a hen-run. But for all his brisk information and quickness to learn, he is temperamentally incapable of sharing the organic character, lovingly described by Higgins, of the Springfield demesne and its surroundings. Were the sisters more closely identified with the landscape we might read *Langrishe* as a parable of sexual politics in the larger, ecological sense; but they too are parasites. The family money came not from the land but from the stock market (American mining shares); their father was no good at running the estate, and now the place is going to rack and ruin. 'Such filth and disorder in the old rooms, a smell of poverty, disuse, rotting wainscotting and dirty beds. Wind echoing in the deserted cottage . . . It looked as if someone had been living there.'

'Killachter Meadow' first appeared in book form in *Felo de Se* (1960) and reappears in *Flotsam and Jetsam* (1996), a collection of shorter fiction, travel notes and miscellaneous pieces, as 'North Salt Holdings' (the Barony of Salt is in Co Kildare). Another five of the original *Felo de Se* stories reappear there too, together with reworked material from *Balcony of Europe* (1972), *Helsingor Station* (1989) and *Ronda Gorge* (1989). 'Lengthening Shadows', a grim view of the present state of England, is adapted from a series of 'Texts for the Air', a BBC radio commission. *Donkey's Years* (1995), *Dog Days* (1998) and *The Whole Hog* (2000), remarkable memoirs now available in one volume as *A Bestiary* (published, with *Flotsam and Jetsam*, by Dalkey Archive), received less attention than they deserved first time round, and in those reviews that did appear a hostile note was sometimes audible; for Higgins is an austere and often difficult writer, more than a touch old-fashioned, with a lordly astringency that can stir the bile of whippersnappers. He is known for an elaborate and exigent style derived from, among other sources, Elizabethan and Jacobean prose, Swift, Joyce, Djuna Barnes and Beckett. He can be expressionist and baroque, lyrical and grotesque, fastidious and colloquial by turns, and presumes a like-minded 'browser' of comparable erudition and unsentimentality. His whole practice and attitude are about as far as one could get from current aesthetics, though it would be wrong to think of him as conservative. Not at all: he is, paradoxically, the most blithely subversive of writers, though grandly aphoristic on occasion: 'Absence makes the heart less fond, *au fond*'; 'Notions of vulgarity vary from vulgarian to vulgarian' — not that we bother much about such things now.

Barnes, in *Nightwood*, a sacred text for Higgins, likens a row of buttons to 'the obstetric line seen on fruits'. He learned his graphic art from her example, and added his own quizzical tone. Two instances of his picturesque and comically vehement technique. 'Asylum' is rife with startling similes: 'She sat upright with knees drawn together, her spine curved back like a bow; from the waist up she was as unadorned as the town of Trim, not a stitch anywhere

Gin and Cloud

to spare her blushes.' (That Trim, Co Meath, is actually quite decorative needn't detain us here.) 'Berlin After Dark' has this:

> As certain burrowing creatures, in order to gain their ends or to exist at all, are resolved down to one anxious or bitter form of themselves, so his features seemed to narrow down to one place and one gesture; his face was a falling back to function. As winds in their persistence stretch and sharpen boulders, and as these in turn indicate free access to territory beyond, so his features spoke of only one preoccupation, and that preoccupation, venery.

The mock-heroic simile ('As . . . , so . . .') we associate with Pope and Fielding, and it's good to find it alive and kicking in modern Ireland. But what's the theme, gist or drift?

'We shift about, all that great glory spent' (Yeats, 'Coole Park and Ballylee, 1931'). Higgins's theme is the decay of a putative old decency, the atomization of life personal and social, the centrifugal impulse. Our decline is figured in sexual chaos, wickedness in these matters being a traditional sign of the end of civilizations. His settings, when not Irish, are typically peripheral London and rural Spain; seaside resorts out of season; winter golf-links, *rentier* havens and expatriate watering holes — wherever there is a last ditch for the odd and singular, the marginal and the disregarded, where talk of winners and losers makes no sense. Alternative lives; and this is where his moral value resides. While business proceeds in the financial centres and the post-industrial zones, somewhere an eccentric 'spinster' slips Ophelia-like, for the last time, into a river, or a disconsolate exile studies cloud formations, adrift in gin and Unamuno's 'pure ether of speculative contemplation'.

He is good on Spain, about which he wrote so well in *Balcony of Europe* (there is such a place): 'All that long wet winter in Andalucia, and all over Spain, which is no more part of Europe than Ireland is part of England, during the worst winter in living memory, the lights failed with predictable regularity, and in tempests of wind and rain the village (10,000 *habitantes* as in Guernica before the bombing) vanished into Stygian darkness. The bars laid in stocks of candles. The effects were ghastly and eerie as in a painting by De Chirico, shadowy faces lining the counter.' Wise to expatriate decadence, like Durrell, Bowles and many another, Higgins, coming later, is attentive too to the newer and even more pernicious decadence of universal package tourism ('We shift about'), as here in 'Ronda Gorge': 'Midway between Málaga and Nerja lies the tax refuge of Torre del Mar with a powerful stench of open drains, its foreshore as grim as the wasteland of Buñuel's *Los Olvidados*. It has become a German colony. A beach has been cleared and named; it will look fine in a colour brochure.' He is good too on Scandinavia: 'It was one of those grey overcast afternoons in Copenhagen, where my true love lies' (*Bornholm Night-Ferry*); the 'folkless fields' of Sweden; 'Cyclists not waving mounted on high old bikes drift alongside the train'.

I am a guest, you are a visitor, he or she is a tourist; and vulgarity is everywhere, above all in 'The Opposite Land' with its lengthening shadows, the one across the Irish Sea, the one right next door, about which he is elegiac: 'Soccer hooligans are uneasily contained behind moats and barbed-wire stockades, written about daily in the over-familiar parlance of the gutter press. Chat shows are popular, a cheap form of commercial radio: old ladies flirt, the accents various, posh to semi-literate, records of social disharmony and frustration.' There is an apocalyptic undertone in everything Higgins writes, however circumstantial or debonair. He always seems to be saying, or implying, something extremely ominous — which may be one of the reasons he appeals to the so-different Irish young on whom he has exercised an immense if largely unacknowledged influence. The same could be said of Maurice Leitch, the inventor of contemporary Ulster Gothic. Whatever is unusual or ambitious in Irish fiction today owes much to their very different examples. A writer's writer — even, as was said of Henry Green, a writer's writer's writer — Higgins has taken more seriously than most Beckett's injunction to 'fail again, fail better', in that he works continually at the same material; for all is autobiographical, 'life as story told'. *A Bestiary* is the summation of this project, a getting closer to the bone, the persona now that of a curmudgeonly if witty recluse. Although the author of a dozen previous titles of distinction, his reputation is still a muted one, a thing of hearsay among initiates, for he is unfashionably 'literary' (his friend Beckett, alas, thought *Langrishe* 'literary shit') and detached from the more obvious contemporary fixations, which he views with horror — as he views the 'loudly pictorial' future being prepared for us, when the writer's trade will be 'extinct as falconry'.

The Whole Hog is good on Kinsale, Co Cork, where Mountjoy scattered Hugh O'Neill's Hispano-Gaelic confederacy on Christmas Eve, 1601, and where Higgins now lives. He reports the famous battle as an international rugby match. But the best of *A Bestiary* is in *Donkey's Years* (the account of his mother's death) and in *Dog Days*. The author, in search of peace and quiet, returns to the Wicklow coast where he spent part of his youth — perhaps to live there, make it once again his home. But the idea of 'home' is problematic, and even accommodation needs thinking about. This was true even in his younger years when the Higgins family left Springfield House, Co Kildare, for lodgings in Greystones, 'the seaside resort where Protestants come to die', a locale he recreates here in the fine opening section, 'First Love'. This 34-page overture is a virtuoso short story in itself, remarkable chiefly for its portrait of the severe though sensual Philippa, some years senior to our young and randy protagonist who spends his days contriving occasions of intimacy in trains, sheds and sand dunes, 'the pair of us naked as salmon on the sea-shore, panting, our unchained bikes propped up against the broken fence, one lying on top of the other as if engaged in rapt and silent copulation, the heavy Raleigh model on top, the dainty female model underneath'. Only once do they attain 'bungalow bliss', in a lumber room where 'I had rigged up some bookshelves and there was my library, the Shakespeare, the Schopenhauer, the Huxley novels in uniform edition, Burton's *Anatomy of Melancholy*'. These makeshift conditions prefigure the contemplative but half-housed lifestyle of his whimsical reincarnation, Rory O'Hills (Rory of the Hills) as he calls himself. After considering 'a mobile home propped up on bricks in the lee of a dripping pinewood, a Dublin tram cut in half hauled there by tractor', the Brother arranges for him to sublet Ballymona Lodge, Brittas, and there he remains for two years.

He quotes Henry James: 'Next to great joy, no state of mind is so frolicsome as great distress' — and there is much here that is frolicsome, notably the flashbacks to Dublin in the forties and fifties, the Royal Hibernian and the Grafton Street Picture House; to Connemara, Hampstead, Berlin, Spain and South Africa. The country life around him is frolicsome too, including the behaviour of closely observed locals, some slightly mad. Rory has an ear for pub talk; like Beckett he is good on the seasons ('the fields in frantic stir at lambing time, placentas blowing about like refuse; saw bullfinch in bush') and times of day and night: 'Mist obscures the valley to the door. Downpour at 4 am, lightning over hills, moon scudding through clouds; in pitch darkness I hear firm footsteps passing by on the road: who? Slept ill; difficult to rise.' There are frequent light-readings: 'Clear sky again after three consecutive overcast days. Snow on nearer hills. Dark by 4 pm, bright evening star. Lit wood fire at five, night comes down early.' The old mordancy is still there ('Retained semen turns to poison'). He will quote you Hesiod at the drop of a hat ('Crows live nine times longer than man'); he hears blackbirds, 'music that would have delighted Messiaen', and there is life yet in the old art simile: 'Combine harvesters working in the dark with powerful headlights. A glow of stubble burning in the fields, smoke swirling up: a nocturnal Turner.' Aside from these things he is mostly alone, except when his teenage son comes to visit, or his friend Anastasia from Austin, Texas, where he once taught Creative Writing ('Don't make me laugh').

As for the modern world, he is unbothered with modish views and conventional appurtenances: 'The brother let in the clutch, or whatever it is you let in (I don't drive).' High tech is a typewriter; radio, not television, relieves the rural silence. Hollywood movies he finds 'alarming', pop music he associates with 'servitude'; for, in a gregarious, coercively polyphonic era, his is the tradition of solitary inquiry and reappraisal; of time out and negative capability; of mystical attention even: 'A wren on the fence in the rain; inky clouds at sunset; a white breast feather falls from the sky. Boom of rising wind in the chimney. Saw sickle moon.' This is the higher vagrancy, out of tune with the world of getting and spending, in tune with an older and larger reality. *Homeless*, he suggests, is one of the saddest words in the language; yet this is not a sad book so much as a waiting book, a book of mysteries, 'revealed truths we cannot comprehend'.

Life as Story Told

Balcony of Europe (John Calder, 1972), its author Aidan Higgins reported in 1995, was out of print and would so remain. It was a failure; 'it presumes too much'. But better thoughts prevailed and here it is again, reduced by a fifth from the loose baggy monster it once was. Gone are fifty pages of Dublin prologue and Aran epilogue, for use elsewhere; gone the 'rejected epigraphs', some of the epistolary matter and nine shortish chapters by my count. The result is a much more manageable book, one that reads more like a novel and less like a demanding literary experience. Higgins's object, evidently, was to highlight the central narrative, and in this he succeeds admirably. No longer overwhelmed with information and digressions, we can concentrate on the people, the story and the picture of Spain in the 1960s. Everything is in clearer focus and moves more briskly, though not so briskly that we lose the ruminative dimension. This new, trim *Balcony* was an inspired initiative by Dalkey Archive (Illinois), his current publisher. Their list, dedicated to keeping important work in print, contains Henry Green, Céline and American authors including Creeley, Barthelme and Higgins's heroine Djuna Barnes — from whom, in part, he learned his spirited, ceremonious prose.

We're in the seaside town of Nerja, east of Málaga, where the Ruttles, Dan and Olivia, are spending a year or two. Dan is an Irish artist, Olivia a New Zealander. Nerja has the makings of an artistic colony. Expats of various nationalities have settled there including some Americans. Dan, the first-person narrator, gets involved with one of these, Charlotte (*née* Lipski), a married woman with a small daughter. The affair takes its course. Olivia is not pleased. The husband, Bob, divines the truth; eventually Bob and Charlotte move on. Did I make it all up, wonders Dan: 'I dreamed her as she dreamed me.' One of Higgins's principal themes, the fictionality of the past, is in play here: *Gone with the Wind* ('*con* Clark Gable *y*

Derek Mahon

Vivien Leigh') is showing at the Cine Olympia. Also the fictionality of the present, the idea that events are imagined even as they happen. Dan has a life-altering experience, but is it real life or a vivid yarn, 'life as story told'? Introspective to the point of solipsism, he seems quite capable of inventing the whole thing; you wouldn't put it past him. But Charlotte is real, so palpably real that you wonder why Dan hasn't painted her many times over. An air of hallucination hangs over much of the rest despite, paradoxically, the sharp resolution of individual scenes and objects. We could be watching an arthouse movie (Buñuel? Polanski?): 'The house flies were sinking and rising, going at odd tangents, and a bluebottle banged against the walls like a charge of electricity. I too felt charged and heated. On the draining-board a halved lemon was decomposing.'

Dan is undoubtedly a painter. He has a Crucifixion on his easel, his art-historical expertise is noticeable; but he lives like a writer, filling pages rather than canvases. His word pictures are in high definition: 'Terraces in chromatic colours, never dull, even on overcast days. Three or four breaks in the cliff, sable and greens, a windbreak of high cane. A couple of long-boats, their fishing days over, disintegrate on the sand. They have, in the prow, the rough outline of the jaw mandibles of gibbons, a design prevailing unchanged since the Phoenicians occupied Málaga.' He describes events as they occur; his desk (his easel) is a café table. Much of the action takes place around the old Balcón de Europa bar, now a hotel; the book is as boozy as *The Sun Also Rises* if not quite *Under the Volcano*. This is all very much of its period, though the expatriate frolic was already an old story when *Balcony* first appeared. Higgins writes elsewhere: 'The Nerja of that time no longer exists. Gone the way of Torremolinos, gone the way of the world.' But the American dimension gives him a means to look at a broader canvas, the Cold War era. (The US military presence in Spain commenced in 1958, with an air-force base at Morón de la Frontera, within reach of the Algerian rising just in case.)

One recurrent feature is Dan's fascination with Charlotte's Polish-Jewish family background, and there's a horrible old Nazi in the opening section who inveighs against 'over-tender' humanistic feelings: 'The Jews have only themselves to blame' and so on. We never forget that this is Franco's Spain. History and geopolitics are constantly in evidence; the roar of warplanes is frequently heard, especially at moments of lovemaking. As always with Higgins we see the larger picture, the personal in the context of the political. Which raises the question of Dan's attitude to women. These were pre-feminist times, Dan's gaze is that of an artist: 'I entered and found her lying naked on the covers, reading a book and smoking a Celtas through a long amber holder, her bison-brown hair confined in two braids as the Andalusian girls wear it. Her dimpled back, her bare backside, conferred a look of innocence that her posture and physical development denied.' Boucher and Gauguin are mentioned. *Balcony* is a profoundly erotic work, thoughtfully erotic, the eroticism contained by a *devotional* disposition towards women — towards, in fact, the phenomena of the world and what he calls, in a striking phrase, 'the seminal substance of the universe'. Striking phrases abound, as you would expect from Higgins: 'The elegant poverty of Mediterranean fishermen'; 'Apostles snoring in Gethsemane'. He excels at the poetic moment, and there are many here, some perfectly simple: one chapter begins, 'As we walked in Málaga in the Alameda Gardens, her hand touched mine.' This highly charged novel is made up of these moments. Episodic, shaped and framed by a fastidious consciousness and lit by the Andalusian sun, it glows with lyrical chiaroscuro and would indeed make an excellent film.

Wild Bunches

It's always helpful to read Montague's prose together with the poetry: the fiction, the memoirs and *The Figure in the Cave*, where we get the back story. 'A Primal Gaeltacht', he calls it in a childhood reminiscence of that title — his original Tyrone landscape, Garvaghey and environs. 'I was brought up,' he says, 'among the hill forts of the Clogher Valley', and he recalls 'the wet lushness which excited me' after ten years abroad. Here are the sources of his erotic archaeology, his devotion to the earth as wife and mother, his ecology and politics. He evokes and invokes various incarnations of this figure as identified by Robert Graves (an acknowledged master) in *The White Goddess*. 'Do you believe in the physical presence of the Muse?', our friend Desmond O'Grady once asked. (Yes of *course*, I replied.) People don't talk like that any more, but it made sense for a generation born into a deeply Catholic culture. Mostly it takes a secular form with Montague. Women of all ages are of crucial significance: thrice married, he is also a considerable love poet. His own *Sean Bhean Bhocht* trope, earth as woman, recurs constantly, perhaps most obviously in 'The Wild Dog Rose' but also *seriatim* in 'Like Dolmens . . .', 'The Rough Field' (Garvaghey, a 'rough field') and incidental pieces like 'Deer Park', where François Boucher's nude portrait of Marie-Louise O'Morphi, Louis XV's Irish mistress, represents the girlish beauty of Ireland as 'royal property'. This connects a seemingly decorative and exotic exercise with more local concerns and aligns it with explicitly ecological work like 'Hymn to the New Omagh Road' and 'Mount Eagle'.

'Demolition Ireland', a later poem, is a further extension of this line of thought. One of the pleasures of reading Montague is to watch how things tie up. Everything is present, or at least implicit, here. Even the dedication to his younger daughter ('for Sibyl') seems to suggest a magical dimension to this brief meditation on industrial

Wild Bunches

development. Again the 'naked earth' is a woman, her 'contours' to be 'trampled', her 'lushly formed' rivers and 'dark trout pool' distorted or destroyed. The 'coiled mysteries' of her 'tangled clefts' take us right back to the beginning where natural wonder mingles with sexual awe. The poem can be read like that or taken, superficially, as a polemic against the 'Celtic Tiger', the 'smart' economy (the *smart* economy?) we enjoyed or endured for a few brief years. The phrase, you recall, was invented by a New York financial journalist predicting rapid 'growth' for Ireland similar to that of the 'Asian Tiger'. But the species isn't native here; it has to be imported, and exported again when its time is up and the 'rushes', if any are left, can 'rise again'. Some think poets should avoid politics. It's not a position to which Yeats would have subscribed — or Kavanagh, or MacNeice. Poetry, like everything else, is political in the widest sense, and it's greatly to Montague's credit that he has kept this knowledge alive — while at the same time giving us some of the finest poems we've seen in the last half-century.

I first saw the name in a Belfast newspaper. He'd won a local poetry prize for which I too had naively entered. This was in May 1960. I was eighteen, in my last year at school, and had sent in one of the Dylan Thomas pastiches I then wrote (before Bob Dylan there was Dylan Thomas), confident I would win. After all, I'd be the only entrant, wouldn't I? Nobody wrote poetry any more — or rather, there were no new poets; it had all come to an end with Dylan Thomas. So I was more surprised than disappointed when a John Montague from Co Tyrone beat me to it. I never knew how many entrants there were: dozens perhaps. The posh-sounding name Montague was surprising in itself, coming from Tyrone where people (his own joke) had names like McTeague. I knew about Tyrone and Fermanagh, where they were for ever trying to blow up police 'barracks'; I'd been down there on the bike.

The title of his poem was a puzzle too: 'Like Dolmens Round My Childhood, the Old People'. What was a dolmen? A heap of stones in a field? Or wasn't that a cairn? The stand-alone first line, and the last: what was going on? We were in a strange place, the 'dead kingdom' of the Clogher Valley, which might as well have been in the 'South', so foreign did it seem to the mind of a loyal Belfast youth; but we live and learn. I was up there recently and took note of the still quiet glens, the rather desolate moors and the many rushy fields to which he more than once refers. Garvaghey, his 'rough field', was little more than a filling station and pub, Kelly's Inn, a modern sort of establishment. Where was the Montague place, we asked Montague the story teller? Oh, long gone. So we went to Fintona, emphasis on the first syllable, and found the post-office shop where his aunts had once been in charge. A modern sort of establishment; but there was a pub, closed up as if closed down, with an intriguing bunch-of-wildflowers motif painted in beside the name above the door: 'The Wild Bunch'. (The town used to have a curious reputation. Were you never married? No, but I was once in Fintona.) We drove east to Armagh, through Beragh, Carrickmore and Pomeroy:

> *placenames that sigh*
> *like a pressed melodeon.*

I first met the man in Dublin during my student days. He was living in Paris then, and later I saw him there too; also in London, where he turned up once in a while. But, however great his sophistication, however cosmopolitan his style of life — France, America, India, Japan — I've always seen him as a shy if contentious and history-haunted fellow lately emerged from the shadow of aunts and neighbours. 'Like Dolmens' was his great debut piece. It was the first important 'Ulster' poem since Kavanagh, Hewitt, MacNeice? And it was the prologue to the new wave of Ulster poets who started publishing in the sixties. He himself started in the fifties, with *Forms of Exile* (Dolmen, 1958), shortly subsumed into *Poisoned Lands* (MacGibbon and Kee, 1961), which first charted his Tyrone background. After studies in Dublin he went on to Yale and Iowa, then taught at Berkeley, but returned constantly in life and imagination to his home ground. His culture of origin was a 'Gaelic' one, though not really Irish-speaking. He wrote his postgraduate thesis on Goldsmith — together with Carleton, one of his favourite authors. 'Like Dolmens', for example, owes something to 'The Deserted Village', that earlier survey of a dying landscape. Goldsmith's 'Auburn' is said to be a composite of the Irish midland places of his youth transposed to an English location, the enclosures of English common land a simile for the Penal prohibitions imposed on 18th-century Ireland; the 'tyrant's hand' has made a desolation of erstwhile happy scenes. So too in Montague's Tyrone:

The whole landscape a manuscript
We had lost the skill to read,
A part of our past disinherited.

Clergyman, old soldier and schoolmaster appear in Montague's work as in Goldsmith's; but one vital figure noticed by Goldsmith will be of special importance to the Tyrone poet — 'yon widowed solitary thing', a poor old woman living on wild herbs. This figure, Goldsmith's 'sad historian of the pensive plain', is also the *Sean Bhean Bhocht*, the *cailleach* Montague so often invokes, often with religious overtones.

She is named twice in 'Like Dolmens': Maggie Owens, 'reputed a witch', and Mary Moore, 'a by-word for fierceness'. The poem, though bleak, is warmly populated. There are four principal characters — Jamie MacCrystal, the two women mentioned, and Wild Billy Eagleson — but the Nialls ('all were blind') must number at least three; then there's Eagleson's wife, the servant girl, who doesn't appear; 'Curate and doctor', at least two burglars, various neighbours, and the poet himself as a boy. That makes at least fourteen dramatis personae before we start counting the other children ('We danced round him shouting'), Orangemen and animals, of which several species are represented: 'winter birds', 'a mongrel bitch and shivering pups', a she-goat, crickets, cattle. The poem cries, gossips, chirps, bangs, gulps and chants; it breathes the intimate life of clothes, beds and dreams. Heather bells and 'clumps of foxglove' add splashes of colour. The whole thing is tremendously alive. The people are eccentric and marginal but instantly recognizable, also the period details: money box (you can see it), Blind Pension and Wireless, the 'rocking hearthstone' and the 'crumbling gatehouse'. The poem itself is a ring of dolmens, a 'standing circle of stones', more human than a circle of standing stones, its kindly conversational tone — casually assonantal, rhyming as if by chance — both anecdotal and authoritative. The poet here, man and boy, casts a druidical magic over these old people, preserving them in his role of *seanchaí* and 'chronicler of a whole countryside'. The poem, achieving its own 'dark permanence of ancient forms', is a triumph of form, destined for permanence, and already part of the antiquity it celebrates.

He has the trick of framing the significant image with such supernatural clarity that it remains unforgettable: spring water so cold it falls like 'manacles of ice on the wrists', an 'enormous osiered banquet hall' imagined at Tara, wolfhounds 'lean as models', the 'white mosque' of a cinema in Bundoran. *Poisoned Lands* is packed with phrases like this, brisk and exact: a 'draught-whipped' candle, a pantry 'silent with milk', the 'hissing drift' of winter rain — and the list continues. An intensely sensuous poet, he gets touch, taste and sound, and excels at the visual. These come together, famously, in 'The Trout', a poem which has been as closely studied as the narrator, 'lord of creation', studies the actual trout itself. Sound and taste are implicit but potent; sight and touch create the surface action, the 'photographic calm' and 'lightly pulsing gills'. He is 'so preternaturally close' he is almost one with nature, as so often. The erotic ramifications are many and various, and the poem ends on a brilliant synaesthesia of touch and taste, hand and tongue. The sexual content ('sensual dream', 'visible pleasure') is unmistakable and has invited much comment, but it may not be too far-fetched to read a political, even a journalistic subtext into this poem of the 1960s. The 'slow-motion calm' that 'grows before action' seems to predict what he calls elsewhere 'coming events', i.e. the Troubles. The 'taste of terror' would become familiar to many in Ulster.

Montague's America. He spent his earliest years as an emigrant child in Brooklyn, sent home as a youngster to grow up in Tyrone, and Brooklyn in the thirties remains etched on his mind, together with old comics and westerns. Tough times, and he would humorously half like us to believe he ran with a tough crowd, a wild bunch; but it wasn't really like that. I think they were 'lace curtain' Irish. In any case the American component has stayed imaginatively active for him, and he taught for some years at Albany, New York, where he was a friend and colleague of the novelist William Kennedy, a 'tough' writer if you like. At Berkeley in the fifties and sixties, at a time when American poetry enjoyed considerable prestige, he had frequent contact with another wild bunch, the California poets: Rexroth, Snyder, Duncan, McClure, Spicer. I too was in America in the late sixties and noticed the high regard in which these West Coast types were held. Donald Allen's *The New Poetry*, anthologizing the rangy verse of that era, was hugely influential. As Montague describes it in the memoirs, he admired Kenneth Rexroth's seven-syllable line and later 'adopted and adapted' it in

Wild Bunches

The Dead Kingdom: 'Something about the cadences made his poems very readable.' He was intrigued by Robert Duncan's belief in magic, unfortunately derived from the teachings of Aleister Crowley (brrr!), once expelled from the Golden Dawn, but found a more positive hint in Duncan's *The Opening of the Field* (1959), with its diffuse and 'non-linear' (though written in lines) 'composition by field', the poetic equivalent of an artistic method then fashionable in New York; popular physics gave the idea some 'scientific' validation. Montague associated the notion, roughly speaking, with his own private field, Garvaghey, and made this parochial space an exemplar and synecdoche of the global, even the cosmic: 'the rough field of the universe'. Reticulated lines of energy, it was believed, held the imaginative sphere like a ball in a net, perhaps anticipating the 'wired world' of today.

Duncan lived in San Francisco proper, but Gary Snyder was a Berkeley resident. He had studied in Japan and favoured a Buddhist aesthetic, as a teacher was interested primarily in his students' spiritual lives and, says Montague, 'the need to develop a discipline of contemplation from which poetry might be distilled, aiming to improve their souls so as to improve their verses'. As part of this programme Snyder urged friends and disciples to join him in orgiastic partner-sharing experiments — 'but his sense of discipline was so stern that it was nearly puritanical, and it was astonishing how much scholarship could be applied to everything, even sex and drugs'. I think Montague gives too much credit to these California poets, but an inferior poem or theory can often help point a good one in the right direction. Take Snyder's 'Water' (*Riprap*, Origin Press, 1960), one unconscious source, I suspect, for his *own* trout:

> *Pounded by heat raced down slabs to the creek*
> *Deep tumbling under arching walls and stuck*
> *Whole head and shoulders in the water:*
> *Stretched full on pebbles — ears roaring*
> *Eyes open aching from cold and faced a trout.*

These notes are themselves an example of composition by field, if I understand it. I'm too close to the work ('preternaturally' close, you might say) to treat it in a linear or otherwise systematic fashion, so I'm dashing here and there over the surface. My comments on

Derek Mahon

sight and light, for example, take us straight into his second collection, *A Chosen Light*: indeed, we are there already with 'The Trout'. The 'witch-bright glow' of 'A Bright Day', recreating experience by 'ritualizing its details', becomes a sought-after illumination, its 'slow exactness' momentarily replacing

> *the accumulated richness*
> *Of an old historical language.*

The poem is one of a short Ulster series that switches suddenly to Paris, where he lived for many years. (He now lives in Nice.) His Paris address, '11 rue Daguerre', itself points fortuitously to a photographic calm and a preoccupation with light. He was a film critic at this time too. These were the bright days of the cinematic 'New Wave', with its existential lyricism, and of *Tel Quel*. This was the atmosphere Montague breathed in Paris, where he was a friend of *Tel Quel* contributors like Michel Deguy and lit upon the work of Guillevic and Francis Ponge, both of whom he has translated. He could hardly have avoided it: Ponge, together with the hermetic Yves Bonnefoy, was one of the most admired poets of the day. Not Saint-John Perse, for example, with his 'old historical language' and rhetorical manner, but Ponge the student of soap and snails whose *poèmes en prose* rely on 'a slow exactness' of observation and an air of scientific method. So it's no surprise that Montague translated him: 'If speaking of earth like this makes me a minor poet, an earth tiller, that's what I want to be! I do not know a grander subject.' Or, as Montague puts it in a poem for Kathleen Raine, with whom he shares a belief in a 'magical' universe:

> *the same above as here below,*
> *the galaxy a holy show.*

But the author of *The Rough Field* is much more than a minor figure. A vital and defining influence in contemporary Irish poetry since the fifties, he also helped facilitate two other important developments, the Dolmen Press and Claddagh Records. He dedicated the volume *A Chosen Light* to Liam Miller who started the one and to Garech Browne who started the other. The significance of these ventures can scarcely be exaggerated. The nexus sustained indigenous culture at a difficult time. The Dolmen Press *was* Irish poetry in those days, backed up by Claddagh which, besides its great revival of traditional music, initiated a distinguished 'Spoken Word' series. This included and includes many well-known contemporary names. Kinsella was a director of Dolmen, Montague of Claddagh. Artistic and musical contributors to the joint enterprise included Louis le Brocquy and Seán Ó Riada. It even extended to the stage, with *The Rough Field* 'playing' to full houses in Dublin and London in a programme devised and produced by Liam Miller. The Chieftains were part of it in the beginning, taking their group name from Montague's short story 'Death of a Chieftain'. Thirty years before *Riverdance*, from his base at Luggala, Co Wicklow, Garech Browne and his circle made traditional music sexy; and Liam Miller produced such beautiful books that he made Irish publishing, such as it then was, glamorous. The overlap between Dolmen and Claddagh extended to graphics and visual motifs, many derived from Montague who chose, for example, John Derricke's Elizabethan woodcuts to illustrate *The Rough Field* on its first appearance — bard and piper not only invoked but portrayed, besides much curious and often grisly period detail. Ten years later I wrote, and Michael Heffernan produced, a Montague programme, 'A Grafted Tongue', for BBC Radio 3. His English audience was largely confined to certain circles — readers of the magazine *Agenda*, for instance, and of Kathleen Raine's *Temenos*, neither of them mainstream. He is better known in Scotland and Wales, and certainly in France, where he was recently elevated to the Légion d'Honneur.

He always had a gift for sudden, explosive action: 'The Trout', 'A New Siege', and that moment from his time in Armagh when a past pupil buzzes the school in his RAF plane which

> *Rose out of a hole in the hedge,*
> *Sudden as a flying swan, to circle*
> *Over the school in salutation*
> *And fold into cloud again.*

But the lure of peace is stronger. *Odium theologicum* and vehement nationalism have receded; he's more relaxed now in his old age. Ever since 'Woodtown Manor', with its 'Franciscan dream of gentleness', he has been drawn to a contemplative mode, increasingly so in the

Derek Mahon

later volumes. Tension relaxes. You might say he renounces virtuosity except that, perhaps one effect of his mytho-poeic stammer, his line has always had an edgy relationship with euphony. Has he found what Edward Said called a 'late style'? Not in Said's meaning of the phrase, for there is no struggle. What we have instead is a philosophic repose curiously akin to Kavanagh's 'true note on a dead slack string'. He quotes Hokusai: 'At ninety, I should penetrate the mystery of things; at a hundred I should have reached a remarkable stage . . .' He has long been interested in Indian religion, the Hinduism once described by the British journalist James Cameron as 'flesh of India's flesh and bone of her bone', and has visited ancient sites there — at least partly, I suspect, in a spirit of pilgrimage. The outcome has been not so much individual poems, though these exist, as an abiding spiritual curiosity of a kind that seizes upon any manifestation of magical or mystical significance. The supernatural is never far away in Montague's work. Though not obviously a conventional believer, he is in that sense a religious poet, and as such joins the old Irish tradition of *plein-air* eremitical nature poetry and its intense communion with the things of this world:

> *The air rinsed clear,*
> *bright with potency,*
> *as if some magic figure —*
> *a stooped gardener,*
> *or a friendly giant —*
> *might suddenly appear,*
>
> *but only the self*
> *listening to the self,*
> *awash with stillness,*
> *taut with anticipation,*
> *bright with awareness,*
> *far from the botheration.*

J. G. Farrell

The novelist J. G. Farrell, who died in 1979 in Co Cork, was a remarkable writer and a remarkable man. He published six novels, of which the last three — the 'Empire Trilogy' — brought him celebrity and financial security and enabled him to retire from his little flat in Egerton Gardens, SW3, to a farmhouse on the shore of Dunmanus Bay. That was in April of this year. Four months later he slipped from a rock while fishing and was swept out to sea. He leaves behind an echo of charming and brilliant conversation, and three superb novels. Not an immense output, perhaps; but Jim found his voice slowly. Stricken by polio while at Oxford, he spent some time in hospital — an experience recorded in *The Lung* (1964) — and emerged prematurely white-haired, hands in pockets and shoulders hunched. His mature personality combined melancholy and wit in a uniquely Jim-like way. His weary drawl, paradoxically expressive of continual surprise, sometimes of 'alarm' or 'dismay' — two of his favourite words — lent itself to affectionate imitation; and the voice of the man is exactly the voice of the narrator of *A Girl in the Head* (1967), *Troubles* (1970), *The Siege of Krishnapur* (1973) and *The Singapore Grip* (1978).

His death came as a blow to his friends, and for a solitary he had a great many — but it comes too, as a blow to literature. He was forty-three when he died, and in his prime. Who knows what magnificence he might have given us? Marvellous as the 'Empire Trilogy' is, it was only the beginning of something. One sensed that his artistic ambitions were large, although he himself would have repudiated the idea. No question of a routine reissue of the famous whimsicality every few years; he would have attempted something more demanding. He measured himself, I suspect, against the giants of modern literature and, given time, he might have joined them. Many readers found the *Grip* disappointing, but not this reader. True, the military bits sometimes become hard work, as they do in *War and Peace*; but his central metaphor, the 'grip' of European capital on the Far East at that period, and the sense of life as an expanding-and-contracting organism, are ingeniously explored. This 'organic' motif (he had an X-ray vision of society), and the recurrent symbolism of vegetable decay and animal encroachment, make these books poems in prose as well as historical reconstruction and comic masterpieces, with their distinctive narrative music. They are also a belated swansong for the British Empire, whose still-visible remains Jim Farrell contemplated with qualified affection. Like many Anglo-Irish people, he loved Ireland and was yet intensely English. Consider the Major, perhaps Farrell's best-known character, lecturing dog-lovers on how to handle their pets during the Japanese air-raids, or wincing at the sight of a French diplomat using his (the Major's) old school tie as a belt.

The Singapore Grip is, I believe, his finest book; but, like most Farrellites, I lost my heart to *Troubles*, that strange, haunting story set in a crumbling hotel in Co Wexford during the War of Independence, in which the Major, a younger man than in the *Grip*, makes his initial gloomy appearance. On the first page occurs the sentence: 'A few years later still the Majestic itself followed the boats and preceded the pines into oblivion by burning to the ground.' It was that 'and preceded the pines' that hooked me. Here was a novelist who stood back, who took the long view. There is nothing meretricious or merely topical about Farrell's work; it has the detachment and repose of great art. Which is not to say that it lacks humanity. On the contrary, an important part of Jim's make-up was a vivid and compassionate humanism that embraced Dives and Lazarus, the choleric tycoon and the indigent 'coolie'. And always there is the sense that in the midst of life we are in death. In *Troubles*, the love-sick Major writes a long letter to the object of his affections, pouring out his heart on every conceivable subject, and Farrell remarks that it will never be posted because 'the kind of letter the Major was writing is seldom voluntarily finished before the Grim Reaper bids us lay down our pens'. Well, Jim Farrell has laid down his pen; but the books remain. The books, and the memory of a treasured friend.

1979

Everything for Keeps

The novelist J. G. Farrell (1935-1979) inspired great affection and esteem in his lifetime, and a mystique survives — owing, in part, to the tragic nature of his early death. (He drowned in Dunmanus Bay at Kilcrohane, Co Cork, where he had moved just months before.) His biographer Lavinia Greacen (*J. G. Farrell: The Making of a Writer*, Bloomsbury, 1999) has also edited a fascinating and generously annotated selection of his letters to family, friends, agents and publishers, and added vivid passages from his diaries. The result is a moving and memorable portrait of the man, one that his many fans will want to have; and not only fans but, increasingly, students — for Farrell's fiction, a big hit in its day and never out of print, is now recognized as an important contribution to the post-colonial, or perhaps post-imperial canon, with special reference to the famous 'Empire Trilogy': not really a trilogy but, his own word, a triptych: *Troubles* (1970), *The Siege of Krishnapur* (1973) and *The Singapore Grip* (1978).

An English-born Anglo-Irishman, he spent most of his working life in London, with much travel: France, Spain and Morocco, Mexico, India and South-East Asia. His 'Indian Diary', first published posthumously in 1981, is particularly fine, and perhaps reveals more about the author than anything else he wrote. At one hotel he considers tipping the staff 'in inverse ration to their place in the caste system'. The elegance of the phrasing, and of the thought, is typical. Watching a funeral at a burning ghat in Benares: 'Presently the attendant turned one of the legs over. It was when it went right over against the natural articulation of the joint that the body really stopped being a person for me and became an object.' Again, that elegant phrasing, of a piece with a personal elegance amusingly described by John Banville as 'slightly sinister'. Anatomy and economics were two of Farrell's chief preoccupations. Anatomy because, stricken by polio while at Oxford, he was always conscious of physical inadequacy; and economics as he pursued his imperial researches and drew his own trenchant conclusions. The two preoccupations came together in a pathological, but warmly pathological, vision haunted by such old-fashioned things as mortality and unavailing love. Lavinia Greacen is tactful, but there was no shortage of women in Jim's life, and several of them feature here as regular correspondents — notably Gabriele, a mystery girl from his early years; Sarah Bond, another early flame; and his later soulmate Bridget O'Toole — besides fellow writers Margaret Drabble and Alison Lurie, Sonia Orwell, and various agents including Deborah Rogers, one of the first to see the brilliance of *Troubles*. He was mischievous, but had great empathy, with women. With men he could be a firm friend — for example with fellow sportsman Jack Kirwan (rugger mostly) of the then 'Dalkey Set', to which Jim too belonged; and with Russell McCormmach, an (American) Oxford contemporary. Or he could be a formidable sparring partner, as with the legendary 1960s publisher Tom Maschler ('of Cape'). With his parents he was a devoted and dutiful son. 'Warm, and sometimes full of self-doubt,' says Greacen, the letters trace his daily life and literary development through the 1960s and 1970s, 'recreating a lost autobiographical voice'. It was an unusual voice, speculative and whimsical, and one that those who knew him remember well. Its very timbre is audible here in this 'increasingly companionable' volume.

When he died email was still in the future but the phone was always at hand; so, as with others, those who lived nearest him had little or nothing to contribute of an epistolary nature. Those farther off, with more to show, provided the bulk of the material. Would Jim, in any case, have adopted email? Very likely. Despite his handicap and an air of retro *chic*, he was quite nimble and advanced in some ways. He kept a racy-looking bike in his London flat at 16 Egerton Gardens, a short walk from Harrods, and to 'Russ' McCormmach shows a surprising interest in the martial arts. Not so surprising, really, if you think of *The Singapore Grip*: 'Did you go through with the karate idea? I have, in fact, often thought about it myself, my trouble being that I'm not strong enough, as a result of polio, to hurt anybody, no matter how scientifically aimed my blows. It would be refreshing to feel dangerous and arrogant for a change.' Very man-to-man with Russ, he reports that he's met a call-girl 'who decided she was in love with me and introduced me to all her prostitute friends, gangsters, pimps, etc. I had no idea just what the London underworld was like'. Two steps from Stephen Ward and Christine Keeler, for an unworldly man he was remarkably well connected. To Russ and Gaby both he reports that he's reading a life of Tolstoy: 'My amazement and admiration grow with every page. He had the talent I most admire, that of playing everything for keeps . . . What a man! I'm sure genius is largely a question of energy.' It wasn't until the obituaries that he himself was mentioned in the same breath as the author of *War and Peace*, though he must have been aware of the ghostly presence. His own theory of history was very similar.

New York, where he spent two years on a fellowship, was 'intolerably dirty and hostile', so he got out of town a lot. On Block Island he made a fresh start on a new book, 'partly inspired' by the charred remains of the burnt-out Ocean View Hotel, evidently a magnificent place in its day. Diary entry, May 1967: 'This morning I went up to look at the remains: old bedsprings twisted with heat; puddles of molten glass; washbowls that had fallen through to the foundations; a flight of stone steps leading up into thin air; twisted pipes; lots of nails lying everywhere, and a few charred beams. The way the glass had collected like candle-grease under the windows impressed me most. When you picked it up it flaked away in your hand.'

This was to be the Majestic in *Troubles*, its description transferred almost word for word from the Diary. His current reading was fortuitous too, Giorgio Bassani's *The Garden of the Finzi-Continis*: 'I kept recognizing myself in the narrator, vis-à-vis the Kirwans in Dalkey.' What he admired in Conrad he admired also in Lampedusa's *The Leopard*: 'Clear, very concrete images, the characters beautifully portrayed.' Clear, almost hallucinatory images were a striking feature of *Troubles*, and recurred with photographic intensity in the *Siege* and the *Grip*. All his characters, moreover, are 'beautifully portrayed'. Elizabeth Bowen lived long enough to read, admire and review *Troubles*, remarking that it was not a period piece but 'yesterday reflected in today's consciousness; the ironies, the disparities, the dismay, the sense of unavailingness, are contemporary'. Jim met her and writes to Bridget ('Dear Bríd'): 'I had a longish personal chat with her. A tremendously good person, in

Derek Mahon

spite of her stammer and nervousness she is very open and direct. She mentioned that she was about contemporary with the twins in the book though much less enterprising.'

On a research trip to India, while charmed by the elephants and peacocks of Jaipur, he notes 'an encampment of untouchables in a dusty grove just outside the hotel gates, to remind that things are bad here — though it occurred to me today that people here don't actually *look* unhappy. People in England, including Indians, look much more desperate . . .' To his American agent from Kathmandu, then on the hippy trail, he reports that few of the hippies strike him as real people: 'There are any number of maladjusted young Americans drifting around India, though making precious little contact, it seems to me, with any of the Indias.' He himself did no better, he admits, but the poverty and 'unavailingness', now a favourite word, were to leave their stamp on his subsequent work — especially on the *Grip*, with its imaginative immersion in the life of the Singapore slums of the 1940s. The Diary again: 'Glimpsed at twilight on the Singapore River, an old Chinese standing to scull a tiny, frail prau with a lantern on a stick behind him. A vast barge surges by, causing him to rock wildly in its wash.' Even his casual observations carried a metaphorical import, usually political.

The Kirwans reappear in his life when he decides to buy a house at Gortfahane and Jack, a Dublin solicitor, acts for him. It's often thought that, with this move, Jim was withdrawing from the world, but he had friends come to visit. Always determinedly active, he goes window-shopping at the London Boat Show, deferring a decision. He was now quite well off thanks to sales, prizes and film options, and had it in mind to find himself a *pied-à-terre* in Paris, though he never got around to it. The photographs reproduced here include several of the man himself at different ages, an old one of the Ocean View Hotel in decline, the Gortfahane house, and the adjacent rock where he fished and where a freak wave swept him into the water in the third week of August 1979, the week of the disastrous Fastnet Race when 15 died. He was the 16th. His grave is at St James's (Church of Ireland), beyond Durrus.

A House Remembers

'In the morning on the way to school you saw things, tracks, furs, feathers and once a paw with its cloven hoof and its long nail intact. You skirted the fork of dark trees. It was a pagan place and circular' (*A Pagan Place*, 1970). The person addressed, the author herself perhaps (Edna O'Brien), is a young girl growing up in Co Clare in the 1940s. Her father is the then traditional drunken brute, her mother the traditional long-suffering woman of the house, devout and overworked. An unmarried older sister, Emma, comes back from a job in Dublin dressed in the height of fashion, muttering 'this dump, this dump', and is soon found to be pregnant. The father responds with fury, the mother with anguish, and the townspeople with self-righteous avidity. The younger girl, the 'you', otherwise nameless, responds not so much to the fact of Emma's pregnancy as to the responses of the others — or so it appears, for no explicit view is ascribed to her. Only later, after she has been sexually abused by a young priest, does she make her position clear, and then not in words but in action. She decides to take the veil, and this short novel ends with her departure for a convent in Belgium. The unusual second-person narration captures the painful, contributory *immanence* of everything, as if the very bread on the table, the rain on the window, conspired to inflict injury. People are perceived instinctually, as sources of trepidation or reassurance. Things happen, and the girl sees. Sometimes she is frightened, sometimes she must be happy: 'It was like a summer's day inside your head. No sooner had the nun stopped than you raised your hand and said you would go.'

O'Brien belongs to an Irish generation who still thought seriously about the religious life. Convents, and the shadows of convents, have loomed large in her memory and imagination — even, perhaps, her romantic imagination. A story like 'Sister Imelda', for instance, is in a tradition of conventual eroticism which includes

215

her namesake Kate O'Brien and Antonia White and goes back at least as far as Diderot's *La Religieuse* (1796). This dates her, of course, since the conventual life is dying out everywhere. Put another way, she was lucky as a young writer to catch the tail end of an important phase of Irish social history, when clergy and 'religious' were a prominent feature of the national life and psyche; though her own emphasis falls elsewhere. Kate Brady and Bridget ('Baba') Brennan, the cheeky one, belong already to the new secular Ireland whose first stirrings occurred in the 1960s. Life really begins for them when, in *The Country Girls* (1960), they get to 'the neon fairyland of Dublin'. The neon signs of Dublin, in those days, were known individually, and the moving ones were famous: the Bovril sign at the north end of D'Olier Street, 'Player's Please' on the roof of Kapp & Peterson (Tobacconists) roof in College Green. Those who were young in Dublin then remember the dancehalls too, in Harcourt Street and Parnell Square where Kate and Baba go.

Her admiration for Joyce is well known, and she often adopts a stream of consciousness, most notably in *Night* (1972). Frank Tuohy claims that while Joyce was the first (hardly the *first*) Irish Catholic to make his experience and surroundings recognizable, 'the world of Nora Barnacle had to wait for the fiction of Edna O'Brien'. Coming down to more recent times, we might liken Kate not to Nora but to Chris, the laundry girl in *The Ginger Man* (1955), who complains about the young Dublin men she meets; or to the unhappy young women in the work of William Trevor — those in 'The Ballroom of Romance' or 'Teresa's Wedding'. These were pre-feminist days, but conditions were ripe for change, and Edna was a notable agent of change; to us of the sixties generation she was an 'icon'. *The Country Girls* and *The Lonely Girl* (1962) were both banned in Ireland. She pays her farewell to one tradition with the perfect story 'Irish Revel', often compared to *Dubliners*, though the real comparison, I think, is with George Moore's *The Untilled Field* (1903): 'Walking again, she wondered if and what she would tell her mother and her brothers about it, and if all parties were as bad. She was at the top of the hill now and could see her own house, like a little white box at the end of the world, waiting to receive her.' O'Brien, a resolute and glamorous figure, refused the long-suffering victim role to which so many women of the era, real and fictional both, were condemned in the 'land of shame', as she

A House Remembers

called it in 'A Scandalous Woman'. Instead she set her own standards and created her own life, first with a rich international arty set in Wicklow, and later in London.

'So off I went on the boat and train as thousands had done before me . . . I arrived at Euston at six one perishing February morning . . . Even at that early hour I noticed that, while Dublin had existed for me in black and white, London was decked out in all-singing, all-dancing technicolour' (Marian Keyes, 'Swinging London'). O'Brien, who had made a similar move forty years before, will not be pleased to hear that she is the unwitting mother of Irish 'chick lit', yet it seems obvious. *Girls in their Married Bliss* (1964), though a sombre and serious read, introduces many of the now familiar themes of the bright pink, formulaic fiction that fills contemporary bookshops, the strain of 'having it all' and the rest. But there's a difference. The early work, at first reading, has a 'naive' charm, and was so marketed, but this *faux-naïveté* disguises an artfulness barely distinguishable from art; and it's really quite a 'literary' performance. Baba provides most of the funny stuff ('You're a right-lookin' eejit'; 'Go down and tell him I'm having a haemorrhage') while Kate is the serious one: 'It was a beautiful book, but sad. It was called *Tender is the Night* . . . All the nicest men were in books — the strange, complex, romantic men, the ones I admired most.' Her first love is a man called Du Maurier, and Daphne du Maurier's *Rebecca* shadows Kate's reception at Eugene's fine house in the Wicklow hills. 'You're like Anna Karenina in that coat,' he tells her. Anna Karenina? 'She must be some girlfriend of his,' thinks Kate, 'or an actress.' A hundred pages later, without comment, she's reading *Anna Karenina*. 'Where's Chekhov?' asks Baba, meaning the foreign-born Eugene. And, like so many books of this kind, it all goes back to *Jane Eyre*, condemned in its time as the outpouring of a disgracefully 'natural' (irreligious) heart. She takes the epigraphs to later books from Keats and Emily Brontë, Mandelstam and Brecht. It won't do, if it ever did, to think of O'Brien as a naive author, writing as the bird sings — though she can, when she wants, sing with a beautiful, lyrical simplicity: 'It was rainy lilac April weather — sun and squally showers, and then a wind rose to dry the rain off the hedges and blow the white apple blossom all about, so that it seemed to be snowing flowers.' These books delighted us in the sixties because they were so magically real: this was the Ireland we knew, or some of it. Louis MacNeice was a fan; Dymphna, a nurse I met at the Shamrock Ballroom, was a fan.

The London novels (*Girls in their Married Bliss, August is a Wicked Month*, 1965) broke new ground for O'Brien, and now the English critics were annoyed, for she had ceased to be a mysterious country girl and become a Chelsea sophisticate — one with a sharp tongue too, and a brisk line in sexual candour. The sex 'n' violence of the new work estranged some who had warmed to the innocent cheek of the Irish books. We're not allowed to say 'stridency' or 'hysteria' any more, but her new women, looking to have it all, sometimes sailed perilously close to these hazards. Some developed new character traits, swinging wildly between cynicism and gushy metaphor: 'The river of his being flowing into the pasture of her body. She was thinking of that when she got to the restaurant.' Some of her best work at this time was in the short story. 'The Love Object', a complex and subtle study of a short-lived affair between a divorced woman and a suave, dominant older man, covers a remarkable emotional range. There are anomalies: an evidently clever and beautiful woman with a good job and two sons at boarding school, how can she seriously entertain thoughts of suicide? But the graph of enchantment and disenchantment is beautifully drawn; and her final, thoughtful transition from rage to absolution marks a doubly significant advance for the O'Brien heroine.

'A house remembers. An out-house remembers.' Julia Kristeva once observed that the problem with academic feminism is or was 'its too frequent lack of a truly radical content, being bourgeois, self-promoting and without political purpose in the real sense'. O'Brien took on the radical content. Besides *The Country Girls Trilogy* there is now a quartet touching on themes of Irish public interest. After some years of apparent creative disorientation she turned to a new topicality, focusing once more on Ireland and Irish 'meaniacs', as an early landlady calls them. Among her memorable meaniacs are McGreevy in *House of Splendid Isolation*, James McNamara in *Down by the River* (a novel about child abuse) and Michan of *In the Forest*. McGreevy is based on Dominic ('Mad Dog') McGlinchey, a crazy gunman whose doings intrigued the papers some years ago; and Michan on Brendan O'Donnell, convicted of the murders of a young woman, her son and a priest in

O'Brien's own Co Clare, also a prominent news item in its day. Abandoning sun, sand and liberated sex, she now turned or returned her attention to more recent Irish experience, beset as it was by violent politics and sexual pathology. It's to her credit that she should explore these new (old) themes, but there's something slightly forced about the attempt, a predetermination, a chasing after contemporary relevance. She evolved a fine rhetorical turn of phrase: 'To go right into the heart of the hate and the wrong . . . That is the future knowledge. The knowledge that is to be.' A vatic way of saying that we must question ourselves closely if we are to arrive at any sort of serviceable truth. Unlike earlier work, the later novels are not an easy read. Sometimes a linguistic tremor dislodges words from their usual meanings. Style, structure and artifice have a random, speculative, dicey air, as if she's looking for a new mode of discourse, a new way of seeing and understanding that resists her importunate efforts. The future knowledge, perhaps.

The Lonely Girl was published in the States as *Girl with Green Eyes*, a title also used for the film of the book. Her filmography is a study in itself. She scripted, for example, the accomplished *I Was Happy Here* (1965), starring Sarah Miles. But the one we remember best is *Girl with Green Eyes* (1963), with Rita Tushingham and Peter Finch, a classic of sixties cinema, as important to Ireland as Godard's *Vivre sa Vie* (1962) to France or Schlesinger's *Darling* (1965) to England. Since, as in most adaptations, the film took various liberties with the book, I suspect Edna never liked it much, but it meant a lot to cinema-goers in those days and stands up even now. The first signs of Irish secularism and feminism appeared about then, and her early work, besides reflecting them, contributed to these developments. It contributed too to a new cosmopolitanism, as in Eugene, and anticipated the rise of consumerism in the acquisitive role of Baba — though Baba has her own problems. O'Brien's books and films, together with her intriguing personality, combined to achieve something beyond literature, cinema or biographical mystique. They caught a historic moment, one in which obvious realities and pent-up aspirations demanded release; and created a myth.

If Only

Fool's Sanctuary (1987) was Jennifer Johnston's eighth novel, and one of her best. One of her three best, I should say, together with *How Many Miles to Babylon?* and *The Old Jest*, both of which it resembles in many respects. It shares certain features with other Johnston novels too: plot configurations and even characters reappear, subtly transformed, in book after book, as they do in Turgenev, so that there is now a recognizable Johnston novel as there is a recognizable William Trevor; like him she has created a world of her own. This is a great strength, for it raises emotional compulsions to the status of archetypal patterns, even of myth; and of such material is the finest literature made. Johnston's gift is poetic; it is also dramatic. The sanctuary of the title is Termon, a Big House in Co Cork. As in previous books, a no-longer-young woman remembers, and what she remembers is the story, though the nature of her recollection is the substance. Typically the narrator is bedridden or at least sedentary. The narrator of *Fool's Sanctuary*, Miranda Martin, is evidently bedridden, and dying at Termon surrounded by doctors and nurses who seem to think her slightly mad. Miranda, who never married, is nearly as old as the century; she bobbed her hair just after the first world war, at much the same time as Lois, in Elizabeth Bowen's *The Last September*, appeared in her white skirt on the steps at Danielstown and the twins in J. G. Farrell's *Troubles* learned to foxtrot. Termon, says Miranda, is 'a romantic ruin full of ghosts', and she names her ghosts before slipping out of the first person and into the third, where most of the story takes place: her father, a dreamy old fellow obsessed with drainage schemes and the like; her severe officer brother Andrew; Andrew's bumbling English friend Harry; and Cathal Dillon, with whom she was in love. She has only the vaguest memories of her mother, who died young.

When young herself, Miranda was a bit of a tomboy, fond of

If Only

gratuitous gestures like climbing up on a rock, stretching out her arms to the sun and bursting into song — a style of behaviour that irritates Andrew but endears her to Cathal, a local lad studying in Dublin who came down 'that weekend'. Cathal, who has 'pale city skin' and takes great care not to wet his new city shoes, is a favourite of her father's but not really the sort Miranda's sort would consider one of their own. There is an obscure harshness between him and Andrew, and Cathal resents the presence of Harry, who is owlishly attentive to Miranda, the resentment springing not only from amorous rivalry but from the fact that Harry, like Andrew, wears a British uniform. Harry and Andrew, we later learn, are in Ireland not on holiday but on active service, their orders similar to those of the officers hand-picked in 1920 to destroy Michael Collins's intelligence network and soon shot in their beds. Cathal, by contrast, is in the Republican movement. He too has orders, to facilitate the abduction of the British spies, which is why he was there 'that weekend'. 'They've done their homework very well,' the obnoxious Andrew admits; 'I am a sort of glorified spy, though I can't say I like the role very much.' When men in trench coats come looking for Andrew and Harry they've already gone, tipped off by Cathal — a friend of the family, after all. For this breach of discipline, Cathal is taken out and shot; and the story comes to an end.

But if the story is at an end, the novel is not. Miranda, drifting towards death, hasn't yet finished. She wonders what would have happened had Cathal lived: 'We might have outfaced the ghosts together; raised a spreading brood to fill this house.' On the other hand, 'he might have moved towards politics after the fight was over, shifted into that grey area where expediency nudges truth out of its way, where freedom becomes a slogan rather than a possibility. I would have hated that.' She has kept faith: 'I have known the embraces of no man; I wait now with deep impatience for the deep embrace of death.' She speaks of 'motors' and 'the wireless', recalls the men drinking port while she played the piano, and hums a seductively mournful Anglican hymn: 'The day thou gavest, Lord, is ended; the darkness falls at thy behest.' She remembers, lingering on the phrase, an Indian summer: 'We lived for a few days, a week even, through an unearned respite.' A respite from what? Not from autumn only, but from the onrush of events, private and public; in a word, from history. Miranda, who by marrying Cathal might have helped history on its way, is left with the recollection of a lost opportunity — not that the loss was her doing.

This is Jennifer's recurrent theme: 'If only . . .' If only things had been different, if only people could live in peace — a familiar liberal lament, redeemed from platitude by her irony, vitality and sense of the ridiculous. Yet the pain is there, book after book, as the flag comes down: a regimental Union Jack on which is somehow superimposed the Starry Plough of the Citizen Army. The lyrical plangency of this lament (a lament, also, for personal honour of an old-fashioned kind: consider Cathal's torment) is the Johnston hallmark; it's one of the things we cherish in her work. I would like to suggest though that, having made herself perfect through practice, she consider once more an option briefly taken up in *Shadows on Our Skin*, that of contemporary life and the problems we face now. It will be objected that these are implicit in everything she writes; and so, in a sense, they are. You can't tell a poet what to do next; but I can't help feeling there is something bigger and riskier to be tried than she has yet set her hand to. 'There are no new days ahead of me,' is how Miranda begins; but, in so far as this bears a more than purely personal application, it is not true; it's *historically* untrue. Ireland is crying out for the imaginative departure, and Johnston is one of those who are able for it. I wonder what would happen if one of our finest novelists were to attempt, say, something analogous to Nadine Gordimer's compact masterpiece *The Late Bourgeois World*.

The novels, so reliant on dialogue and soliloquy, aspire to the condition of theatre; and she has written plays too. Of these, none has more than three characters, and all give the impression of having only one. *The Porch*, in which an old lady is taken by relations from her home and packed off to a 'home', is described as 'almost a monologue', but the same could be said of them all. Mamie in *It Was the Nightingale*, another old lady, converses with the shade of her ex-husband; and in *The Invisible Man* an actor preparing to play King Lear uses his gay assistant merely as a foil, as a fool in the Shakespearian sense. The taste for monologue is evident also in the novels where, as often as not, women of advancing years reminisce, talk to themselves or to imagined presences, make tea, smoke, drink and hum snatches of ill-remembered songs. It's not that the

If Only

plays are novelistic, but that the novels are theatrical. In an autobiographical introduction to *Fool's Sanctuary* Jennifer remembers her mother, the actress Shelagh Richards, standing in their drawing room listening to or rather watching the radio, from which came cheers, screams and the raving voice of Hitler: 'She just stood there staring at the wireless, and that was theatre; her face and stance as much as the screaming of the voices.' Daughter also of the playwright Denis, she was stage-struck from an early age: 'The line between the world of theatre and the real world in which we lived seemed very fine.'

War and Peace

Pasternak, like Tolstoy, thought of history as an organic growth, seeing it 'in the form of images taken from the vegetable kingdom, moving as invisibly in its incessant transformations as the forest in spring'. Beauty, he says, is 'the joy of possessing form, and form is the key to organic life since no living thing can exist without it, so that every work of art, including tragedy, witnesses to the joy of existence' (*Zhivago*, tr. Hayward and Harari). Form, imagery, organic life. Even as an undergraduate at Trinity College, Dublin, Michael Longley had a precocious grasp of the sort of stanza favoured by Donne and Herbert, and the first poems included here (*Collected Poems*, 2006) shine with remarkable formal confidence: 'The Hebrides', 'Epithalamion', 'A Personal Statement'. This is one of the benefits of knowing your Greek and Latin. A student of Homer and the Roman elegists, he has worked equally well with compelling anecdote and elaborate lyric shapes. The elaborate shapes are early work, since when he has pursued an increasingly direct mode which dispenses with ingenuity and rhetoric; technique becomes second nature. The achieved personal voice he established with *Gorse Fires* (1991), well travelled, wide-ranging, while rooted in local experience, is now the recognizable Longley sound, relaxed and authoritative.

An old friend, I've a particular soft spot for the poems of family and home (Belfast) and have long envied his eclectic ease with both highbrow and popular taste. He finds analogies for poetry in art and music (Satie, folk, jazz) and, like Yeats, parallels between certain aspects of Irish and Japanese culture; but his principal themes are autobiographical and contemplative. 'The Weather in Japan' which 'makes bead curtains of the rain, / Of the mist a paper screen' is really Irish rain, the rain of Connemara ('Rain and sunlight and the boat between them') and of his adopted parish in Co Mayo, to which he returns constantly. A key text in relation to his own practice is an essay he published in *The Dublin Magazine* — heavens, forty years ago — on the Ulster artist Colin Middleton whose 'constant preoccupations' he identifies as 'the female archetype and the qualities of place' and whose later work he praises for its 'apparent freedom from intrusive neurosis'. (Middleton had affinities with Ben Nicholson and Henry Moore.) These were and are Longley's own priorities, and he adds: 'True art must always be to some extent local.' He would acknowledge descent from MacNeice, Rodgers and Hewitt; also from Kavanagh, who shared Betjeman's love of 'indeterminate beauty': quaint corners, overgrown places, odds and ends. Middleton's studio collection of 'shells, pebbles, feathers, driftwood', bits of landscape, are Longleian furniture too; but his primary concern is 'to make space in my brainbox for the other creatures of the world'.

'What is the use or function of poetry nowadays?' asked Graves in the foreword to *The White Goddess*. 'The function of poetry is religious invocation of the Muse; its use is the experience of mixed exaltation and horror that her presence excites. This was once a warning to man that he must keep in harmony with the family of living creatures among which he was born, by obedience to the wishes of the lady of the house; it is now a reminder that he has disregarded the warning, turned the house upside down by capricious experiments in philosophy, science and industry, and brought ruin on himself and his family.' *The White Goddess* is, in one sense, a political book; and Longley, a poet Graves would have recognized as a kindred spirit, is in that sense a political poet. He is also a Muse poet, a love poet and a nature poet, a celebrant of the female principle; and like Graves he is a war poet, of the two world wars in which his father fought, and of the recent war of nerves in Northern Ireland where he lives. His work celebrates 'the family of living creatures' (birds, beasts and flowers, but people too). 'The lady of the house' (lover, wife, Muse) is a turf-scented locution Longley himself uses more than once; he constantly places himself in relation to landscape as if wondering at his own earthly presence. Whatever about philosophy, science and industry receive their elegiac comeuppance between the lines, in the poems about Belfast and the first world war:

Derek Mahon

> *Now I see in close-up, in my mind's eye,*
> *The cracked and splintered dead for pity's sake*
> *Each dismal evening predecease the sun,*
> *You, looking death and nightmare in the face*
> *With your kilt, harmonica and gun,*
> *Grow older in a flash but none the wiser.*

He has been more successful with the longish poem than most contemporaries; but his natural length is the page, or half the page. A wit once estimated the weight of the human soul as that of a mature snipe, and the same might be said of the most satisfying poems here. They weigh just right; they fit themselves perfectly. 'The West' for instance:

> *Beneath a gas-mantle that the moths bombard,*
> *Light that powders at a touch, dusty wings,*
> *I listen for news through the atmospherics,*
> *A crackle of sea-wrack, spinning driftwood,*
> *Waves like distant traffic, news from home;*
>
> *Or watch myself, as through a sandy lens,*
> *Materialising out of the heat-shimmers*
> *And finding my way for ever along*
> *The path to this cottage, its windows,*
> *Walls, sun and moon dials, home from home.*

Remote landscapes (Co Mayo, the Hebrides), and the imaginative extremities they suggest, are important to him and figure largely in his work, giving it a tough, flinty texture like the prose of Synge and the pictures of Jack Yeats. There's a soft side to him too. It rains a lot of the time, but when the sun breaks through it's a MacNeicean country sun-shower worth waiting days for, a Mississippi sunset or, mixing the hard and soft modes, the clear light of classical antiquity. He is endlessly quotable, by the stanza or by the individual line: 'You sit there writing while the light permits' (to Emily Dickinson); 'Play your guitar while Derry burns!' (to James Simmons); 'Where science ends and love begins' ('The Ornithological Section'). Occasionally, as in 'The West', 'Skara Brae' and 'In Memory of Gerard Dillon', he is quotable by the whole

War and Peace

poem. Or take 'Thaw', a lyric as brief as it is suggestive:

Snow curls into the coalhouse, flecks the coal.
We burn the snow as well in bad weather
As though to spring-clean that darkening hole.
The thaw's a blackbird with one white feather.

A young musicologist, Maria Johnston, compares Longley to Messiaen, who transcribed birdsong and reproduced it in his music. She quotes the French composer: 'Every spring each blackbird invents a certain number of themes which it retains and adds to previous themes; the older it gets the vaster its repertory of melodic motifs becomes.' The same might be said of this self-renewing poet, himself an amateur naturalist. Blackbird, robin, lark and lapwing populate these pages, together with seabirds and house sparrows which 'with precision wheetle and cheep under the eaves', and a 'wind-tousled' wren with her 'brain-rattling bramble-song'. Animals too — fox, badger, hare — enter this Noah's Ark of a book, and all these endangered species join our own in a plea for art and peace, the end of art:

Home is a hollow between the waves,
A clump of nettles, feathery winds,
And memory no longer than a day
When the animals come back to me
From the townland of Carrigskeewaun,
From a page lit by the Milky Way.

'Who was it suggested that the opposite of war / Is not so much peace as civilisation?' Peace yes, and not before time, but there is much violence and war in the background where 'Achilles hunts down Hector like a sparrowhawk'. His father saw action at the Somme as a young man, and the poets of that war are a special interest — among them Isaac Rosenberg who appears here in 'Bog Cotton' and 'No Man's Land', where Longley also speaks of his 'Jewish granny' on the maternal side. It's the granny, I think, who gives their peculiar poignancy to Holocaust poems like 'Terezín' ('No room has ever been as silent as the room / Where hundreds of violins are hung in unison'), 'Ghetto' ('The little girl without a

Derek Mahon

mother behaves like a mother / With her rag doll to whom she explains fear and anguish'). As for those poems about the recent troubles in Northern Ireland ('Wounds', 'Wreaths'), I'm not so sure: these have, in the nature of things, begun to date. But one of them, 'Ceasefire', will surely live — perhaps because, removed in space and time from the poetry of the latest atrocity, it comes to the point obliquely. Achilles and Priam meet after the death of Hector and Priam says: 'I get down on my knees and do what must be done / And kiss Achilles' hand, the killer of my son.' This gesture is probably the finest and most astonishing comment any of the Irish poets have made on the subject.

It has been remarked upon before that this king-size bloke, once a formidable second-row forward on his school first XV, handles his materials with rice-paper delicacy. Though equal to large conceptions, he is a lover of fragility and evanescence and excels at the moth-like lyric and crystal image. These are scattered throughout. The poem in memory of the artist Gerard Dillon describes one of his pictures:

> Cats on the windowsill, birds of prey
> And, between the diminutive fields,
> A dragonfly, wings full of light,
> Where the road narrows to the last farm.

As if from an entry in Coleridge's *Notebooks*, a waterfall slows down to a chandelier; above Chicago, 747s line up beside the moon; he opens a 'galvanised Aeolian gate'; in 'Yellow Bungalow' he hears an accordion's 'bellows wheeze / And fingernails clitter over buttons and keys'. These precise observations (that 'clitter' is spot-on) are of a piece with the conservationist instinct which attends to 'other creatures'. Cloud, linen, flower and snow absorb the blood and dust of the Homeric pieces and the violence the Belfast elegies mourn. The explicit love poems are few, yet they are all love poems. A subtle eroticism pervades everything, for here is a poet in love with the world itself. His relation to it, uxorious and eirenic, is that of a sage at peace. Poetry like Longley's gives something back to eternity.

The Coleraine Triangle

Think of an isosceles triangle, upside down, with Coleraine as the apex and the twin seaside resorts of Portstewart and Portrush as the base angles. During the university term most of the students reside in the base angles. Last year the Writer in Residence resided in Portstewart; this year he resides in Portrush, in a pleasant whitewashed house with flaking pilasters at the front door and a magnificent sea view. From the window where I write I look eastwards along the shore to the ruins of Dunluce Castle (once a MacDonnell stronghold) and the Giant's Causeway. Slightly to my right is the Royal Portrush golf course, slightly to my left the Atlantic Ocean, with a scattering of rocky islands called the Skerries between me and Scotland. On a clear day I can see Jura and Islay. Earth has not anything to show more fair. Since the occasion years ago when I nearly smashed up a friend's car driving back to Dublin from an all-night party in the Wicklow hills, I have been a non-driver; so I take the train to the university — a mere five minutes — and that brings me into contact with the people who live here all the time. They like living here since this stretch of coast is a sort of Ulster Riviera, with Portrush as its Nice. Belfast people flock here at Easter, and in July and August, to stare across the water at Donegal. The locals make a packet. Genteel landladies, the season at an end, go off to foreign parts for a well-earned rest, letting their premises to the students just arriving for the autumn term. Those who work during the holiday season go back on the dole and head for the Harbour Bar where, before an open fire and beneath sepia photographs and advertisements for Craven 'A', the sagacious Peter Scullion serves the best pint for miles.

    At one time Portrush was really quite posh. One has only to contemplate the vestigial Edwardian grandeur of the Northern Counties Hotel to imagine what it must have been like. Cocktail bars, heated swimming pool, palatial lavatories, and even a civil

Derek Mahon

wolfhound called Fingal (must be a Fenian dog) who sleeps beside the revolving door when not on duty at the reception desk or going through the accounts. Alas, Fingal is not long for this world. The lavatories, it's true, continue to sustain their elderly, sibilant murmur; but the swimming pool, although still functioning, hasn't been smartened up for years, and the bars now cater, *faute de mieux*, for the local toughs, some of them uniformed: historical parallels spring to mind. There is an absence of urbanity. A colleague, an Englishman and a brilliant linguist, is convenor of the university Gaysoc. He is not obviously homosexual, but some time ago the boot boys got his number and tried to work him over. Fortunately he had learnt some karate while studying in Japan, and was able to deal with them single-handed. His prestige is considerable.

Hotels play an important part in the social life of the area. Nobody seems to actually stay in them; but there are frequent discos, and they are almost the only places to eat out if one is disinclined to the sombre atmosphere of the Chinese restaurant or the high prices and disappointing curries of the Indian. One of James Simmons' songs begins, 'When I was a young man and hung around hotels', and admirers of his work should acquaint themselves with the peculiar lifestyle of this coast, with its strange combination of derivative hedonism and sabbatarian grimness. Sitting at the bar of the Strand Hotel in Portstewart, with its sea view to the west, surrounded by middle-class people of circumspect and long-standing affluence, and listening to piped music — 'Red Sails in the Sunset', 'Stranger on the Shore' — you realize that you are not in Ireland at all, not even in Northern Ireland. You might be in South Africa, or New Zealand, or California. Well, no, not California: the atmosphere is too constrained, lacking in colour and gusto; although these people probably inhabit some old-fashioned California of the mind, where the Union Jack somehow waves in the breeze over Sunset Boulevard and the natives are deferential. Provincial sahibs, fiercely domesticated, they represent nothing but themselves. The women fascinate me, especially the middle-aged and elderly women. Each one lives, I know, in a large bungalow full of photographs and possessions but few books, and those few by Somerset Maugham; their children have done the expected thing. They are all as tough as old boots, but some are handsome, one or two even graceful. I admire them.

The Coleraine Triangle

I admire them, but I know they read the *Belfast Newsletter* and sigh for the days of Lord Brookeborough. If you were to ask them about the 18th-century rotunda on the cliff top at Downhill, clearly visible from their windows, they would probably tell you that it was built by the eccentric Earl Bishop of Derry in memory of his mistress. It *was*, in fact, built by the Earl Bishop, Frederick Augustus Hervey (1730-1803), and the architect was Michael Shanahan. It was not, however, built in memory of the lady, but in her honour, and Miss Mussenden was not his mistress, although many people (including the Earl Bishop) would have liked her to be; she was his niece. If you then asked them was it true that the Earl Bishop, in Penal times, made the Mussenden Temple available to Catholics for a weekly Mass, and stipulated in his will that the practice should be continued after his death, you would be committing a social solecism, threatening their sense of security. They would know in their hearts that you were quite possibly right, but would dismiss your information as uninteresting, unrelated to their own lives, and yourself as an oddity. Or perhaps not; perhaps you would be providing food for thought.

Portstewart, Co Derry, is a more Catholic town than Portrush, Co Antrim. I feel this to be numerically so, but a single glance is enough to create the impression. Portstewart is dominated by an immense convent school on a cliff, and the stone cross on the roof is visible everywhere, giving the place an oddly Catalonian air. Halfway along the promenade, however, there's a cenotaph commemorating those who died in the world wars; and the pugnacious stone Tommy on top, vigorously bayoneting the sea wind, seems to repudiate the cross which predates him. The memorial plaque lists both Catholic and Protestant names, and some which might be either, yet I can't help feeling that the stone soldier is a bloke from the East End of London.

This is one of the places where 'the Troubles seem far away'. Security is slack; the Taigs keep a low profile; UVF rules OK. (It doesn't, actually; RUC rules.) Even so, that yellow glow to the west at night is not, as some would have it, the glow of Derry but the glow of Magilligan with its arc lights and watchtowers. And there are slogans on every wall. My own favourite, because of its weird poetry, is Ned Carson's: *We shall never forsake the blue skies of our Ulster for the grey mists of an Irish Republic.* This has now

Derek Mahon

been painted over, but I'm glad to have the opportunity of recalling it here, since it reflects one aspect of Ulster Protestant pathology, the querulous recidivism. A traditional French platitude describes Germany as *un beau pays mal habité*, and the same is true of the North. One recent Sunday, a fine October day, I walked the length of Portstewart Strand. The surfing young skated in on the breakers. A low-slung car snarled past, pirate radio blaring, crunching mussel shells and obliterating tide marks with its tyres. On the boot was painted, by oil transfer, a Confederate flag, no doubt in imitation of something seen in a rock movie. I found this significant, with a significance probably not understood by the artist. His instinct was right, however; he wanted to make a defiant gesture, and he had found an appropriate idiom. When the car got stuck in the sand, its wheels churning, one offered no assistance. A light aircraft, privately owned, patrolled the beach at a height of a hundred feet, backwards and forwards, backwards and forwards, its shadow briefly patronizing each upturned face.

The North supports a prosperous bourgeoisie out of all proportion to its real assets. Where does the money come from in a society where security has long since replaced textiles and shipbuilding as the largest industry? Presumably from security. Peaked caps are everywhere, incongruously dignifying the most unlikely people. So many policemen (and policewomen), so many part-time soldiers, prison warders, security guards, car park attendants, porters, janitors and rat-catchers, each with a peaked cap. Last year there was an unemployed young man, not very bright, who stood outside shops, their self-appointed security man, to look you up and down and let you pass. He, too, wore a peaked cap. Where he is now I don't know; but sometimes he appears to me as the spirit of the place, the *genius loci* in a peaked cap. I imagine a hypothetical future in which everyone has departed. The Catholics have all moved south or gone to the States; the Protestants have gone to England, or Canada, or Australia. A stiff breeze through the broken windows scatters antique *Newsletter*s across the carpets of the Northern Counties Hotel. Rats infest the kitchen; Fingal sleeps his last sleep, half submerged in the no longer heated swimming pool, trailed by driftwood and empty matchboxes. A light aircraft, privately owned, rusts on the strand. There is no sign of life. Nothing happens here, and maybe nothing ever happened. And then, in the

The Coleraine Triangle

morning silence, I hear footsteps, and my friend the *genius loci*, in his peaked cap, takes up a new post outside a revolving door. He looks me up and down and lets me pass.

1979

Dublin in the Sixties

I first set eyes on Jeremy Lewis, the author of *Playing for Time*, in October 1961. He was coming down Dawson Street wearing a large false red beard and I thought, 'What a twit!' In those days half the undergraduate population of Trinity seemed to be English, most of them the chinless-wonder variety, much given to shouting, vomiting and whimsical affectations like the false beard. But whereas some were twits, there were happily many intelligent and likeable persons among them; and of these (despite the beard, which he soon discarded) Lewis was one. No chinless wonder he: as a glance at his cover photo will show, he has chin enough for two or three. Chins of this kind are supposed to indicate strength of character and firmness of purpose, attributes Lewis firmly disclaims; yet some resolution must have been involved in putting together the present memoir. The raffishness is here, and the atmosphere of conscious privilege. Whether he really 'gets' Dublin is another question.

I should declare an interest. Jeremy Lewis has been a friend of mine since those days, and a figure bearing my name makes four appearances in the text, three of them friendly enough, one potentially libellous; but even the libellous one is qualified by 'or so the story had it', so perhaps there is nothing in it for me. More interesting are his portraits of other contemporaries like ffenella, 'a handsome, strong-featured girl in a corduroy coat, with auburn hair, an exciting-looking bosom and in one hand a copy of *The Tin Drum*', with whom our hero falls gauchely in love; and of well-known 'characters' like the retired judge who, his last day on the bench, 'had condemned a man to death for stealing a bike, so achieving a lifetime's ambition of donning the dreadful black cap'.

En route to Dublin for the first time from his Sussex home (Euston-Holyhead-Dun Laoghaire), the author falls in with an Irishman in a knobbly white jersey. 'Trinity, eh?' chuckles this travelling

Dublin in the Sixties

companion. 'By God, they'll have your guts for garters!' His first impression of Dublin, as it was a half-century ago, seems to confirm this rackety promise: 'After the sobriety of London, Dublin seemed wonderfully seedy and raffish; for all its 18th-century elegance, the city had something rotten and rancid about it, as though it were built upon a compost of straw and dead rats and old tweed jackets and unmentionable alcoholic drinks.' But this is no reprise of Donleavy or Cronin. Apart from a single visit to the Brazen Head, the city Lewis discovered was one of quiet suburbs and respectable digs.

I might, in recompense for 'so the story had it', reproach him with not discovering Dublin at all. But his obvious Englishness must have been against him there; and he clearly loved Ireland, for the right reasons. A screening of *Mise Éire*, and 'the plangent, heart-rending music of Seán Ó Riada', did funny things to him and, taken with intoxicating doses of Yeats, Synge and Joyce, 'had the schizophrenic effect of giving me a strong if vicarious sympathy for Irish Republicanism, while at the same time regretting that so congenial and familiar a country was no longer "one of us", at least as far as formal politics were concerned'.

He records an instructive visit to the Aran Islands: 'I assumed, in my patronizing, ignorant way, that few of the islanders had been to Galway, let alone Dublin or England, for their distinctive handmade clothes and shoes, their unusual bony looks and their quiet gentle speech seemed to set them apart even in the West of Ireland, as though they were a protected species on some kind of Celtic reservation. To my surprise I found that many of the old-timers to whom I had been speaking in slow and measured tones, wondering if they had heard of trains or aeroplanes or television sets, had, in fact, spent most of their working lives in Boston or New York, returning in old age to the islands they had left in their teens.'

Only half of the book is set in Ireland. Alternating chapters deal with life in England or travels abroad, which makes for a more rounded autobiography, besides setting the Dublin experience in a larger context. Before going to Trinity he worked briefly in advertising, but came a cropper by disclosing a preference for Dickens over Marshall McLuhan.

Student travel in the sense that we know it began in the 1960s, and Lewis was quick off the mark; but his chapters on hitching to

Derek Mahon

Greece and Greyhound Busing around America suffer from a straining after laughs. The joke is generally on himself, the Englishman Abroad; yet I could have wished for more original observation and less of the rib-tickling hilarity. Perhaps the problem lies in the fact that he never seems to travel alone, always in a protective pack. He looks better in Paris, drinking with John Montague; or back in London, with the present writer in Ward's Irish House, a pub which no longer exists. There we met (my fourth and last mention) a pleasant Galwayman called Alan C. Breeze, who was something of a poet. Lewis gives him his due, citing 'Tshombe's Lament', about the Irish UN force in Katanga. Alan C. Breeze, not his real name, died alone in a frozen attic in Camden Town in 1969. It's good to see him remembered here.

A Ghostly Rumble among the Drums

As if to mark its decline from the great days, Trinity took the curious step of appointing the present writer its first 'Writer Fellow' for the academic year 1985-86. I was given 'rooms' the size of a matchbox — which I seldom used, having found a flat in Anglesea Road; also the use of an office in the School of English, overlooking the Provost's Garden. I was to act as 'Writer in Residence', teach 'creative writing', encourage the infants, and generally make myself available. It worked out fine in fact and, thanks to Rita, I actually got paid. Rita as in Lewis Gilbert's brilliant film *Educating Rita* (1983). This was made in and around the College, and Trinity earmarked its share of the dosh for the new Writer Fellowship scheme. The job title was a little puzzling, since it seemed to imply that the real Fellows of the College either didn't or couldn't write, which could hardly be true, now could it; and, as always in these situations, there was reciprocal puzzlement as to my role, with High Table folk wondering quizzically who was this writer fellow and what did he actually *do*. What I actually did, aside from writing and 'teaching', was to re-live in imagination a previous era, the early sixties, when we were undergraduates and often behaved like idiots. I remembered, for example, crashing the Trinity Ball and lying on the lawn in Front Square as dawn broke, listening to the birds while the legitimate dancers paraded out arm-in-arm through Front Gate to breakfast in Jury's of Dame Street or the Red Bank.

The College remained unchanged in many respects, though whether the same is true today I'm not so sure. A poster would announce, 'Dublin University Ladies' Boat Club: Bad Taste Party, Islandbridge: How Low Can You Sink?', and I would be chucklingly back in my own undergraduate years when parties of all kinds were the order of the day and night. Everyone drank as if it was going out of style, at a time when a pint cost 'one-and-six' or so, a bottle of plonk ten bob, and a bottle of hooch two quid. Much

Derek Mahon

time was spent in O'Neill's, the Bailey (the *old* Bailey), the Old Stand and Jammet's Back Bar, no longer there. Drunkenness, in some circles, was not only commonplace but more or less obligatory; conspicuous sobriety was frowned upon. Nor, contrary to tradition, was it us natives who were the most dedicated practitioners (though we kept abreast) but the Sloane Rangers, the tough fops with their silk scarves and snarling red two-seaters. This lot, public school men who weren't bright enough for Oxford or Cambridge, and posh gels not tall enough for the Brigade of Guards, created noise out of proportion to their numbers, bawling 'Charles!' and 'Celia!', *Brideshead*-style, and revving their little roadsters — but you know all that. What you may not know is that some, a handful of belated Bright Young Things, are still in circulation — to be found, little changed, in rackety venues like the Chelsea Arts Club; a 'Fulham Wanderer' will often wear a stringy Trinity tie, as if in mourning for lost youth. By 1985 the air of conscious privilege and London *chic* was already a thing of the past — or rather, the most privileged were now the offspring of the Dublin middle class, not English toffs and residual Anglo-Irish *gratin* as in our time.

Work? I hardly did a hand's turn in four years. Except for Alec Reid, Con Leventhal and others you could count on the fingers of one hand, if you had learnt to count, the faculty were so boring then that exhausted revellers, unshaven and hollow-eyed, some still in dressing-gown and slippers if they lived in Rooms, would snore to themselves in a fractious manner throughout morning lectures. Sometimes lecturers themselves would succumb to ennui or hysteria, like the Philosophy don of advanced years who introduced us to Kant. Gazing out of a window at New Square, trying to summarize the *Critique of Pure Reason*, he paused and gradually, quite gently, started shaking with silent laughter as if at some cosmic joke, which perhaps it was. He smacked his thigh, leered at us, laughed bitterly aloud — a prolonged, self-renewing, slightly crazy laugh, what Beckett calls the *risus purus*, 'the laugh laughing at the laugh', in which we presently joined — and trailed helplessly from the room.

Trinity, in those days, wasn't much about work, though quite a lot of reading got done. The word meant different things. To the question, 'What are you reading?', one might have replied, depending on context, 'Honor Maths', 'the racing page', or even, in exceptional circumstances, *The Decline and Fall of the Roman Empire*.

A Ghostly Rumble among the Drums

The old circular Reading Room, presided over by the good-natured Harry Boveneiser (the name was of 18th-century Rhenish Palatine origin), seemed as much a social focus as a locus of serious study. Packed to the doors like a fashionable restaurant, it was used partly as a pick-up joint. Girls dressed up then to go into College, the cobbles playing hell with their high heels. Men dressed up too, sort of, except for slobs like myself who wore the same sweater and jeans for four years. Front Square was like a Dior catwalk, and the two sexes sat in the Reading Room with blurry volumes before them, sizing up the talent out of the corners of their eyes. The air crackled with sexual electricity. On one occasion a man's voice asked loudly and unchivalrously, 'Gloria Shawe-Taylor' (or something), 'are you playing footsie with me?' Sometimes, if 'readers' got out of hand, Harry had to double as a bouncer.

'Rooms' then were available only to men — or 'gentlemen' as we were called, without obvious irony, by porters and skips. The skips, of whom the most famous was Larry Kelly, a thoughtful figure who would not have been out of his depth in diplomatic circles, brought us pitchers of hot water each morning, emptied the ashtrays, and silently pocketed whatever modest gratuity might be lying on the kitchen table — the gratuity indicating that a guest had spent the night. It was these shrewd, tolerant men, in their navy-blue jackets and jockey caps, who really ran the College. Larry, my own skip for a year, knew everything that went on, and the Provost had him in for a glass of Jameson each Friday evening to get the lowdown on the week's events. When Larry died a very decent obituary notice appeared in *The Irish Times*, to be followed by a letter of appreciation from an American scholar who had spent a sabbatical year in Rooms.

Some of our contemporaries have distinguished themselves in the 'real world', some in private life; and some, alas, are no longer with us. Of those literati who have remained active, many started in Players' Theatre or *Icarus* magazine, published each term and edited in rotation by the writing crowd, a few of whom went on to publish 'seriously' in Dublin proper, London and elsewhere. We look back now on our youthful efforts with horror and shame, as well we might: no question of Swift's 'What a genius I had then!' No, what we had then — Brendan, Rudi, Michael 'n' Edna, Deborah de Vere White and the late, still unappreciated Ronnie Wathen —

was time and leisure to make our first mistakes and perhaps to learn from them. Our four undergraduate years, unlike the urgent three elsewhere, developed in us a slower pace of thought (too slow perhaps), a respect for reverie and the *longue durée*, which is one of the luxuries of the artistic life. John McGahern, asked what he would do with an Arts Council grant, is said to have replied, 'Stare out of the window', and we did a lot of that. Dublin then was full of people staring out of windows or into pint glasses. Not any more: the so-called 'Celtic Tiger' years, coinciding with a revised climate, have banished slowth, silence and rich inconsequence to the mists of time in the interests of greater 'productivity' and enhanced anxiety levels. People are getting up at six in the morning, for heaven's sake. The College is now a 'campus' and we're no longer graduates but 'alumni': where is the pride? The hyphen and semi-colon are in danger. What price the life-enhancing inactivity of yore, its benefits evident only in the longer term?

It was fun, too much fun perhaps. Things turned *fairly* serious, even for us, with the approach of finals — from which, Dr Owen Sheehy-Skeffington warned us, we would never quite recover. He proved to be right, except that it wasn't finals themselves that were traumatic so much as leaving Trinity, which had become, for many of us, a home from home. To be back again twenty years later, too old now to die young, posing as some sort of temporary academic, gave rise to existential problems at first, to do with self-definition and an alarming sense that, despite having lived for years in London, I'd only been away for a term or two. I liked it when the students called me by my first name; but, try as I might, deep down I knew I was a young man no longer, despite appearances. I'd sit in the Senior Common Room with other fogies, read the *TLS* and *The Spectator* and, refusing the port, sip my after-dinner coffee, thinking of Scott Fitzgerald's 'Echoes of the Jazz Age': 'Now . . . we summon the proper expression of horror as we look back at our wasted youth. Sometimes, though, there is a ghostly rumble among the drums, an asthmatic whisper in the trombones . . . and it all seems rosy and romantic to us who were young then, because we will never feel quite so intensely about our surroundings any more.'

1986

Icarus in the Ignorance Age

It wasn't expected to fly long, hence the name; but here we are, still aloft. Reading a recent *Icarus* I'm struck by similarities to, and differences from, the magazine we knew in the early 1960s. Nobody writes sentences like that now, for a start; pedantries of that sort, and semi-colons, have gone the way of fountain pens and typewriters. We could be racy, but our very typefaces were more formal in the hot-metal days. The new one I'm looking at is handsomely produced and evidently innocent of misprints. (The author of this birthday greeting was, and remains, the world's worst proof-reader.) We were quite good at misprints, as I recall, and made a point of having several in each issue. In fact I'd like to take this opportunity, if it's not too late, to correct a certain typo in the one I edited (No. 38, December 1962), where Deborah de Vere White's 'casings of husk' appeared as 'casings of *hush*', and please don't get it wrong this time. (She didn't speak to me for quite a while after that . . .) Maybe this dazzling new efficiency is a feature of the Knowledge Age, computers and so on. We of the Ignorance Age (see *Trinity Tales*, Lilliput, ed. Balfour, Howes *et al*, 2009) could be slapdash at times, but there were those who contributed quite good stuff, and some of these went on to become 'real' writers: Brendan of course, Mike Longley, Edna Broderick, Cheli Duran, Timothy Webb and Jeremy Lewis.

Cheli was a gifted American young woman, of emigré Spanish Republican background, who seems to have given up the poetry at some point; I never see her name in print, though that's not necessarily the same thing. Mike Longley still tells the story of how the present writer, 'short and cocky', introduced himself with the words, 'Are you Longley? Can I borrow your typewriter?' I'd been aware of him, two years ahead of me, at school in Belfast, where he combined poetry and rugby, but sixth-formers take no notice of fourth-formers. I've just re-read (No. 38) Tim Webb's

Derek Mahon

poem 'Lucretius' and am still impressed. (Haven't seen him for years.) Jeremy, slightly younger, now a Consulting Editor at *The Literary Review*, returned to London after graduation and worked for various publishers. He has himself published, among other things, a memoir of those days and an extremely readable life of Cyril Connolly. A name we don't see now is that of the great R. J. (Ronnie) Wathen (like Hiawathan), another Englishman, who published several remarkable slim volumes with the Dolmen Press and elsewhere — *Bricks, Stones, My Shame in Crowds* — but made no attempt to promote the stuff, with the result that he is at the moment largely, and undeservedly, forgotten. I've long had a sort of Hopkins theory, that some of the best work away in relative or even complete obscurity and will one day be brought to light. Please reprint, from No. 38, Wathen's 'Straight Line'.

Regular contributors took turns to edit the magazine. My own issue was notable for a striking cover and a shockingly pretentious 'political' editorial from which I won't be quoting. The cover design, provided by a then fashionable *Observer* artist, showed the 'I' of 'Icarus' taking off like a moon rocket as Yuri Gagarin had done the previous year — a great coup, I thought. Eamonn McCann, to whom I showed a copy on a visit home to Belfast, disagreed. It enraged him. So shiny, so trendy, so phoney, so unlike the deliberately rough-looking radical stuff he and his mates favoured; and he was right. It was all production values, and failed even in that regard ('hush' instead of 'husk'). Alec Reid, our chairman and guru, disliked the general tone for the opposite reason: too *engagé*, as we used to say, though its politics were only a gesture.

Around this time I met the well-known Ulster poet W. R. (Bertie) Rodgers, a BBC features writer, then in his fifties, who came over from London as a guest of the Phil to speak to a paper on Louis MacNeice. Bertie's stepdaughter Nina Gilliam was a college contemporary. A strange, ironic beauty with a tongue that would clip tin (Belfast expression), she went on to work for a feminist group in New York. Nina alerted Hedli, MacNeice's widow, who lived in Kinsale, so Hedli came too and scared the wits out of everyone. Bertie gave *Icarus* a poem. We felt we were meeting the great, and perhaps lost sight a little of our function as an *undergraduate* mag, with all the gaucherie and head-scratching that implies.

'Notes on Contributors': feedback. Do you really want to know?

Icarus in the Ignorance Age

It's like reading reviews and, believe me, that's no fun, though often helpful. (Why do they always assume you think your own stuff is terrific?) What's this about feedback@tcd.ie? The Knowledge Age again? Our feedback took place by word of mouth, and often in pubs. The pubs fed us pints and feedback too, in the form of advertising revenue. O'Neill's of Suffolk Street, the Wicklow Lounge, the Bailey and Davy Byrne's featured regularly front and back. I see there are no ads in the recent issue. No ads? You're spoilt, you lot, with your grants and your subsidies. Or did we have them too? I don't remember . . . Oh, and Elvery's the sports shop. Hodges Figgis of course. Switzer's. Gaj's. *The Irish Times*. Also, in No. 38, Hedli's Kinsale restaurant, the Spinnaker, then just newly opened and still there fifty years on.

It wasn't all poetry. There were short stories, though nobody seemed to read them; and book reviews, often quite cheeky. What a bunch of know-alls we were! There was no in-fighting though. Convinced we were the best, we swanned around in the sure knowledge that the writing life, now begun, would be for ever a bed of roses; learning later . . . There was a time, I've noticed, when *Icarus* lost its way, failed to appear, appeared rarely and in altered formats. But we seem to be in flight once more. Alec's original modest vision has survived, prevailed. Even in the sixties with their callow pretensions, my own included, *Icarus* was the voice of a community that knew how to waste time and think about the important things. Most had no intention of being writers. They just wanted to scribble a bit, and that's all right; in fact, that's better than ambition. As for the 'serious' ones, I for one remember long smoky afternoons in Rooms beneath cloudy skies and think of Yeats's line, 'The arts lie dreaming of the life to come.' Happy birthday.

2010

Anne Madden: A Retrospective

'I imagine,' says Anne Madden, 'most artists, whatever their medium, are trying to uncover or discover a reality beyond actuality, trying to make visible invisible aspects of the world. Of course many things that are real to us are invisible: imagination, feeling and consciousness itself which defines us as human, as well as the unconscious psyche which houses our dreams, symbols, intuition and instinct.' She is a poetic artist. Dreams, symbols and intuition are her themes; instinct, the quick flick of knowing what to do next, inscribes itself decisively in her work like a watermark. 'I use the image as an emotive charge,' she says, 'even when it becomes very abstracted . . . [and] the symbolic aspect of myth sometimes as a pretext, just as I use figuration, then abandon all narrative.' Yet narrative lingers, and a distinctive feature of her work is its transparency-in-opacity, its almost paraphrasable 'meaning'. It's not only 'about paint', as the saying goes, but about recognizable subjects of a more general nature. If sometimes formidable, it asks us in; often we can even tell what's going on (her titles help), though this is not to suggest that she isn't, above all, devoted to her raw materials. It would be a mistake to think of her as primarily a cerebral artist, for she is a very physical one: 'I want to not know,' she says. The canvases correspond to her height and reach; she lays them on the floor and moves around them. Watching her in her Dublin studio, or on documentary film, you notice how she handles them like life-size models. She works on a more than domestic scale. Deeply engaged in her materials, a friend to the saturated colour field, she identified once with the New York School of the fifties, conceded 'the autonomy of the medium', set aside illusion and anecdote but, crucially, 'retained the image', a frozen narrative. Her work is, in fact, quite autobiographical, and often refers explicitly to recent events and bereavements seen at a short distance in time. The megalith paintings of the seventies, for instance, based on the Stone Age

Anne Madden: A Retrospective

tombs of the Burren, Co Clare, 'seek out the symbolic order and hidden secrets of the . . . Burren of my youth'. These try to 'find or extract light from the dark places of grief'. A lick of paint is worth a thousand words.

Not everywhere is dark with grief by any means. The delightful early pictures 'Meadow with Sun' and 'Blue Landscape' (both 1958) seem bright with the summery youthful ease that precedes the difficulties of later life (but not the proleptic crimson sphere top left in each, dripping like a severed head in the second of these). Even her grimmest episodes have an exuberant formal panache. An uncomplicated, high-definition daylight illuminates the 'poured paintings' of Burren rock formations done in the sixties — 'Land near Kilaboy' (oil and sand), 'Transformations' (both 1964) — the bony limestone of Clare lending itself to an almost scientific clarity. 'Stony hills poured over space,' says Betjeman in 'Ireland with Emily', thinking of the Burren ('far and foreign'). No living presence, it seems, disturbs the geological silence of this realm, and it's not until the *Megalith* series of the seventies that human drama begins. The stage curtains (acrylic on cotton duck) are sheets and ribbons of openable stone. Dolmens, menhirs, stone circles and passage graves, an Easter Island in the Atlantic, provide these powerful arrangements with their structural rationale, but they are at a remove from literal representation, being primarily about colour and form. We meet for the first time her signature midnight blue, an ultimate ultramarine gazing starlessly back at us through the funerary uprights: 'ignorance, silence and the motionless azure', as Beckett put it. These monumental blocks, stove red or chimney black, act perpendicularly as the mystic blurs act horizontally in Mark Rothko's classic works. 'One doesn't read his tiers and veils of paint primarily as form,' says Robert Hughes of Rothko. 'They are vehicles for colour sensation.' Not quite the reverse is true of Madden's standing stones. They are most definitely form, a celebration of form, a formal principle made paint; but the restrained colour blocks (no question of 'sensation' in the popular sense), both bold and subtle, are forceful and imposing as only restraint can be. Tension, yes, but there is no conflict between *disegno* and *colore*; each is an achieved, authoritative object containing in itself, as Coleridge said a poem should, 'the reason why it is so, and not otherwise'. ('Authoritative' is hardly the word though, since these are questions as much as statements.) To adopt Clive Bell's phrase, they are 'significant form', a sign language like language itself; but that intense midnight ultramarine, once seen, is never forgotten. As in Rothko, there is mystery, a rich asceticism, but mystery with a sharper edge and a clearer vision.

'Iam dies alibi,' wrote the younger Pliny to Tacitus, *'illic nox omnibus noctibus nigrior densiorque; quam tamen faces multae variaque lumina solvebant'*: 'Elsewhere there was daylight by this time, but (we) were still in darkness, blacker and denser than any ordinary night, which (we) relieved by lighting torches and various kinds of lamp' (tr. Radice, Penguin Classics). He is describing Pompeii on 25 August, AD 79, the day after the eruption. 'At last,' he writes later, 'the darkness thinned and dispersed into smoke or cloud; then there was genuine daylight, and the sun actually shone out, but yellowish as it is during an eclipse. We were terrified to see everything changed, buried deep in ashes like snowdrifts.' He and his mother have made their escape and are staring back from the road. There were no reports from those trapped in the city, many in their homes, but the fatal experience can be and has been imagined, its artisan houses and airy villas swiftly inundated by cooling pumice and volcanic ash. It was reading Pliny's description of the calamity that gave Anne Madden the idea for the magnificent Pompeiian group she produced in the early eighties, exchanging Clare for a Graeco-Roman setting. This was not an entirely new departure, since these paintings and drawings came as a natural extension of the megalith motif. 'By then,' she says, 'theory went out of the window, literally, with a series of window forms made of colour bands, thresholds between interior and exterior space.' These colour bands, and the partitioning of the canvas, are a favourite device, indeed almost her autograph. If we look again at the diptychs and triptychs of the seventies with titles like 'Megalith' (1974), 'Alignment' (1975) and 'Menhir' (1978), we can see ground plan and elevation taking shape: strong rectilinear uprights, ember red and midnight blue, bisected or trisected by vertical inset 'pages' of eloquent 'text', tonally pure, silent and motionlessly azure. These manuscript 'pages', glimpses of infinity framed by classically formal columns on either side, frames within frames, increasingly come to resemble windows and doors. Through a thin blue slash in 'Alignment', an initial chord which is not exactly a quotation but perhaps derived from Matisse's 'Porte-fenêtre à Collioure' (1914),

Anne Madden: A Retrospective

almost shyly introducing the idea of an opening, we leave or enter the house of historical memory. 'Door into the Dark' (1982), the title borrowed from Seamus Heaney, picks up the theme, frames the aperture with doorposts, lintel and threshold, blows smoke, cuts with vertical median strip-lighting, and we're looking at the inside of a garage door with exhaust fumes and a slice of the sky beyond. If we're looking in, as in the Heaney poem, we're looking at a Sibyl's cave or a tabernacle, but I don't think we are; I think we're inside trying to look out. It's we who are in the dark, trapped in the garage, shed or house. Those fumes are disturbing; something is very wrong. Either a car engine has been left running or there's a fire somewhere — outside perhaps, smoke trickling in at the ever-so-slightly open door: a rich and alarming image composed of sombre, shifting blues and greys, one crack of light admitting narrative and paraphrase. It's a short step from here to Pompeii.

Frances Yates researched 'the art of memory', a mnemonic technique practised by hermetic philosophers of the *cinquecento*, based on the idea of the soul as a house, a metaphor later adopted by C. G. Jung; and Gaston Bachelard, in *The Poetics of Space*, studied the poetic evidence for rooms as 'abodes for an unforgettable past . . . the topography of our intimate being' (tr. Maria Jolas). Chapter nine, 'The Dialectics of Outside and Inside', incorporates the suggestion that a door presents 'the temptation to open up the ultimate depths of being' and imagines, 'incarnated in the door . . . a little threshold god'. The thought was familiar to the ancient world: in Roman times the god was called Janus, he of the two faces looking before and after — otherwise Gennaro, patron saint of Naples, of openings, doors and corridors. 'How concrete everything becomes in the world of the spirit,' says Bachelard. Menhirs and megaliths, dolmens and passage graves, abodes of souls, transform themselves under Madden's hand and hazel gaze into the open graves of Pompeiian houses. The eruption has taken place, and now we have the irruption into these private spaces, each decorated with mural art, of the boiling volcanic ash described by Pliny.

She concentrates on one house in particular, perhaps the most famous, the House of the Mysteries, with its spectacular, life-size shining frescoes of gold and black on a ground of cinnabar red. Apart from the fine proportions of her interiors, squared-off and faintly 'baroque', with their remote echo of Leonardo's architectural perspectives, there are, so to speak, depths without perspective, flat surfaces haunted by anecdote. There is a ghost of patrician reserve, even a gnostic hauteur, in these distinctive panels of darkness and light so reminiscent of long-ago Georgian tenements; but if we take these memory boxes as life-size too we are visiting the sort of modest artisan houses most people used to inhabit in Dublin and Belfast. The connection is not immediately obvious, but becomes so when we remember the 'elegiac' megalith stones referring, in part, to events in Northern Ireland during the seventies. Here too we have the remembered dead, overcome by disaster, their private space invaded, homes desecrated, lives destroyed.

The original frescoes, done by a Campanian painter working from Greek models, depict the initiation of a young woman into the Dionysian mysteries (whence the name of the house), and Madden dwelt at length on this figure, studying her posture in a series of graphite drawings. Read to and scourged, the weeping girl is 'a metaphor of enlightenment and illumination'. Anne herself speaks quite naturally of art as 'vision' and 'revelation', spiritual in its impulse and mysterious in its force. 'Smearing mud on cloth', in Hughes' trenchant phrase, painting is primitive magic, a transformative alchemy in its effort to transmute 'its primary material into another reality', says Anne; even factory paint, like the globe itself, comprises 'earths' and minerals, some relatively uncommon. A highly literate and articulate artist, she has noticed that quantum theory shares with the Upanishads 'an order which links everything to everything else, us to the stars for instance'. *Tat tvam asi*: that too are you. The universe is a woven text, a web of particles; space and time are inseparable. She recognizes 'a dynamic continuous present opening into luminous spaces I can enter and move through to a beyond, the void; the void is my canvas'.

One luminous space that now opens for her is the garden, another the sea. The two announce themselves simultaneously with the moonlit triptych 'Night Paths' (1988), where a white wave breaks in a vigorous arc between two leafy midnight lanes. The illuminist 'Chemins éclairés', light shining out of darkness, belongs to the same year, as does 'Le Jardin'. The related 'Entrance to the House of the Tragic Poet', one more Pompeiian piece, was started at this time and finished two years later; meanwhile 'Le Bateau' (1989) and 'Night Garden' (1990) are in hand, the whole group aglow with deep greens and blues, dark leaves, bright steps and quiet immanence. The garden pictures, beautifully lit and easy on the eye, are among the most thrillingly restful and watchful things she's done. At a difficult time Beckett urged her to 'tackle her dark', as he had tackled his own. 'So I tried,' says Anne, 'to paint my way back to the studio, along the paths to a box of light' — a space she and her husband Louis le Brocquy shared for many years at Carros (Alpes Maritimes) before moving back to Ireland. That 'box of light' is a place of peace and work, a house of the soul Bachelard would have acknowledged. How concrete everything becomes.

With the Pompeii and garden series we stand a few steps from the subject, door or tree; with the Odyssey pictures we soar, startlingly, to a considerable height and, in a species of aerial photography, look directly down on a solitary boat at sea — the sea 'an image', says Anne, 'of the unconscious on which we sail'. The vertical sectioning of the canvas in now replaced by diagonals and vortices, rectilinear structure by a fast, dabbing, rotary action, monumentality by flux, *disegno* by *colore*, saturated fields of blue: a sea-change, literally, into 'something rich and strange'. Odysseus' boat, a vague skiff in most of the pictures, has the proportions of a ship's lifeboat in 'Le Bateau' and 'Transposition' (1995), seemingly unmanned or manned perhaps by that 'No One' who tricked the Cyclops. It lies down there athwart our line of vision between sand and water, sun and shadow, light and dark, not exactly Rimbaud's 'drunken' boat but evidently adrift, 'at sea', perhaps literally a 'life' boat. The swirling density of the picture surface, an extreme weather of violent storm and shocked respite, points up the lonely poignancy of the boat and the heroism of the voyage, one moment thrown about in the dark, next moment helplessly at rest in some transitional trough:

> *As idle as a painted ship*
> *Upon a painted ocean.*

The boat is usually at the centre of the composition, the eye of the storm, like a shaped consciousness peering up and back at us, a keyhole into the light. Take away that chink of light and we have the void, 'chaos and old night', a random universe of elemental forces. The boat and its double in 'Vortex' (1995) skirt a black hole

Derek Mahon

that looks like a 'black hole' in space; the crowded, dimly shining brushwork of 'De Profundis', the same year, bespeaks frantic supplication and a faint hope of relief. The quick, importunate strokes, paint laid on thick, the almost audible crush of turbulent souls, or so I read them, are fanned by an impersonal luminescence, the rich tactility of the chiaroscuro heartfelt and urgent. Darkness visible: ambient blue-black but somehow 'a dark white', as in the 'Addenda' to Beckett's *Watt*: 'The sky and the waste were of the same dark colour . . . the source of the feeble light diffused over this scene is unknown.' The boat itself perhaps, a white chip of thought in the cosmic confusion?

A reader of Mircea Eliade, she sees myth as a door into notional worlds. It helps to lie in the sea, out of season, in the floating world between Nice and Cap d'Antibes, away from the traffic on the N7, and watch a hazy sun shine down through the wings of a spread gull. This is the Baie des Anges, the Côte d'Azur of Bonnard, Matisse and many another drawn by the colour and light. Anne and Louis lived in the hills and colour fields of Provence proper. Icarus struck the sea, says Ovid, between Mykonos and Samos, but Madden's *Icarus* paintings take place, I think, in the Baie des Anges, where the flier and author Antoine de Saint-Exupéry vanished in July, 1944. 'I was the boat,' says Anne. '(It) grew wings to negotiate another dimension in space. Birds play the part of the artist here; for Saint-John Perse a migrating bird was a sort of seaplane or flying boat (*Oiseaux*, illus. Georges Braque, 1962), its life a perpetual quest; 'consuming solar energy like a plant, driven by two strokes to the spectral limits of flight', his bird 'seems close to losing its wings up there'. Madden's tough paraclete, gull or hawk, is seen at a distance but from below, already at the point of coming unstuck before dropping like a bolt from the blue. We can't look for long at death or the sun, said Rochefoucauld; but gold, the sun's representative on earth, can be contemplated at length. Think of the mosaic art of Byzantium, St Mark's Basilica, the Book of Kells, the work of Klimt. Madden too risks working in gold paint. The mud-yellow tesserae of 'Aran Field' (1957) prefigure this. Icarus' vast sun ('Transition', 1997) is a roaring globe of coppery gold, a permanent explosion of throbbing solar activity. Gold plays a part in the *Garden of Love* series (2001-2) and is the active principle in 'Winged Figure' (2004) and 'Aurora' (2005). Her angelic winged

Anne Madden: A Retrospective

figures share a genetic code with the Northern Lights of the *Aurora* series, a festival of cosmic creativity and renewal. Spun, fiery coils of electricity wave about in rag-painted space, as seen from the Wicklow hills or in transatlantic flight. What with its whirling, breezy hues and igneous exultation, it almost looks like the birth of a new planet.

She asks 'the old Berkeleian question: does an objective reality exist and, if so, what is its nature? Does it lie in fact and appearance or in an invisible order of things? And does the face of things hide or reveal this invisible order?' She is trying, she says, 'to make sense of being-in-the-world'. This is a philosophical task, but philosophy has always been a useful resource for artists, and it's a measure of her ambition that she should think in these terms. An alchemist, she has worked with the four elements (earth, fire, water and air in that order), but earth and air are her main coordinates, the elements Simone Weil identified with 'gravity' and 'grace', the sticking fast and the letting go, the weight of the past and the flight of the heart. A vicarious Icarus, author of durable images rooted in traditional symbol and myth, she has spread her wings and flown to aleatoric space: 'Icarus, an artist figure reaching for the out-of-reach and failing, dies into the immaterial . . . Art seeks the sun, the light, enlightenment, always out of reach.' Growing initially from a specific landscape, her work has taken flight into a variety of lyrical abstraction. Not only beautiful but sublime in Burke's sense of the word ('I want to not know,' says Anne), it nonetheless keeps faith with reality. Though still girlishly eager to 'bound off into the universe', she keeps her feet on the ground or perhaps on the threshold. Yves Bonnefoy, another poet of thresholds who has also lived in Provence, has a two-line poem that goes like this:

> *Tu as pris une lampe et tu ouvres la porte.*
> *Que faire d'une lampe, il pleut, le jour se lève.*

> You took up a lamp and now you open the door.
> What use is a lamp, it is raining, the day breaks.
> (tr. Kinnell and Pevear)

The Mystery Intact

A photograph, said Susan Sontag (*On Photography*, 1977), is 'not only an image (as a painting is an image), an interpretation of the real; it is also a trace, something directly stenciled off the real, like a footprint or a death mask. While a painting, even one that meets photographic standards of resemblance, is never more than the stating of an interpretation, a photograph is never less than the registering of an emanation.' Photography revives, she suggests, the primitive status of images: 'Our irrepressible feeling that it is something magical has a genuine basis. No one takes an easel painting to be in any sense consubstantial with its subject; it only represents or refers. But a photograph is not only like its subject; it is part of, an extension of the subject.' One might argue, of course, that paint, like any material thing, is ultimately consubstantial with human bodies. So too is light, as when St Matthew says the light of the body is in the eye. We may speak, in both cases, of 'an extension of the subject'; and it's in this sense that John Minihan's systematic record of Irish writers, *An Unweaving of Rainbows: Images of Irish Writers* (1998), like John Butler Yeats's graphic work a century ago, may be said to contribute to literature itself.

Irish literary photography too (both of and by the writers) goes back a hundred years, though not the full one-hundred-and-fifty; for we had no inspired innovator to capture James Clarence Mangan, say, as Félix Nadar and others captured Baudelaire — though, in *The Mangan Inheritance* (1979), the novelist Brian Moore tries to rectify this omission by having his protagonist Jamie Mangan, a young journalist, find a fictitious daguerreotype of his poetic ancestor, in a loft in Montreal — 'a portrait in a scrolled brass frame preserved under glass, a small, shimmering, mirror-bright picture on silver-coated copperplate. It measured about three inches by four and showed a man facing the camera, a head-and-shoulders portrait taken against a plain background . . . What made Mangan

The Mystery Intact

stare as though transfixed by a vision was that the face in the photograph was his own. He turned the daguerreotype over. On the back of the frame, written in a sloping looped script in the top right-hand corner, was the notation: (J. M., 1847?).'

But if there were no Irish commercial photographers to compare with the big European names, there were inspired amateurs — some of them writers themselves like Edith Somerville, Shaw and Synge. The authors of *The Real Charlotte* (1894) bring out the magic, indeed the alchemy, of the thing in their description of Christopher Dysart at work in his darkroom: 'There was no sound in the red gloom except the steady trickle of running water and the anxious breathing of the photographer. His long hands moved mysteriously in the crimson light among phials, baths and cases of negatives, while the uncanny smells of various acids and compounds thickened the atmosphere.'

Shaw, writing in 1885, ten years before his own first experiments with the camera, had already decided photography was in some respects superior to fine art: 'Artists are sticking to the old barbarous, difficult and imperfect processes of etching and portrait painting merely to keep up the value of their monopoly of the required skill. They have left the new, more complexly organized, and more perfect, yet simple and beautiful method of photography in the hands of tradesmen, sneering at it publicly and resorting to its aid surreptitiously. The result is that the tradesmen are becoming better artists than they, and naturally so; for where, as in photography, the drawing counts for nothing, the thought and judgment count for everything.'

Wilde, who understood the power of the image (think of *Dorian Gray*), was much photographed, notably during his American tour by the New York society portraitist Napoleon Sarony, whose twenty-seven studio shots of the great self-publicist have been frequently reproduced. Wilde sat too for the Julia Cameron studio; and Merlin Holland, in *The Wilde Album* (1997), published for the first time some remarkable late snaps of his grandfather taken in Rome, probably in the spring of 1900, with Wilde's own camera. Wilde himself wrote to a friend: 'My photographs are now so good that in my moments of mental depression I think that I was intended to be a photographer.'

Of the various Irish writer-photographers at the end of the 19th century, none achieved more lasting results than Synge, whose twenty-three surviving studies of life in the Aran Islands were eventually published as *My Wallet of Photographs* (Dolmen, 1971), arranged and introduced by Synge's niece Lilo Stephens. The author of *Riders to the Sea* and *The Aran Islands* used a Lancaster Instagraphic 'plate-and-bellows' camera of polished mahogany in a black leather case with eyeholes for lens and viewfinders, an apparatus now in the library of Trinity College, Dublin.

'Only a fadograph of a yestern scene' (*Finnegans Wake*). Joyce, though himself no photographer, was famously photographed at different stages of his life, usually by the most fashionable practitioners. Portraits of the artist abound — as precocious student, intense young man, *flâneur*, father, convalescent and sage. His striking looks helped, and his dandyism. Bow ties and waistcoats, gym shoes and walking sticks contributed to an indelible composite image, and even the tinted specs and eyepatches he wore to save his failing vision were somehow less functional than decorative. All this and more is evident in Gisèle Freund's late studies done in Paris. Surprisingly, given his interest in the 'ineluctable modality of the visible', Joyce didn't have much to say about photography as such, except in terms of popular culture: 'The *Bath of the Nymph* over the bed. Given away with the Easter number of *Photo Bits*. Splendid masterpiece in art colours . . . Three and six I gave for the frame.' Photo bits, like advertising jingles and music-hall songs, recur throughout *Ulysses*, often with voyeuristic undertones — pictures cut out of papers, those lovely seaside girls ('your head it simply swurls'). Bloom himself is a camera; to Gerty McDowell in the Nausicaa episode he is 'the gentleman opposite looking'. He is even a film camera; for his day, as Joyce describes it, is a home movie of the domestic city. Harry Levin speaks of 'cinematic montage' and 'the optical illusion of reality obtained from a continuity of discrete shots'; and we remember that Joyce was involved (1909) in Dublin's first cinema, the Volta, where too 'projections tended to slow down and at times stop altogether, suddenly arresting the action and suspending the characters in mid-air'. Photography as commercial landscape, moreover, is already widespread in Dublin of 1904: 'All kind of places are good for ads.'

Context is established in the *Unweaving of Rainbows* album with formal portraits of literary venues: the Shelbourne (its generational revolving door), Davy Byrne's 'moral pub', Doheny & Nesbitt's, and the old Pearl Bar, once a haunt of journalists. Finn's Hotel is here, where Nora Barnacle worked in youth; Hubert Butler's Maidenhall in Co Kilkenny, a generic portrait of a Georgian country house; and St Colman's (Church of Ireland) at Farahy, Co Cork, spiritual home of Elizabeth Bowen. Here too, appendices to Minihan's *Samuel Beckett* (1995; introduction by Aidan Higgins), are the Beckett homes in Kerrymount Avenue, Foxrock, and the Boulevard Saint-Jacques, where both the 'Cooldrinagh' name-plate and the Paris mailbox have extraordinary presence. Minihan is not a studio artist; consistent with his long London experience as a press photographer, a 'snapper' on the *Daily Mail* and the *Evening Standard*, his effects are generally extramural and extemporaneous.

Stephen Joyce, in dark specs like his grandfather, attends the unveiling of a plaque at 28 Campden Grove, Kensington ('Campden Grave', Joyce called it), where James and Nora briefly resided in 1931 in order to get married, 'for testamentary reasons', in England; while Edna O'Brien, with a Molly-esque gesture, smiles in furs from an upstairs window. Ulick O'Connor emerges from the National Library where Joyce and his cronies gathered. The London dimension expands to include three generations of MacNeice women, George Barker and Eddie Linden taking refreshment, and Michael Mannion, the modest 'Bard of Kensington', at work in his bachelor pad, a man-about-town's evening rig airing beside the kettle. John Ryan and Anthony Cronin are here, veterans of the first commemorative Bloomsday pilgrimage to the Sandycove tower in 1954; but it's a younger crowd who take up most space. One knows these people, the handsome and the ravaged, the gorgeous and the quaint, the beautiful and damned. A rainbow of personality is rewoven here; from all eyes — well, from most — shine soul and sensibility, and these shine back at them from a loving lens, a private and innocent eye.

The title, chosen by the publisher, is unfortunate. It derives from Keats: charm flies, Keats complains, at 'the mere touch of cold philosophy'. The 'woof and texture' of a rainbow, he says in an industrial metaphor, have been reduced to scientific data (perhaps he's thinking of Luke Howard's taxonomy of clouds) in 'the dull catalogue of common things':

Derek Mahon

> *Philosophy will clip an angel's wings,*
> *Conquer all mystery by rule and line,*
> *Empty the haunted air and gnomèd mine,*
> *Unweave a rainbow . . .*

To ascribe to Minihan a coldly scientific 'unweaving of rainbows' is peculiarly inappropriate. Alive with mysteries and haunted air, his work is no dull catalogue, and even his 'common things' are made uncommonly mysterious ('sublimely gloomy', in the words of one critic) by his devoted attention. See his Athy pictures, *Shadows from the Pale* (Secker, 1995), especially the 'Wake of Katy Tyrrell' series and fortuitous curiosities like the decrepit 'Armstrong Siddeley Motor Hearse', itself a corpse, with its sphinx radiator cap. His method is to know the woof and texture, rule and line, but leave the mystery intact. Unlike, say, *The New Yorker*'s Richard Avedon, whose ultra cool, harshly lit and decontextualized theatre people Avedon calls 'symbolic of themselves' ('I'm never really implicated; I don't have to have any real knowledge'), Minihan is intensely personal, participatory and idiosyncratic. This is what so distinguished the Beckett book, where the great clinician is clearly in a humorous relation to the camera, so that serendipitous occasions present themselves spontaneously: the patient cup, the gnarled hands, the walking-away shot from behind.

When we think of great portrait photographers, among the names that spring to mind are those of André Kertész and Bill Brandt (Kertész's Eisenstein, Brandt's Pound and Graves, his Dylan and Caitlin Thomas); Rollie McKenna; Jane Bown's work for *The Observer*. Minihan's best results resemble theirs in their human warmth; more than that, he snaps immortal souls. Toting a Nikon F3, motor drive, a range of lenses from 21mm to 200mm, he has established himself as one of the finest snappers of his generation; and his work is a vivid extension of the literature it illustrates. His famous shots of the famous — Beckett, Edna O'Brien, Gloria Swanson, Ray Charles, Joseph Brodsky, Diana Spencer, the list is endless — are famous in Ireland and elsewhere. Many of his subjects are literary or artistic figures, but he's by no means exclusively, or even primarily, a 'literary' artist. Life above literature: like the Athy series, recording the works and days of an Irish country town (his home town in Co Kildare), his Irish Arts Center photos, taken in

The Mystery Intact

the course of a week in New York, New Jersey and Philadelphia, are concerned with real people untouched by 'celebrity'. What they have in common is that all immigrated from Ireland in the early or middle decades of the 20th century, which means they are now mostly 'senior citizens', in years if not disposition. There are no young people here, actuarially speaking. Sorry, young people, but older folks are important and interesting too, as you will discover in time.

First up is Sister Victor Waters, 104 this year, of Tenafly, New Jersey. A native of Galway, she arrived in New York in 1925 and spent three years as a governess in Chicago before joining the Franciscan Sisters, with whom she has remained. Minihan loves nuns and knuckles. Sister Victor, obviously as bright as a button despite her venerable age, leans over in attentive conversation, one well-worn hand on the arm of her chair. Consider that hand. Bony and bumpy, it resembles the gnarled, arboreal hands in the Beckett series. A working and giving hand, may it never waver. The eyes and mouth speak volumes. A hundred years' experience: Coolidge was in the White House when she stepped off the boat. Rose Cosgrave too, though younger, shares those hands. She uses them to hold up, in the photograph, a framed photograph of herself as a beautiful young woman with strong features and a modest, resolute smile. This one lives up almost literally to Minihan's favourite description of photography as 'a mirror with a memory'. The picture of the younger Rose is undoubtedly black-and-white; that of the present Rose is certainly black-and-white, which Minihan prefers to colour. This exhibition, like previous ones, is entirely in black-and-white, as a glance will show. Why? *'Everything* is in colour,' he points out, meaning most contemporary imagery (cinema, TV, internet) but also the 'real' world. 'Colour is all about *now,*' he says, meaning ephemeral. 'The solemnity of black-and-white makes you really *look*'; and so we do.

Writing in *The Recorder* (Spring, 1998), the journal of the American Irish Historical Society, about what he calls the Irish Republic's recent 'identity crisis', Darcy O'Brien observed: 'Old friends and family are left behind; familiar experiences of the past recede. Once known for her poets, revolutionary zeal, and piety amid poverty, Ireland is now celebrated in the pages of *Time* as the Celtic Tiger . . .' No such crisis seems to afflict the *American* Irish

Derek Mahon

community, which (except perhaps for the 'undocumented') is secure in its proud sense of identity. To put this show together the Arts Center worked with four other community groups, including the Aisling Center in Yonkers and the Commodore Barry Club in Philadelphia.

The Irish, says the novelist Mary Gordon, 'have always in the back of their eye a vision of the ideal', and this is magically borne out by these portraits. The eyes, looking *beyond* the real world, retain ghosts of a previous world, Ireland itself. Everyone has been 'here before' in the folkloric sense. Many began their American lives with minimum-wage jobs in the service industries, started families, and joined local County-based organizations to strengthen the home connection. Some have never gone back, though it must be a rare one who has never *looked* back. Some have been back to visit only to find the old country, like all old countries, changed by the tiger economy we used to hear so much about. These people, once Irish, are now American, and have been for decades. Just look at them. Whatever age they are, you'd think they're a bunch of youngsters. Eyes twinkle, as Irish eyes are supposed to do; vitality and warmth abound. Look at Pat Tominey, a kid of sixty-seven (but a strapping kid). John snapped him first in his NYPD patrol car in 1972, and again this year. Born in Armagh, Pat sailed in 1958 and spent years with 'New York's finest', working the 18th Precinct on West 54th Street between 8th and 9th Avenues, near the Arts Center indeed, in what used to be known, in tougher times, as 'Hell's Kitchen'. He's seen it all, but the years have done little to his appearance except to grey his hair.

Looking at these photographs, I wonder what the subjects themselves will make of the show. Will it reinforce the sense of solidarity? Will it remind them of a shared history, grounded initially in hard times so many years ago? John Montague, born in Brooklyn in 1929, therefore roughly their contemporary, remembers his father, from Co Tyrone, trying to keep the household together in 'a crumbling brownstone' amid 'a clatter of garbage cans':

> *Christmas in Brooklyn,*
> *the old El flashes by.*
> *A man plods along pulling*
> *his three sons on a sleigh;*

The Mystery Intact

soon his whole family
will vanish away.

My long lost father
trudging home through
this strange, cold city,
its whirling snows,
unemployed and angry
living off charity . . .

That was then; this is now. 'In the new ontology,' says Jay McInerney, a mere child in his fifties, 'nothing exists until it has been reproduced on film stock; or videotape.' Well, here we are on film stock. But far from reducing the existence, the real life, of those portrayed, these pictures enhance it by sun-writing them into the record. The black-and-white solemnity Minihan recommends gives these people historic status. Not only are they your grandmother, your aunt, your father, brother or sister, they are up there now with the immortals, captured for ever as they were one day in April. 'The illiterates of the future,' said László Moholy-Nagy in *New Vision* (1935), 'will be those who know nothing of photography rather than those ignorant of writing.' Photography: 'sun-writing'. Unknown to formal history, these faces will be reproduced in books for generations, framed in the mirrors of memory not as illustrations but as people who once really were, like those of Matthew Brady in their day; and that's the best kind of celebrity.

The Pied Piper

The poetry of Joseph Brodsky is both addictive and exasperating. Addictive because, hooked but never satisfied, the reader keeps going back for more; exasperating because it eludes every attempt to pin it down. What was he saying? Russians are quick to remind you that the October Revolution was no sudden break with a feudal past, that the previous twenty years had seen significant changes: a new liberalism, industrial advance and so on. Culturally, of course, these years saw extraordinary achievements in music, art and literature that hardly need enumerating. The poets of that 'Silver Age' are read, both there and here, more widely than ever before, now that everything is available: Akhmatova, Pasternak, Mandelstam, Tsvetaeva (a great favourite with Brodsky). There's a continuity here, a renewal of the tradition. It was Mandelstam who spoke of a 'nostalgia for world culture'. Brodsky (1940-96), raised in some of the hardest times, shared this nostalgia; when the thaw came, with the worst constraints removed, he was somewhere else. He too was a provincial, or so he claimed, in search of world culture, hence all those poems set abroad (Rome, Paris, London). He insists on his provincialism: 'I was born and grew up in the Baltic marshland.' To be exact he was born in Leningrad, where his father was a news photographer; Joseph and his mother were evacuated to a district north of the city during the siege of 1941-4. Describing his first visit to Venice many years later he writes, 'The sky was full of winter stars, the way it often is in the provinces,' a charming thought not really impaired by its ambiguity (what, even in summer?). It was a windy night, he says, and his 'nostrils were struck' by the smell of happiness — of 'freezing seaweed'. The Baltic littoral, he says, is not the source of this epiphany but something beyond biography, 'somewhere in the hypothalamus' where our 'chordate' ancestors stored their impressions of 'the very ichthus that caused this civilization'. It comes to the same thing, but note the vocabulary. A driven autodidact, who at fifteen just walked out of school, he liked unusual words (chordate means vertebrate) and worked at his English and his spiritual survival: 'From the grey, reflecting river flowing down to the Baltic, with an occasional tugboat in the midst of it struggling against the current, I have learnt more about infinity and stoicism than from mathematics and Zeno.'

His English is impressive, sometimes even showy. During his later years he was known for his essays as much as his poetry — and these, despite a maddeningly breezy tone, are often brilliant. Several, like those on Frost and Auden, are masterpieces of critical exposition. The autobiographical ones are among the best ('Spoils of War', 'The Condition We Call Exile'); and *Watermark* (1992), his book about Venice (yet another book about Venice), has wonderful moments of delighted imagery. Noting the violin necks of gondolas, he says 'the whole city, especially at night, resembles a gigantic orchestra', and he records memorable reflections about water, time and monsters (basilisks, sphinxes, winged lions, chimeras) — 'our self-portraits, in the sense that they denote [our] genetic memory of evolution'. On Ezra Pound: 'For someone with such a long record of residence in Italy, it was odd that he hadn't recognized that beauty can't be targeted, that it is always a by-product of other, often very ordinary pursuits.' (He disliked the idea of Pound, but is buried near him in the island cemetery of San Michele.) Aphorisms abound: 'If there is a substitute for love, it is memory.' An exile 'is thrust from, he retreats into, his mother tongue'. 'Art is not a better, but an alternative existence; it is not an attempt to escape reality but the opposite, an attempt to animate it.' 'Exile makes a writer more conservative.' Brodsky himself is sometimes guilty of targeting beauty, a by-product of exile as it was for Pound. He was certainly a location snob, no doubt one result of early hardship and 'internal exile' in the mid-sixties. The episode was a formative one. Sentenced by a rigged court in Leningrad to five years' hard labour for 'social parasitism', he was roughly treated in prison before being transported to the remote village of Norenskaya, Archangel, where he spent eighteen months while influential names campaigned for mitigation. Norenskaya, where he worked the land, was bleak, though he later described this period as one of the best times of his life. He lived in a log cabin with a desk made of boards, an oil lamp, a typewriter and a baroque inkwell given to him by Akhmatova. He read the Anglo-American moderns and seems to have experienced a revelation about his own poetic project.

He emerged with renewed confidence. Subsequently exiled from the Soviet Union itself he moved, with Auden's help, first to Britain, then to America where he lived thereafter, teaching in Michigan, Massachusetts and New York — 'like a snake-charmer, like the Pied Piper of old'. America paid the piper. Some thought him the best American poet of his generation. His work, though written in Russian, was quickly translated by him and others into a racy English notable for ingenious rhyming. His co-translators included Auden and highly regarded American poets like Richard Wilbur and Anthony Hecht, a team that had done the same for Andrei Voznesensky. *A Part of Speech* (1980), the first fruit of this collaboration, remains his finest verse collection. Included there are such good things as 'Autumn in Norenskaya', 'The End of a Beautiful Era', 'I Sit by the Window', 'Lagoon' and 'Lullaby of Cape Cod', perhaps his single greatest achievement. Translated by Hecht, it's ten pages long and relates Brodsky's flight from Russia and the anomie of a hot American night:

> From the empty street's patrol car a refrain
> of Ray Charles' keyboard tinkles away like rain.
> Crawling to a vacant beach from the vast wet
> of ocean, a crab digs into sand laced with sea lather
> and sleeps. A giant clock on a brick tower
> rattles its scissors. The face is drenched with sweat.
> The streetlamps glisten in the stifling weather...

A Coca-Cola sign 'hums in red' like the writing on the wall at Belshazzar's feast. Sometimes Brodsky is right on, sometimes verbose, sometimes he loses the reader in a riff of knotted cleverality; he gives his inner cod full play. All his strengths and weaknesses are evident in this era-defining lament, a turning point in his own development: the drama, the lyric thrust, exact and meaningful description, casual insights; but also the obtrusive wisecrack, the too obvious Lowell note, the apparent lack of direction. The lack of direction, though, is a function of his exile theme, the sobering thought that some things stay the same wherever you go. The

The Pied Piper

elaborate stanzaic pattern clearly owes much to a world of Russian prosody known only to the specialist. With his fondness for mirror images, the exile has already noticed a surprising East-West correspondence in the 'change of Empires', and his primary intended readership still seems to be the folks back home, to whom his work was not then available (but who are now enthusiastic):

> *I write from an Empire whose enormous flanks*
> *extend beneath the sea. Having sampled two*
> *oceans as well as continents, I feel that I know*
> *what the globe itself must feel: there's nowhere to go.*

Nowhere to go? And perhaps nothing much to say except that western civilization is a good thing and freedom more than the knowledge of necessity. An apocalyptic undertone suggests a notion like Fukuyama's ill-timed 'end of history', but there's more to Brodsky than that. It never quite emerged clearly in his work (he died in his fifties) but there are large philosophical questions lurking behind the cultural travelogue. He was married twice and had two children, but his poetic voice is a lonely one, that of a man with no home, no family, a 'nobody in a raincoat', an existential hero. Exceptionally for a poet, he made music of this condition. Whatever about his American fame, he is *the* Russian poet of his disillusioned generation:

> *A loyal subject of these second-rate years,*
> *I proudly admit that my finest ideas*
> *are second-rate, and may the future take them*
> *as trophies of my struggle against suffocation.*
> *I sit in the dark. And it would be hard to figure out*
> *which is worse: the dark inside, or the darkness out.*

Going the Distance

Harry Clifton lives in a church, a deconsecrated Dublin church converted into flats: 'the ruins of religion'. This seems appropriate. A 'worshipper of sky-lights', a post-Christian existentialist and an experienced nomad in deft touch with the contemporary world (postmodern Ireland and elsewhere), he is nostalgic, if not for the forms of religion, for a spiritual dimension absent from serious Western discourse since Teilhard de Chardin and Thomas Merton, to each of whom he more than once refers. The Clifton spirit is ascetic but engaged, knowing but idealistic. One of the finest poems here, 'God in France', takes its title from an interview with Saul Bellow in *Le Monde*. Asked what he would like best the old boy replied, 'To be God in France, where no one believes any more; to have no calls, to sit all day in cafés . . .' Not *abscondicus* exactly, more *emeritus*. (To have no calls: see Clifton, *Berkeley's Telephone and Other Fictions*, 2000.) As for cafés, those 'lit conceptual cages', Clifton and his wife, the novelist Deirdre Madden, lived for ten years in 'unfashionable' Paris. Previously he had taught in Nigeria, administered aid programmes for Cambodian refugees in Thailand, travelled in North and South America and spent a winter in Italy. He is home now, one of the most respected Irish poets, if too long *abscondicus*, and evidently absorbed in the perennially fruitful themes of 'exile' and return. *Secular Eden*, his first general selection since *The Desert Route* (Gallery, 1992), brings together the poems of his Paris period, including some set elsewhere (Qatar; Co Derry) — which, together with earlier volumes still in print, represents a substantial and imposing body of work.

Though not the other Harry Clifton to whom Yeats dedicated 'Lapis Lazuli', he has an interesting family history. His great-grandfather was a well-known Irish nationalist politician; his mother is Anglo-Chilean. The poet has taken the world as his province. Like MacNeice, like Yeats indeed, he benefits from a certain journalistic facility, which added salt to early poems like 'Monsoon Girl' and 'Death of Thomas Merton'. Merton's death took place in Bangkok during the Vietnam war. The complex sanctity of the worldly Cistercian is presented against a backdrop of blazing jungle where 'Spiritual masters shrunken to skin and bone / Await you in silence on a natural ground of Buddhas'. There's a 'switch' in the poem 'from corruption into wisdom', which re-enacts the configuration of Merton's life and glances at the nature of his death. (He was electrocuted in his bath by a faulty light-fitting: such deftness is a little hair-raising.) A great one for jungles, Clifton is also drawn to deserts, literal and figurative, positive deserts whose emptiness and clarity offer not desolation but points of departure: blank page, *tabula rasa*, post-modern site, peopled perhaps with a few shapes like those of Giacometti — 'an exemplary figure', said Clifton in an interview, one of those who see the artistic life as 'an austerity and a dedication'. The sense of vocation is evident in Clifton's work, the single-mindedness required to pursue 'absolute values in a world of relative values', the contemporary global force-field of finance and information. Always aware of the world-historical dimension, he exercises a semblance of impersonal control over chaos — a control embodied in the formality of generally regular, rhymed stanza forms, some simple, some quite elaborate. He has been criticized for this seeming impersonality — by, for example, the American poet and critic Richard Tillinghast who, noting a fondness for 'geometry and abstraction', questioned the 'disengagement'. The explanation, as Tillinghast concedes, lies in the cool consciousness of one who has been to the war zones. Cool but deep, Clifton himself speaks warmly of detachment, 'the cold element in art', while putting great faith in the idea of species solidarity. 'Euclid Avenue', in *The Desert Route*, recreates the world of Hart Crane in a fierce lament for the underside of America, its 'night bus-stations, galaxies of strays — / The sons and daughters of the human race'. Old-fashioned rhetoric still has its place, as also the old question of how to live on Earth.

Crane appears again in *Secular Eden*, this time playing jazz records in 'the cranked-up ecstasy / Of latter days'. Other triumphs are 'Reductio', about Giacometti; 'Icy Pandemonium' (Simone Weil: 'What the soul needs is silence and warmth. What it gets is an icy pandemonium'); and 'Noosphere', where the poet, reading Teilhard

Derek Mahon

high above India and 'the scattered lymph of earthlight, stadium-glow in the Himalayas', questions his own ability to 'go the distance'. One of his principal themes is the artistic life itself, the means of creation:

> *Between two worlds, suspended in mid-flight,*
> *I dream of a bare table, the warmth to come,*
> *A silence at the heart of Paris, a room,*
> *Detached, anonymous, nothing to do but write.*

What is big now, he asks Giacometti, what is extended in space? The answer: a lean-to shed, 'a single tungsten bulb', the memory of figures glimpsed in revolving doors, while 'from table to wooden chair / Saharas spread'. He is at his best in the large, 'Yeatsian' block stanza bristling with wit and stricture like middle-period Geoffrey Hill. Here's God *emeritus* in Paris, in the person of his fraught, irascible Son:

> *Was I to kneel before him, the tramp at the station,*
> *Unpeel his stinking trainers, wash his feet,*
> *Amaze the wage-slaves? In the name of what*
> *Would I drive the midnight circle of philosophers*
> *Out of their TV studios, swivel chairs,*
> *With hempen fire, the rope of castigation?*

'Benjamin Fondane Departs for the East' shares this vitality and panache — as did, according to contemporary reports, the Paris-based Romanian Jewish poet and *cinéaste* who died in Auschwitz. Trains, so often transports of delight in Clifton's work, here play a different role. This is the 'public' Clifton, but there is a quieter one besides, devoted to the consolatory and redemptive private life — one who prefers a shorter line and a lighter touch as in 'Bare Arm', the title poem and 'The Bird-Haunt' ('Their high, piping cries / Barely audible / In the uproar of the world'), or a more fanciful idea as in 'Rabbits at Orly Airport' ('quivering in our turbo-blast') and the great 'McCrystal's', where he takes the limpid playfulness of Elizabeth Bishop to an all-night general store in, I think, the north-west corner of Lough Neagh, Northern Ireland:

Going the Distance

All night, on the opposite shore,
The lights of McCrystal's glitter.
You could walk on water
To get there, and be drowned,
Or take the long way round . . .

This is Heaney country — the filling station that 'Blazes like broad daylight', the old airfield 'Overgrown since the last world war' — but where Heaney's landscape is tactile and fathoms deep, Clifton provides some philosophical fun:

There, where sky and water meet
And none are strangers to themselves
Or the land beneath their feet,
McCrystal, quietly stacking shelves,
Open infinitely late

On the universe, picks you out
From the fixed and wandering stars
Of sailmakers' cottages, nightbound cars
Forever approaching, the only man
Driven by supernatural doubt.

There is something Berkeleian, even Platonic, going on here ('veil of phenomena'; 'optical, an illusion'), yet the poem skips along with such seeming inconsequence that we can, if we like, ignore the hidden depths and enjoy the visuals. He is not all austerity and dedication, in other words, but a poet ringing the changes on sound and rhythm. Seriousness and drollery, adventure and achievement, are all here. He's already gone much of the way and looks set to go the distance.

Indian Ink

Rajbag ('Ragbag' to us fans) is a strip of shops and houses behind the shore some four miles south of Goa's crowded Patnem Beach. The train from Bombay to Bangalore stops at Chaudi (Chowdy), the nearest town, and a 'tuk-tuk' makes the trip in fifteen minutes. (The ubiquitous tuk-tuk is the rickety auto-rickshaw, a sort of motorized gig.) I'm staying in a house of holiday flats belonging to friends; mine gives on to the back garden. Dusty lanes lead inland, sandy lanes to the shore where I 'swim' daily. Between village and sea, in its own sixty acres, stands the elaborate, pricey and gated Intercontinental Hotel 'Resort' with a James Bond poolside and a simple nine-hole golf course — not a 'links' by any means, despite the brochure. Theory: the name of the game was originally *golfes* (gulfs; water hazards), a French idea imported to Scotland by Mary Stuart, who wielded a mean wood. The few Americans, for whom the place was presumably designed, play a slow game in the considerable January heat, attended by local caddies; but most of the guests are rich Russians, fit and prosperous-looking families, beneficiaries of *glasnost* and *perestroika*, exuding easy confidence as if this is the Crimea — or as if, after all, they've finally won what Kipling called the Great Game, the 19th-century Russo-British cold war for Afghanistan and, by extension, the subcontinent. A shark fin in the water is a Russian nipper's goofy inflatable shark.

Goa was Portuguese for centuries, and I'm told some people still speak the language. 'Manueline' church and domestic architecture survives in and around Panaji (formerly Panjim), the state capital, and there's a trade in *azulejos*, those decorative blue and white tiles depicting maritime scenes. Names in the Goa *Herald*, an English-language daily, will include Dias, Souza, even Braganza. The Lisbon spice traders often married local girls. Many Goans are light-skinned; others share the dark Dravidian look of the South. Most are Hindu, many Christian. This was never part of the Raj, and the place has a distinctive laid-back character rare in busy India. Sometimes you could think yourself in the Greek islands. Goa, like Greece, is full of temples and tiny churches; also shrines devoted to the Vedic pantheon. A great favourite, here as elsewhere, is Ganesh the elephant god who looks after peace and prosperity. Ganesh has been good to Goa. So too is the love goddess Radha, blue Krishna's favourite *gopi* (groupie), and lovely Saraswati, shown with a sitar and a fistful of cash, in charge of the music. Old temples (11th century) dot the red earth of the Western Ghats (hills; steps). The languages: local Konkani, official Hindi, English and, at the moment, Russian. There are Konkani writers, but the best-known Goa poet must be Camões, author of *Os Lusíadas*, who spent time here on his way to China with Vasco da Gama, and lingered on his way back.

Except for the Intercontinental, which has a conference centre and globalized facilities, and pipes the sinister voice of Sinatra into its lounges (Sinatra, now as then, the poet of mobster kitsch and market-driven brutalism), Rajbag is a quiet spot and largely unspoilt. Perhaps it could use a little spoiling, like India generally despite the new tigerish times. Clean water, for example, is still a problem. The electricity fails five times a day. But noise and light pollution belong in tourist slums like Patnem where beach raves go on into the 'wee hours', says the *Herald*, and the coppers shut down bars on a regular basis. Those who prefer to watch TV, a riot of noisy options, get Bollywood musicals with singin' and dancin' (no kissin'), wet saris and innocent fun; even the violent stuff is operatic. Goa has its own Konkani channel, and the usual satellite menu is there: Sky, Fox, that sort of thing. On the subject of electricity, could India not run the grid, like France, on its nuclear power, together with solar energy? (Perhaps it will one day: this could be photovoltaic heaven.) As for truly unspoilt, you have to head even farther south to find beaches with the real 'Bounty' look: palms bending right over white sand in *namaskar* (obeisance) to the ocean, and scarcely a soul in sight. Turtle Beach, for instance, not far as the kite flies, beyond the Talpona River with its great railway bridge. Turtles lay there once a year, at their *own* birthplaces, take off to Hawaii, and return to hatch their chicks. When the young emerge from the sand they dash down to the sea, maybe a hundred at a time. This happens at night to elude predators. The forestry

Derek Mahon

department, in a beach hut hung with sperm-whale vertebrae, is on hand to help.

Here in India you're closer to the heart of the natural world. The very dust of the road is alive with intimations. Cows, who *know* they're sacred, mingle freely with people, sometimes nudging you out of the way. Insect life makes no distinction between field and room, outside and in; bushes and trees have a speaking presence. After dark, forest life gathers round, rustling and squeaking. There's always something going on: birds shrieking, cats fighting, plants almost audibly growing. You're part of all this, *tat tvam asi*, only human by chance; it's easy to understand the old belief in serial reincarnation. We resist the mosquitoes with Deet and other insecticides, but traditional Hindu teaching says we're all involved in *atma*, the world breath or soul. All this ties in with Gaia theory, which reminds us that we belong to nature. We're cleverer than monkeys in most ways, but one with them in spirit at some level; one too with all organic and even inorganic life. Which doesn't mean that we love mosquitoes: there are few less edifying sights than that of an Ulster poet stalking mozzies.

Saw elephants in Delhi, but not here. No monkeys either — though Liz, an English wildlife snapper met by chance, tells me the forests are full of them; and there's one old tiger hanging on in the Cotigao nature reserve. But we've seen these things in zoos over the years. Peacocks too, beloved of Saraswati, which were once sacred in Goa; now, their habitats destroyed by forest clearance, they are in danger. Liz has seen a news item about intercontinental druggists using decommissioned Soviet submarines, and my thoughts stray to the *glasnost* types at the hotel. I'm reading *Under Western Eyes*, the one Conrad novel where women call the tune, a sort of Henry James yarn about revolutionary intrigue. The 'desperate loquacity' Conrad ascribes to the 'Russian temperament' isn't evident in daylight hours (no doubt it's different when the evening vodka flows). Instead, a certain grim preoccupation as if someone is about to sell a submarine to the cocaine interest.

A white-headed, red-brown Brahminy kite (*Haliastur indicus*) darkens the garden with its broad wingspan, scaring the usually bold crows, who shriek and scatter; it swoops grandly away over fields to a rubbish dump. Serious, scrubbed youngsters in school

Indian Ink

uniform (blue shirts, grey shorts and skirts) with old-style schoolbags on their backs, in twos and threes: Ireland in the 1950s. A rare thundery crackle in the hills comes to nothing: pity. I'd love one brief thunderstorm to freshen the air, briefly of course. Meanwhile everyone walks around with a broad grin, for India have beaten Oz by 72 runs in the third Test match at Perth . . . Indian light: a Scots 'gloaming' at end of day; in the morning, everything in fierce definition, near and far. Seen through half-shut eyes on the beach, Natashas and Tamaras, the red and green Ghats; also Mr and Mrs Donovan Grant. Robert Shaw in the movie, Donovan ('Red') Grant, aka 'Capt Nash', was conceived behind a circus tent in Aughmacloy (*sic*), Co Tyrone, joined the British Army, defected to the Russians at a Berlin checkpoint, and finishes up as a hitman for Smersh in *From Russia with Love*. Here he is, on the beach at Rajbag in his white shorts.

A post-colonial moment, one of many. Leaving the hotel grounds after a dip, I'm faced as usual with about two dozen animated taxi and tuk-tuk drivers mad for a fare. 'Bapa!' they shout unignorably to any distinguished-looking foreigner who walks, meaning 'Grandad!' if you please. Hailed constantly in this fashion, I've grown cowardly and started avoiding the main gates. Instead I sneak round behind the bike sheds and power plant to a staff exit and reach the road unbothered. Which is fine since I distrust pretentious gates that have to be opened by uniformed men with sticks and am always interested in power plants and the like. (Hasn't Hart Crane a poem called 'The Power Plant', written in the Isle of Pines? No, 'The Air Plant', a different thing.) I don't get off entirely though: torpid, untouchable dogs groan at my white shins — as I do myself . . . Seen in Chaudi, a ghostly *sadhu* (holy man) buying a lottery ticket. A sacred but bony cow chews on a cardboard box.

Chandra, the moon god, is shown with a rabbit. *Mare Imbrium*, Sea of Rains, contains the souls of the dead. Moonlight, says Plutarch, is 'a moist and pregnant light which promotes the generation of life and the fructification of plants'. Black laterite outcrops divide the beaches, though these can be climbed. Inland, Neolithic cave drawings, as old as the monkey wars, said to equal those of Lascaux. Of modern Indian art I know little; film and music flourish of course, as they've done since Satyajit Ray and Ravi Shankar. The novel thrives: the Desais, mother and daughter; Rohinton Mistry, a *Canadian* Indian, or rather an Indo-Canadian, born in Bombay and living in Toronto: so much more real than Rushdie ... Durrell words (*Justine*): hircine, banausic. Two phrases from the Katha Upanishad: 'the razor's edge', 'the blind leading the blind'.

Anandu, a local man, looks after the garden and the garden gods, Shiva etc. In his own house, pix of Krishna and Radha; in his yard, peahens. His wife in line for an eye operation in Paniji. There are two kinds of coconut, the brown we know and the green, both potable. The green look like big mangoes; out here the unkempt brown look even more like severed heads. The locals, some of their own heads severed by the Portuguese in earlier times, have conflicting views about 'development'. It 'creates jobs' of course, if you want a job, but seems to be in the hands of outsiders and foreigners. The government wants to set up SEZs (Special Economic Zones) for this purpose, which will upset local agriculture. Someone cynically suggests that what's needed is Special Entertainment Zones, but Goa has enough of those already. The *Herald* Bollywood page: 'Kareena Kapoor in Hot New Avatar!'

Anandu, to my surprise, bids me good trip with Indian courtesy of the old kind: a brisk springy bob to tap my grimy sneakers. We exchange *namaskars*. I'm off to Panaji and the historic quarter, a square mile of colonial houses including the Panjim Inn and quiet, picturesque St Sebastian Square. Panaji keen on cinema since opening sequences of *The Bourne Supremacy* were shot here some years ago. Iberian art-deco; dusty marble of public buildings, an air of neglect and desuetude: the sort of place to which Casement might have been sent in his consular days. Conrad; Graham Greene; John le Carré. Contemporary Panaji, along the Mandovi river with its old forts and lighthouses, is notable chiefly for the Kala Academy, a multi-purpose arts centre which, together with the Inox Cinema in nearby Gandhi Road, serves as a focal point for the annual film festival. Now showing at the Inox: *Bombay to Bangkok* (Hindi). The Inn gallery shows local artists, figurative and abstract, with names like Sonia Rodriguez and Frank de Souza, strong on the blue faces and tropical hues. Many expats and yoghurt-weavers here as in West Cork. Republic Weekend: Indian and Western concerts in Old Goa, a heritage spot a few miles out of town and burial place of St Francis Xavier.

Indian Ink

The real object of this Indian jaunt is an Irish festival at the Habitat Centre in Delhi, organized by Ireland Literature Exchange; so now back to Delhi (Deccan Air) to link up with the rowdies. There's been a fire at the Grand Hotel. Nobody hurt, and Minihan's negatives are safe, but we've all been relocated to yet another Intercontinental, a big corporate-style place in the diplomatic neighbourhood. Early next morning, from my 17th-floor window, I watch the city wake up under its yellow fug. A solitary dawn tuk-tuk chugs past in the road below. Light goes on in a pineapple-shaped office building: corporate homage to the organic. Schoolboys on a parched football field, white light on a sudden thick rush of traffic, the constant tooting at this height a reminder of Manhattan — though Delhi, or at least New Delhi, with its wide tree-lined thoroughfares and 'circles', resembles not New York but Washington. I'm only here for four days, so won't be seeing Agra or Jaipur this trip; but I spend a morning in and around immense, circular Connaught Place, the heart of Delhi. Now showing at the Regal: *Atonement* (English). Good bookshops here. Galgotia & Sons stock things you might not easily find in a London shop: J. K. Galbraith for example, not much read now in the turbo-capitalist West, but evidently agreeable to the pleasantly left-liberal Indian world view, Nehru's enduring legacy. It was Galbraith, Kennedy's man in Delhi, who pointed out that boom is *always* followed by bust though the market *always* says it will be different this time. Lutyens' huge arch, India Gate, commemorates those Indians who died in the first world war: Sikhs in the trenches. Postcards to Anandu, Liz and other friends in Rajbag.

Delhi's *Time Out* runs a piece by Ranjana Dasgupta on the non-existent Great Delhi Novel: 'We still have to wait for that magic moment when Delhi becomes a city of the mind.' At the Habitat Centre students, journalists, writers: full houses for the visitors. Recently charged with a lack of interest in Indian poetry, I've been trying to catch up. Aside from the *Bhagavad Gita* and so on, this means going back, in modern times, to Rabindranath Tagore (1861-1941), the Yeats of Bengal, whom Yeats himself admired. Both names keep coming up, since we're talking about Indo-Irish literary and historical links, of which there are quite a few when you think about it. Indians like to say their Independence movement was inspired by the Irish example; and there are certainly similarities. It was Edmund Burke who first made the Indo-Irish comparison.

The Connaught Rangers mutinied at Jalandhar in 1920. (Jim Farrell's *The Siege of Krishnapur* is about the real *Indian* Mutiny, so-called, based on contemporary reports from Lucknow.) Gandhi and De Valera had much in common as regards economics; religion led to partition in both countries. Yeats's politics resembled those of Tagore, and his praise of the Bengali poet was both an anti-imperial gesture and a statement of caste solidarity.

Tagore came to notice in the anglophone world with his own translation of *Gitanjali* ('Song Offerings'), first published by the India Society (London, 1912) with a rather fanciful introduction by Yeats, who spoke of 'a tradition where poetry and religion are the same thing' and endorsed Tagore's brahminical priorities. 'Dream of the noble and the beggarman' didn't rule out 'the book of the people' and 'the common tongue'; and both, despite their 'elitism', have had their popular following. Both were dramatists too, and both have had their songs set to music. Indian reverence for Tagore seemed 'strange in our world', says Yeats, 'where we hide everything under the same veil of obvious comedy and half-serious depreciation'. Rabindranath was and is a sitting duck for the reductive impulse, especially in (prose) self-translation. When God tells him to sing, he says, 'it seems that my heart would break with pride; and I look to thy face, and tears come to my eyes. All that is harsh and dissonant in my life melts into one sweet harmony, and my adoration spreads its wings like a glad bird on its flight across the sea.' The tone is elevated throughout, too unrelievedly so for contemporary taste, though the Penguin versions by William Radice create a better impression. Besides, Tagore's subsequent work, like Yeats's, grew stronger and more complex, the imagery sharper: 'Ink-black clouds banked in the north-east, the force of a coming storm [Independence?] latent in the forest, waiting as quietly as bats hanging in the branches . . . ' (Radice).

Tagore is still a presence in Indian literature despite the subsequent appearance of the modern 'Nayi Kavita' (New Poetry) and later 'Bhit Kavita' (Beat Poetry): see *New Poetry in Hindi* (2003), edited and translated by Lucy Rosenstein. Among the Hindi poets at Habitat: Kunwar Narain, the grand old man, with wife and son, and Ashok Vajpeyi, critic and *animateur* — who works, as we all do, for 'the other reality, the republic of imagination'. Narain, one of the outstanding figures of the last half-century, studied at Lucknow and has lived for most of his life in Delhi. A great traveller in his time, he has worked in theatre and film and edited magazines. A humanist, touched by Marx and Buddha both, he is very much a 20th-century man, an Aragon or a Montale. His work negotiates cryptically between tradition and innovation, past and future, spirit and the material world (all very Indian):

> *Water falling on leaves means one thing,*
> *leaves falling on water another.*

Amrita Bharati, a Sanskrit scholar who has spent much time in ashrams, shares this dialogue of matter and spirit. Sometimes described as a mystic, she has translated Hölderlin and Kathleen Raine into Hindi. Her woman's voice, 'silent for centuries', has something cloistered about it in the best sense ('far into the silence the sound of my footsteps'), and indeed there seems to be a spiritual quest taking place. While 'He' walks on mountains, she flies to 'the high chasms of the sky'. Maybe, she thinks, these 'two paths' will meet one day 'in the stillness of the word'. She is political too, though: in good Nayi Kavita fashion she keeps her feet on the ground. India, someone said, is really very down-to-earth. Narain, faced with mutability in 'Changing Posters', notices how an advertisement hoarding with 'a beauty bathing in Liril soap' or 'children thriving on Dalda oil', new bikes or fertilizers, changes from month to month:

> *But what never changes*
> *is that sad, quiet boy*
> *who puts up posters for a pittance.*

Kipling's Kim is an O'Hara, his father an ex-sergeant in an Irish regiment. With Ulster connections, the irascible poet of Anglo-India secured for his own son Jack a commission in the Irish Guards during the first world war. Jack died within hours on the western front. Louis MacNeice was in Delhi in 1947, one of a BBC team covering the Independence celebrations, and later visited other parts of the country. At the Shore Temple in Mahabalipuram, outside Madras, he wrote a poem about the erotic rock sculptures

Derek Mahon

'where worship comes no more'. These are the dreams we've needed, he says, since we forgot how to dance. There's now a dance festival there each January, as perhaps in ancient times, but MacNeice's 'we' wasn't an Indian 'we'. John Montague praises 'the ripe-thighed temple dancers' similarly immortalized at Konarak; and Harry Clifton, in *Comparative Lives* (1982), has an 'Indian Sequence' including 'Magnetic and True North' written in a 'region of clouds', Sikkim perhaps:

> Into this otherworldliness
> History steams, like a Himalayan toy train,
> With its Times of India, *news of Madras and Cawnpore,*
> And its goldenhaired Western children, dope on the brain.

Which brings us down to the present, or nearly. It's many years, in fact, since the hippies hit the road to enlightenment, peace and love; now a new generation is fighting it out in Afghanistan. We stare down there on the return flight to Heathrow; grey ridges stretch away into the distance.

A year on they're still at it, and the violence has spread to India itself — always a violent country in any case. (The police too are very bad.) This time I'm here for the week-long Jaipur Literary Festival in Rajasthan's 'pink city', some 200 miles west of Delhi. Now four years old, this takes place at the Diggi Palace Hotel, up a lane off Sawai Ram Singh Hospital Road, not far from the city centre. The hotel, set in ten acres of garden and woods, is a 19th-century two-storey compound. With its peacocks and Durbar hall, it has the air of a Rajput country house: solid old-fashioned furniture, verandah with cane chairs, regimental and sporting prints, stone floors, no frills. Camel carts deliver market produce, cars and tuk-tuks hoot at the end of the lane; but within all is quiet, except after sunset when traditional Rajasthani music plays at low volume to candlelit tables in the night air. The Diggis are adding an extension (bricks come in bullock carts), and festival time brings out the fairy lights. Open-air stage, tents, pool ('tank'); lectures, panel discussions and poetry readings: a sort of Indian Hay-on-Wye. A moving spirit behind the show is the laird-like William Dalrymple, author of *City of Djinns*, *The Age of Kali* and much else besides,

Indian Ink

together with his wife Olivia Fraser, fluent in Urdu; over a hundred participants in all, and a thousand visitors coming and going. Special guests: Amitabh Bachchan, 'King of Bollywood', who draws a huge crowd, and Vikas Swarup, author of the novel *Q&A*, source of the controversial Danny Boyle movie *Slumdog Millionaire*, which we get to see. Boyle was good at home with *Shallow Grave* and *Trainspotting* but this new rags-to-riches fairy tale, with its box-ticking, chocolate-box eclecticism, is remarkable chiefly as a harbinger of the imminent globalization of the Indian film industry. National opinion is largely hostile; there are complaints about poverty porn, slum tourism, squalor dollars, the infamous Western eye, as if Mira Nair's *Salaam Bombay* (1989), let alone Satyajit Ray, never happened. Still, the objectors are right: an extreme tackiness attaches to the whole enterprise. The actors have indeed been exploited. An op-ed piece in the *Hindustan Times* comments: 'We had no business trying to break free of our karma. Now divine retribution has caught up with us. Poverty is our commodity, and that's all the world wants from us.'

I'd formed my idea of modern Indian poetry by reading anthologies of English-language verse and Hindi verse in English or French translation, much of it ironical and restrained like so much recent English (and French) verse itself. Take Dom Moraes who died in 2004. Once described as 'an Englishman with a brown face', he was the son of the legendary newspaper editor Frank Moraes, won the Hawthornden Prize at Oxford and enjoyed a brief London fame in the 1950s; later he lived in Bombay and wrote travel books. He had a great lyrical gift and an eye for imagery ('the sea like soap-suds in the night', 'pines like wire brushes', 'a skylark in each eye') yet never rose to the larger subjects. In 'Tibet', where he went as a reporter during the Indo-Chinese hostilities in the 1960s, he writes:

> *Today the raw pale sun*
> *Appears, and the mules snort;*
> *Das writes his report.*
> *We have seen no Chinese,*
> *No fighting has begun.*
> *Hawks sleep in the trees.*

Derek Mahon

Nothing happens, and it turns into a 'missing you' love poem: much better that way perhaps, though he might have found something to say about the offstage conflict. A private poet finally. The clipped, sardonic lines signal detachment and a reluctance to engage with the world. But exposure to Indian poets performing their own work set me thinking. One group reading by Rajasthani, Urdu and Telugu poets proved particularly thrilling: intense, incantatory renditions of exuberant, musical verse, much appreciated by the largely Indian audience — like having Yeats, Dylan Thomas and Joseph Brodsky on the platform, though of course beyond us Westerners.

The West loves the sublime, the East the beautiful: how's that for a generalization? The distinction, as old as the hills, was memorably formulated by (again) Burke in *A Philosophical Enquiry*, part three, where he speaks of the 'remarkable contrast' between these 'ideas of a very different nature, one [the sublime] being founded on pain, the other [the beautiful] on pleasure'. The thought has infinite ramifications. 'True art,' says Tolstoy in *What Is Art?*, that late and eccentric work which dismisses so much including, presumably, his own sublime *War and Peace,* is modest. 'Life is full of art of various kinds,' he writes, 'from lullabies, jokes, mimicry, home decoration, clothing, utensils, to church services and solemn processions.' He is recommending the beautiful as opposed to the sublime, peace as opposed to war, level contemplative calm as opposed to the compulsive sex 'n' violence we cherish in Western art: 'ideas of a very different nature', based on very different temperaments, dispositions. There is a sublime Indian art of course, and much war in the *Ramayana* and the *Mahabharata,* but the predominant soundtrack, initially puzzling to the Western ear, seems to evade European notions of structure. The European mind, used to Platonic ideas of form and Aristotelian ideas of dramatic shape, the tensions and releases of the post-Romantic era, keen on climax and closure, is a bit at sea when faced with the conventions of, say, Indian traditional music as described by Forster: (Godbole's) 'thin voice rose, and gave out one sound after another. At times there seemed rhythm, at times there was the illusion of a Western melody. But the ear, baffled repeatedly, soon lost any clue, and wandered in a maze of noises, none harsh or unpleasant, none intelligible. It was the song of an unknown bird. Only the servants understood it. They began to whisper to one another . . . The sounds continued, and ceased after a few moments as casually as they had begun — apparently halfway through a bar, and on the subdominant.' Hindi poetry is like that: a different music, one we listen to closely, hoping perhaps for 'the illusion of a Western melody'.

Iris Murdoch on Hindu art: 'The imagery is usually less highly specialized, less rationally clarified, less relentlessly literary. The magnificent Hindu deities, however clearly and lovingly rendered, are more mysterious. Eastern religions lack the terrible historical clarity of Christianity. Eastern art is humbler, less grand, and has a quieter and perhaps for that reason deeper relation to the spiritual.' Arundhati Roy on Development Aid 'exported to the Third World along with their other waste like old weapons and banned pesticides. Indian governments rail self-righteously against the First World but actually *pay* to receive its gift-wrapped garbage. Aid is just another praetorian business enterprise like colonialism. It has destroyed most of Africa. Bangladesh is reeling from its ministrations.' But have no fear, the Maoists are winning.

William Radice, reviewing a recent anthology of Indian poets in English, observed that 'the dominant impression is gloomy: perhaps because they are deprived of the mass readership and packed audiences at readings that Indian-language poets can command, Indian poets in English seem lonely and self-absorbed . . . exuberance is what is missing . . . what Kathleen Raine called the tabla-beat of India'. Indian languages, says Radice, are an immensely rich rhythmic and metrical resource. 'To any Indian poet in English I would say: close your eyes, think back to the old songs and rhymes and see what magic can emerge.' This has a familiar ring. It's the voice of our own Irish Literary Revival, the voice of George Moore, Hyde, Yeats and the first modern Gaelic scholars. 'What infuriates Indian-language writers,' says Radice, 'is the implication that the writers in English are somehow representative of the whole literary scene.' Tagore, after all, wrote in Bengali. On the other hand, says Radice, 'I've yet to meet an Indian who cares whether his compatriots — those living in India and abroad — write in English or not, and only the most mean-minded would begrudge the international success Indian novelists in English have achieved.' The mention of 'abroad' is significant since many, even most, seem to live or aspire to live in London or New York, the centres of literary business if not necessarily of literary inspiration. That same

Derek Mahon

anthology, edited by Jeet Thayil and published in England, is notable for the high proportion of authors already established in British and American universities; and that too resembles recent Irish experience. It's all about finance and buying into a global market India itself has traditionally resisted, though perhaps not any more. As I understand it, official Hindi, originating in the north-central region — the Delhi area, western Uttar Pradesh and eastern Rajasthan — is a relative latecomer compared to, say, Urdu or Tamil: which may explain in part the cool, cerebral quality of Hindi poetry, its detachment from the traditional sources and creative enthusiasms evidently available to poets in the older languages. What's needed is a generous anthology of work in the many Indian tongues with facing translations for us poor Westerners. It might even reinvigorate our own notions of what poetry can do.

2008-9